The Capitalist and the Entrepreneur

The Capitalist and the Entrepreneur

Essays on Organizations and Markets

Peter G. Klein

Ludwig
von Mises
Institute
AUBURN, ALABAMA

Ludwig von Mises Institute
518 West Magnolia Avenue
Auburn, Alabama   36832

Ph: (334) 844-2500
Fax: (334) 844-2583

mises.org

10 9 8 7 6 5 4 3 2 1

ISBN: 978-1-933550-79-4

The entrepreneur hires the technicians, i.e., people who have the ability and the skill to perform definite kinds and quantities of work. The class of technicians includes the great inventors, the champions in the field of applied science, the constructors and designers as well as the performers of the most simple tasks. The entrepreneur joins their ranks as far as he himself takes part in the technical execution of his entrepreneurial plans. The technician contributes his own toil and trouble; but it is the entrepreneur qua entrepreneur who directs his labor toward definite goals. And the entrepreneur himself acts as a mandatary, as it were, of the consumers.

—Ludwig von Mises, *Human Action* (1949), p. 300

Contents

Foreword
by Doug French

Entrepreneurship has been a hot buzzword recently. Classes in entrepreneurship are being taught at both the high school and college levels. The Ewing Marion Kauffman Foundation: The Foundation of Entrepreneurship has big fancy websites advertising that its President and CEO will give a "State of Entrepreneurship Address." There are global entrepreneurship conferences being held in far-flung places like Dubai. Learning programs are offered to test your "Entrepreneurial IQ." The United States government even has an entrepreneurship website, advertising a Presidential Summit on Entrepreneurship, Entrepreneurship Law, and a Global Entrepreneurship Week.

Is it that simple? If more classes, websites and conferences are offered will we really have more Ewing Kauffmans? A man who as a child was bedridden for a year with a heart ailment but used the time to read 40 books per month. After WWII he worked as a pharmaceutical salesman until, with a $5,000 investment, he started Marion Laboratories. Company sales were just $39,000 in the first year of operation but four decades later Kauffman's company would have revenues totaling $930 million. In 1989, Kauffman merged Marion with Merrell Dow Pharmaceuticals, making more than 300 millionaires of Marion investors and employees.

Kauffman himself would likely have not stepped into the role of entrepreneur if not for the stupidity of his employer, Lincoln Laboratories. A natural salesman and hard worker, Kauffman in just his second year earned more in commissions than the company president did in salary. In response, the president cut Kauffman's commissions. Despite the reduction, Kauffman still out-earned the Lincoln head man the following year, so "he took away some of my territory, which was the same as taking away some of my income," Kauffman related later. "So, I quit and I started Marion Laboratories in the basement of my home."

The government can talk about entrepreneurship and act like it is promoting it, but all of what government does by taxing and regulating impedes the entrepreneur. It's hard to imagine that even Ewing Kauffman could make a similar initial investment today (roughly $44,000 adjusted for inflation), start a firm in his basement, and build it to a billion dollar company. The local authorities in Kansas City were not all that concerned about a fledgling pharmaceutical company operating from Kauffman's home in 1950. Today, there would be permits to obtain, approvals to be gained and license fees to pay. The majority of the legislation that has given the Food and Drug Administration (FDA) its enormous power was enacted after Kauffman's company was up and running.

But as long as there is some shred of a market available, entrepreneurs find a way. They see opportunity others don't. They take financial risks that most people would consider unfathomable. The government edicts, bureaucratic roadblocks and oppressive taxation that discourage the hardiest of souls only serve to challenge and inspire creative entrepreneurs while weeding out potential competitors. All of the wonderful goods and services that we enjoy are due to entrepreneurship and the firms that are created to carry out the dreams of the entrepreneur and serve customers.

It is the firm where most people work. Maybe its a small firm or a big one or one in-between, but unless one is a solo contractor most people trade their time and talent for a paycheck to pay the bills. The vast majority of working people don't give much thought to this framework. They clock in, they clock out. Payday every couple of weeks. At the same time most people will spend the majority of their non-sleeping hours on the job, working for a firm or series of different firms. And work life maybe the single most important part of a person's life. Reportedly 95% of the people who are happy on the job are happy with their life as a whole. But salaried workers, from the lowest paid to the highest, take no risk. And although they are critical to the production of products and services, they are a cost of doing business.

Conversely, the entrepreneur is only paid when the market accepts his or her product. If the market rejects the product, the entrepreneur is not only not rewarded, but most times will lose capital that had been saved previously and was invested in the idea and production. As Kauffman explained, "The odds were strongly against me when I started. There were two or three thousand pharmaceutical businesses started after World War II, and only three ever really succeeded."

As vital as entrepreneurship and the firm are to the working of the market and lives of virtually all working men and women, most schools of economic thought are silent on the subject. Even the work that has been done is incomplete and contradictory. Economists can't even agree on what entrepreneurship is or what exactly entrepreneurs like the late Ewing Kauffman do. And the apparatus that facilitates the manifestation of the entrepreneurial vision—the firm—is but a "black box" where inputs enter and outputs emerge, like so much magic.

But like so many market phenomena that modern economics chooses to ignore or get wrong, an Austrian economist has entered the black box, examining its contents for a better understanding of not only what entrepreneurs are, but what they do and why they do it. Peter G. Klein has devoted his entire career to understanding the entrepreneur and the firm, bringing a distinctive Austrian approach to the problem while drawing from what all schools of thought have to contribute.

This book contains the fruit of Dr. Klein's labors. And while the majority of the book was taken from articles appearing in academic journals, this book should not only be read by students and academics. Klein provides valuable insight that business owners and managers will find useful. As heroic as the entrepreneur may appear or thoughtful as the manager may seem, they don't operate in a vacuum. Often they have no one to talk to and nothing to keep them in check but their own egos, which in many cases offers no check at all but the opposite.

The yearning for knowledge in this area is considerable. Considerable space at most any bookstore is provided for the many and varied management books. There are nearly as many different management books offered as diet books, with each genre being as faddish as the next. Management theorists crank out a continual stream of books full of business advice that "readers find unreadable," writes *The Economist*'s Adrian Wooldridge, "and managers find unmanageable."

While many great entrepreneurs cash in by writing books about their management secrets and entrepreneurial exploits, their supposedly keen insights are often weathered by time and selective memory. But most importantly, these books imply that capital is homogeneous, that the would-be entrepreneur can do what Jack Welch did, or emulate T. Boone Pickens, or apply Ewing Kauffman's strategies and expect the same result. These kind of books are good for inspiration but nothing more.

As Klein makes abundantly clear, capital is instead heterogeneous. Entrepreneurship can't be formulated in equations and sprinkled like pixie dust on the masses by government initiatives or well-meaning foundations with the hopes that the inner-entrepreneur in every citizen will be summoned. Although the brilliant Mr. Kauffman supported the use of his accumulated wealth to support programs promoting entrepreneurship, such programs are often a malinvestment of capital. And the use of tax-payer dollars towards such an endeavor is doubly wasteful.

It is however vital that we understand the function of the entrepreneur and the process that is so critical to the advancement of society and well-being of its members. As Klein pries open the entrepreneurial black box, the glories and special talents of the entrepreneur are exposed, along with the limitations of the firm. The market environment that allows entrepreneurs to thrive is revealed. It is not that the society requires multitudes of entrepreneurs, but only that those with this rare talent be allowed to flourish unfettered. And for those readers who work for an agreed-upon wage helping some entrepreneur become wealthy, an appreciation is gained with the realization that ultimately it is only by satisfying customers that their entrepreneur bosses become successful.

Introduction

As far back as I can remember, I always wanted to be an Austrian economist. Well, not quite, but I was exposed to Austrian economics early on. I grew up in a fairly normal middle-class household, with parents who were New Deal Democrats. In high school, a friend urged me to read Ayn Rand, and I was captivated by her novels. I went on to read some of her nonfiction works, in which she recommended books by Ludwig von Mises and Henry Hazlitt. I don't remember which economics books I read first, maybe Hazlitt's *Economics in One Lesson* or Mises's *Anti-Capitalistic Mentality*. I didn't understand the more technical parts of their analyses, but I was impressed with their clear writing, logical exposition, and embrace of liberty and personal responsibility. I took a few economics courses in college and, while they lacked any Austrian content, I enjoyed them and decided to major in the subject. I had a very good professor, William Darity, who himself preferred Marx and Keynes to Mises but who appreciated my intellectual curiosity and encouraged my growing interest in the Austrians.

As a college senior, I was thinking about graduate school—possibly in economics. By pure chance, my father saw a poster on a bulletin board advertising graduate-school fellowships from the Ludwig von Mises Institute. (Younger readers: this was an actual, physical bulletin board, with a piece of paper attached; this was in the dark days before the Internet.) I was flabbergasted; someone had named an institute after Mises? I applied for a fellowship, received a nice letter from the president, Lew Rockwell, and eventually had a telephone interview with the fellowship committee, which consisted of Murray Rothbard. You can imagine how nervous I was the day of that phone call! But Rothbard was friendly and engaging, his legendary charisma coming across even over the phone, and he quickly put me at ease. (I also applied for admission to New York University's graduate program in economics, which got me a phone call from Israel Kirzner. Talk about the proverbial kid in the candy store!) I won the Mises fellowship, and eventually enrolled in the economics PhD program at the University of California, Berkeley, which I started in 1988.

Before my first summer of graduate school, I was privileged to attend the "Mises University," then called the "Advanced Instructional Program in Austrian Economics," a week-long program of lectures and discussions held that year at Stanford University and led by Rothbard, Hans-Hermann Hoppe, Roger Garrison, and David Gordon. Meeting Rothbard and his colleagues was a transformational experience. They were brilliant, energetic, enthusiastic, and optimistic. Graduate school was no cake walk—the required core courses in (mathematical) economic theory and statistics drove many students to the brink of despair, and some of them doubtless have nervous twitches to this day—but the knowledge that I was part of a larger movement, a scholarly community devoted to the Austrian approach, kept me going through the darker hours.

In my second year of graduate school, I took a course from the 2009 Nobel Laureate Oliver Williamson, "Economics of Institutions." Williamson's course was a revelation, the first course at Berkeley I really enjoyed. The syllabus was dazzling, with readings from Ronald Coase, Herbert Simon, F. A. Hayek, Douglass North, Kenneth Arrow, Alfred Chandler, Armen Alchian, Harold Demsetz, Benjamin Klein, and other brilliant and thoughtful economists, along with sociologists, political scientists, historians, and others. I decided then that institutions and organizations would be my area, and I've never looked back.

The essays collected in this volume reflect my efforts to understand the economics of organization, to combine the insights of Williamson's "transaction cost" approach to the firm with Austrian ideas about property, entrepreneurship, money, economic calculation, the time-structure of production, and government intervention. Austrian economics, I am convinced, has important implications for the theory of the firm, including firm boundaries, diversification, corporate governance, and entrepreneurship, the areas in which I have done most of my academic work. Austrian economists have not, however, devoted substantial attention to the theory of the firm, preferring to focus on business-cycle theory, welfare economics, political economy, comparative economic systems, and other areas. Until recently, the theory of the firm was an almost completely neglected area in Austrian economics, but over the last decade, a small Austrian literature on the firm has emerged. While these works cover a wide variety of theoretical and applied topics, their authors share the view that Austrian insights have something to offer students of firm organization.

The essays in this volume, originally published between 1996 and 2009, deal with firms, contracts, entrepreneurs—in short, with the economics and management of organizations and markets. Chapter 1, "Economic Calculation and the Limits of Organization," first presented in Williamson's Institutional Economics Workshop in 1994, shows how the economic calculation problem identified by Mises (1920) helps understand the limits to firm size, an argument first offered by Rothbard (1962). It also offers a summary of the socialist calculation debate that has worked well, for me, in the classroom. Along with chapter 2, "Entrepreneurship and Corporate Governance," it offers an outline of an Austrian theory of the firm, based on the Misesian concept of entrepreneurship and the role of monetary calculation as the entrepreneur's essential tool. "Entrepreneurship and Corporate Governance" also suggests four areas for Austrian research in corporate governance: firms as investments, internal capital markets, comparative corporate governance, and financiers as entrepreneurs. Chapter 3, "Do Entrepreneurs Make Predictable Mistakes" (with Sandra Klein), applies this framework to the problem of corporate divestitures.

Chapter 4, "The Entrepreneurial Organization of Heterogeneous Capital" (with Kirsten Foss, Nicolai Foss, and Sandra Klein), shows how Austrian capital theory provides further insight into the firm's existence, boundaries, and internal organization. The Austrian idea that resources are heterogeneous, that capital goods have what Lachmann (1956) called "multiple specificities," is hardly surprising to specialists in strategic management, a literature that abounds with notions of unique "resources," "competencies," "capabilities," "assets," and the like. But modern theories of economic organization are not built on a unified theory of capital heterogeneity, simply invoking *ad hoc* specificities when necessary. The Misesian concept of the capital-owning entrepreneur, seeking to arrange his unique resources into value-adding combinations, helps illuminate several puzzles of firm organization.

Management scholars, and some economists, are familiar with Israel Kirzner's concept of entrepreneurship as "discovery," or "alertness" to profit opportunities, typically seeing it as "the" Austrian approach of entrepreneurship. Kirzner, Mises's student at NYU, has always described his approach to entrepreneurship as a logical extension of Mises's ideas. However, as I argue in chapter 5, "Opportunity Discovery and Entrepreneurial Action," one can interpret Mises differently. Indeed, I see Mises's approach to the entrepreneur as closer to Frank Knight's (1921), a view that makes asset ownership, and the investment of resources under uncertainty, the hallmark of entrepreneurial behavior. This suggests a focus not on opportunities, the subjective visions of entrepreneurs, but on investment—on actions, in other words, not beliefs. I suggest several implications of this approach for applied entrepreneurship research. Chapter 6, "Risk, Uncertainty, and Economic Organization," written for the Hoppe *Festschrift* (Hülsmann and Kinsella, 2009), further discusses the Knightian distinction between "risk" and "uncertainty," or what Mises called "class probability" and "case probability."

Chapter 7, "Price Theory and Austrian Economics," challenges what I see as the dominant understanding of the Austrian tradition, particularly in applied fields like organization and strategy. Scholars both inside and outside economics tend to identify the Austrian school with Hayek's ideas about dispersed, tacit knowledge, Kirzner's theory of entrepreneurial discovery, and an emphasis on time, subjectivity, process, and disequilibrium. Despite renewed interest in the Mengerian tradition, the Austrian approach to "basic" economic analysis—value, production, exchange, price, money, capital, and intervention—hasn't gotten much attention at all. Indeed, it's widely believed that the Austrian approach to mundane topics such as factor productivity, the substitution effect of a price change, the effects of rent control or the minimum wage, etc., is basically the same as the mainstream approach, just without math or with a few buzzwords about"subjectivism" or the "market process" thrown in. Even many contemporary Austrians appear to hold this view. Chapter 7 suggests instead that the Austrians offer a distinct and valuable approach to basic economic questions, an approach that should be central to research by Austrians on theoretical and applied topics in economics and business administration.

A final chapter, "Commentary," collects some shorter essays on the nature and history of the Internet, the role of the intellectuals in society, the relationship between management theory and the business cycle, biographical sketches of Carl Menger and F. A. Hayek, and a note on Williamson's contributions and his relationship to the Austrian tradition. Some of these first appeared as Daily Articles at Mises.org and were written for a nonspecialist audience. Indeed, I think scholars in every field, particularly in economics and business administration, have an obligation to write for the general public, and not only for their fellow specialists. Ideas have consequences, as Richard Weaver put it, and economic ideas are particularly important.

In preparing these essays for publication in book form I have made only light revisions in the text, correcting minor errors, eliminating some redundant material, and updating a few references. I think they work well together, and I hope readers will see the end result as an integrated whole, not simply a collection of "greatest hits."

I've been greatly influenced and helped by many friends, teachers, colleagues, and students, far too many to list here. Three people deserve special mention, however. From my father, Milton M. Klein, a historian who taught at Columbia University, Long Island University, SUNY–Fredonia, New York University, and the University of Tennessee, I learned the craft and discipline of scholarship. He taught me to read critically, to think and write clearly, to take ideas seriously. Murray Rothbard, the great libertarian polymath whose life and work played such a critical role in the modern Austrian revival, dazzled me with his scholarship, his energy, and his sense of life. Rothbard is widely recognized as a great libertarian theorist, but his technical contributions to Austrian economics are not always appreciated, even in Austrian circles. In my view he is one of the most important contributors to the "mundane" Austrian analysis described above. Oliver Williamson, who supervised my PhD dissertation at Berkeley, is my most important direct mentor and a constant source of inspiration. Williamson is no Austrian, but he appreciated and supported my interest in the Austrian school and encouraged me to pursue my intellectual passions, not to follow the crowd. His encouragement and support have been critical to my development as a scholar.

I'm deeply grateful to the Contracting and Organizations Research Institute, the University of Missouri's Division of Applied Social Sciences, the University of Missouri Research Foundation, the Coase Foundation, the Kauffman Foundation, and, above all, the Mises Institute for generous financial and moral support over the years. I've learned so much from my university colleagues, coauthors, fellow bloggers, conference participants, and other members of the Academic Racket that it would be impossible to name all those who've influenced my work. My frequent coauthor Nicolai Foss, who thinks and writes more quickly than I can listen or read, keeps me on my toes. I've learned much about Austrian economics, firm strategy, economic organization, and a host of other topics from Joseph Salerno, Lasse Lien, Joseph Mahoney, Dick Langlois, Michael Cook, Michael Sykuta, and many others. Others who offered specific comments and suggestions on earlier versions of these chapters include Sharon Alvarez, Jay Barney, Randy Beard, Don Boudreaux, Per Bylund, John Chapman, Todd Chiles, Jerry Ellig, David Gordon, Jeff Herbener, Stavros Ioannides, Dan Klein, Mario Mondelli, Jennie Raymond, David Robinson, Fabio Rojas, Ron Sanchez, Ivo Sarjanovic, Narin Smith, Sid Winter, and Ulrich Witt. My colleagues have also tried to teach me about deadlines, but I'm still working on that one. I agree with Douglas Adams, "I love deadlines. I like the whooshing sound they make as they fly by."

Special thanks go to Doug French for suggesting this project and to Jeff Tucker, Arlene Oost-Zinner, Paul Foley, and Per Bylund for seeing it to fruition. Most important, I thank my wife Sandy and my children for putting up with my frequent absences, endless hours in front of a computer screen, and occasional irritability. They are my greatest inspiration.

Peter G. Klein
Columbia, Missouri
March 2010

CHAPTER 1

Economic Calculation and the Limits of Organization[†]

Economists have become increasingly frustrated with the textbook model of the firm. The "firm" of intermediate microeconomics is a production function, a mysterious "black box" whose insides are off-limits to respectable economic theory (relegated instead to the lesser disciplines of management, organization theory, industrial psychology, and the like). Though useful in certain contexts, the textbook model has proven unable to account for a variety of real-world business practices: vertical and lateral integration, geographic and product-line diversification, franchising, long-term commercial contracting, transfer pricing, research joint ventures, and many others. As an alternative to viewing the firm as a production function, economists are turning to a new body of literature that views the firm as an organization, itself worthy of economic analysis. This emerging literature is the best-developed part of what has come to be called the "new institutional economics.[1] The new perspective has deeply enhanced

---

[†]Published originally in *Review of Austrian Economics* 9, no. 2 (1996): 51–77.

[1]For overviews of the new institutional economics and the theory of the firm, see Coase (1991); Holmström and Tirole (1989); Langlois (1994b); Furubotn and Richter (1997); Williamson (2000); Ménard and Shirley (2005), and Brousseau and Glachant (2008). For surveys of related empirical work see Shelanski and Klein (1995); Klein (2005), and Macher and Richman (2008).

and enriched our understanding of firms and other organizations, such that we can no longer agree with Ronald Coase's 1988 statement that "[w]hy firms exist, what determines the number of firms, what determines what firms do ... are not questions of interest to most economists" (Coase, 1988, p. 5). The new theory is not without its critics; Richard Nelson (1991), for example, objects that the new institutional economics tends to downplay discretionary differences among firms. Still, the new institutional economics—in particular, agency theory and transaction cost economics—has been the subject of increasing attention in industrial organization, corporate finance, strategic management, and business history.[2]

This chapter highlights some distinctive Austrian contributions to the theory of the firm, contributions that have been largely neglected, both inside and outside the Austrian literature. In particular, I argue that Mises's concept of economic calculation—the means by which entrepreneurs adjust the structure of production to accord with consumer wants—belongs at the forefront of Austrian research into the nature and design of organizations. There is a unique Austrian perspective on economic planning, a perspective developed over the course of the socialist calculation debate. As was recognized in the early Austrian reinterpretations of the calculation debate (Lavoie, 1985; Kirzner, 1988a), Mises's conception of the problem faced by socialist planners is part and parcel of his understanding of how resources are allocated in a market system. Mises himself emphasized that planning is ubiquitous: "[E]very human action means planning. What those calling themselves planners advocate is not the substitution of planned action for letting things go. It is the substitution of the planner's own plan for the plans of his fellow men" (Mises, 1947, p. 493). All organizations plan, and all organizations, public and private, perform economic calculation. In this sense, the calculation problem is much more general than has usually been realized.

With their unique perspective on markets and the difficulties of resource allocation under central planning, third- and fourth-generation Austrian economists have always implicitly understood the economics of organization. In this context, as Nicolai Juul Foss (1994a, p. 32)

---

[2]The framework of transaction cost economics has already made it into textbook form: Kreps (1990b, pp. 744–90), Rubin (1990), Milgrom and Roberts (1992), Acs and Gerlowski (1996), Brickley, Smith, and Zimmerman (1997), and Besanko, Dranove, and Shanley (1998).

notes, "it is something of a doctrinal puzzle that the Austrians have never formulated a theory of the firm." Foss points out that many elements of the modern theory of the firm—property rights, relationship-specific assets, asymmetric information, the principal–agent problem—appeared, at least in elementary form, in Austrian writings since the middle stages of the calculation debate.   Indeed, Rothbard's treatment of firm size in *Man, Economy, and State* (1962) was among the first discussions to adopt explicitly the framework proposed by Ronald Coase in 1937, a framework that underlies most contemporary theorizing about the firm. Mises's discussion in *Human Action* (1949) of the role of the financial markets foreshadows Henry Manne's seminal 1965 article on the market for corporate control along with the recent recognition of finance as an essential part of economics.

Besides anticipating parts of the modern literature, Mises and Rothbard also introduced significant innovations, though this has not yet been generally recognized. Their contributions, while not part of a fully articulated, explicit theory of the firm, deserve attention and development, especially by those working on such issues from within the Austrian School.[3] These contributions are Rothbard's application of the calculation problem to the limits of the firm, and Mises's discussion of how the financial markets both limit managerial discretion and perform the ultimate resource allocation task in a market economy.

The Textbook Theory of the Firm

In neoclassical economic theory, the firm as such does not exist at all. The "firm" is a production function or production possibilities set, a means of transforming inputs into outputs. Given the available technology, a vector of input prices, and a demand schedule, the firm maximizes money profits subject to the constraint that its production plans must be technologically feasible. That is all there is to it. The firm is modeled as a single actor, facing a series of relatively uncomplicated decisions: what level of output to produce, how much of each factor to hire, and so on. These "decisions," of course, are not really decisions at all; they are trivial mathematical calculations, implicit in the underlying data. In the long run, the firm may also

---

[3] Foss and Klein (2010) summarize some of this literature.

choose an optimal size and output mix, but even these are determined by the characteristics of the production function (economies of scale, scope, and sequence). In short: the firm is a set of cost curves, and the "theory of the firm" is a calculus problem.

To be sure, these models are not advertised as realistic descriptions of actual business firms; their use is purely instrumental. As David Kreps (1990b, p. 233)—himself much less sanguine about the merits of the traditional model than most—puts it: if real-world firms do not maximize profits as the traditional theory holds, "that doesn't mean that profit maximization isn't a good positive model. Only the data can speak to that, and then only after we see the implications of profit maximization for observable behavior." However, even granting instrumentalism its somewhat dubious merits,[4] the production-function approach is unsatisfactory, because it isn't useful for understanding a variety of economic phenomena. The black-box model is really a theory about a *plant* or production process, not about a *firm*. A single firm can own and operate multiple production processes. Similarly, two or more firms can contract to operate jointly a single production process (as in a research joint venture). If we want to understand the scale and scope of the firm as a legal entity, then, we must look beyond the textbook model.

Coase and Transaction Costs

Ronald Coase, in his celebrated 1937 paper on "The Nature of the Firm," was the first to explain that the boundaries of the organization depend not only on the productive technology, but on the costs of transacting business. In the Coasian framework, as developed and expanded by Williamson (1975, 1985, 1996), Klein, Crawford, and Alchian (1978), and Grossman and Hart (1986), the decision to organize transactions within the firm as opposed to on the open market—the "make or buy decision"—depends on the relative costs of internal versus external exchange. The market mechanism entails certain costs: discovering the relevant prices, negotiating and

---

[4]For critiques of instrumentalism see Rizzo (1978) and Batemarco (1985). For references to the interpretive literature on Milton Friedman's 1953 essay on "positive economics"—the source of most economists' views on method—see Boland (1979), Caldwell (1980), and Musgrave (1981); all reprinted in Caldwell (1984) along with De Marchi (1988).

enforcing contracts, and so on. Within the firm, the entrepreneur may be able to reduce these "transaction costs" by coordinating these activities himself. However, internal organization brings another kind of transaction cost, namely problems of information flows, incentives, monitoring, and performance evaluation. The boundary of the firm, then, is determined by the tradeoff, at the margin, between the relative transaction costs of external and internal exchange. In this sense, firm boundaries depend not only on technology, but on organizational considerations; that is, on the costs and benefits of contracting.

The relative costs of external and internal exchange depend on particular characteristics of transaction: the degree to which relationship-specific assets are involved, the amount of uncertainty about the future and about trading partners' actions, the complexity of the trading arrangement, and the frequency with which the transaction occurs. Each matters in determining the preferred institutional arrangement (that is, internal versus external production), although the first—"asset specificity"—is held to be particularly important. Williamson (1985, p. 55) defines asset specificity as "durable investments that are undertaken in support of particular transactions, the opportunity cost of which investments are much lower in best alternative uses or by alternative users should the original transaction be prematurely terminated." This could describe a variety of relationship-specific investments, including both specialized physical and human capital, along with intangibles such as R&D and firm-specific knowledge or capabilities.

Economic Calculation and the Limits to Firm Size

Unfortunately, the growing economics literature on the theory of the firm focuses mostly on the costs of market exchange, and much less on the costs of governing internal exchange. The new research has yet to produce a fully satisfactory explanation of the limits to firm size (Williamson, 1985, chap. 6). In Coase's words, "Why does the entrepreneur not organize one less transaction or one more?" Or, more generally, "Why is not all production carried on in one big firm?" (Coase, 1937, pp. 393–94). The theory of the limits to the firm is perhaps the most difficult and least well developed part of the new economics of organization. Existing contractual explanations rely on problems of authority and responsibility (Arrow, 1974);

incentive distortions caused by residual ownership rights (Grossman and Hart, 1986; Hart and Moore, 1990; Hart, 1995); and the costs of attempting to reproduce market governance features within the firm (Williamson, 1985, chap. 6). It is here that Austrian theory has an obvious contribution to make, by applying Mises's theorem on the impossibility of economic calculation under socialism. Rothbard has shown how the need for monetary calculation in terms of actual prices not only explains the failures of central planning under socialism, but places an upper bound on firm size.

The Socialist Calculation Debate: A Brief Review

To understand Mises's position in the calculation debate, one must realize that his argument is not exclusively, or even primarily, about socialism. It is about the role of prices for capital goods. Entrepreneurs make decisions about resource allocation based on their expectations about future prices, and the information contained in present prices. To make profits, they need information about all prices, not only the prices of consumer goods but the prices of factors of production. Without markets for capital goods, these goods can have no prices, and hence entrepreneurs cannot make judgments about the relative scarcities of these factors. In short, resources cannot be allocated efficiently. In any environment, then—socialist or not—where a factor of production has no market price, a potential user of that factor will be unable to make rational decisions about its use. Stated this way, Mises's claim is simply that efficient resource allocation in a market economy requires well-functioning asset markets. Because scholars differ about what Mises "really meant," however, it may be useful here to provide a brief review of the debate.

Before 1920, according to the standard account,[5] socialist theorists paid little attention to how a socialist economy would work in practice, most heeding Marx's admonition to avoid such "utopian" speculation. Then Mises, known at the time mainly as a monetary theorist, published the sensational article later translated as "Economic Calculation in the Socialist Commonwealth" (1920).[6] Mises claimed that without private

---

[5]For examples of the "standard account" of the calculation debate see Schumpeter (1942, pp. 172–86) and Bergson (1948). My discussion of the "revisionist view" follows Hoff (1949), Salerno (1990a), and Rothbard (1991).

[6]Other works that made arguments similar to that of Mises include N. G. Pierson's

ownership of the means of production, there would be no market prices for capital goods, and therefore no way for decision-makers to evaluate the relative efficiency of various production techniques. Anticipating the later argument for "market socialism," Mises argued that even if there were markets for consumer goods, a central planner could not "impute" meaningful prices to capital goods used to produce them. In short, without market-generated prices for both capital and consumer goods, even the most dedicated planner would find it "impossible" to allocate resources according to consumer wants.

Throughout the 1920s and early 1930s Mises's argument became the focus of intense discussion within the German-language literature. Eventually it was agreed that Mises was correct at least to point out that a socialist society could not do without such things as money and prices, as some early socialists had suggested, and that there was no feasible way to set prices according, say, to quantities of labor time. Nonetheless, it was felt that Vilfredo Pareto and his follower Enrico Barone (1908) had shown that nothing was "theoretically" wrong with socialism, because the requisite number of demand and supply equations to make the system "determinate" would exist under either capitalism or socialism. If the planners could somehow get the necessary information on preferences and technology, they could in principle compute an equilibrium allocation of final goods.

The most important response to Mises, however, and the one almost universally accepted by economists, was what became known as "market socialism" or the "mathematical solution," developed by Fred Taylor (1929), H. D. Dickinson (1933), Abba Lerner (1934), and Oskar Lange (1936–37). In a system of market socialism, capital goods are collective property, but individuals are free to own and exchange final goods and services. The system would work like this. First, the Central Planning Board chooses arbitrary prices for consumer and capital goods. At those prices, the managers of the various state-owned enterprises are instructed to produce up to the point where the marginal cost of each final good is equal to its price, and then to choose the input mix that minimizes the average cost of producing that quantity. Then, consumer goods prices are

---

"The Problem of Value in the Socialist Community" (1902) and parts of Max Weber's *Economy and Society* (1921).

allowed to fluctuate, and the Central Planning Board adjusts the prices of capital goods as shortages and surpluses of the final goods develop. Resources would thus be allocated according to supply and demand, through a process of "trial-and-error" essentially the same as that practiced by the managers of capitalist firms. Lange's contribution, it has generally been held, was to show that production under market socialism could be just as efficient as production under capitalism, since the socialist planners "would receive exactly the same information from a socialized economic system as did entrepreneurs under a market system" (Heilbroner, 1970, p. 88).[7]

Market socialism was seen as an answer not only to Mises's calculation problem, but also to the issue of "practicality" raised by Hayek and Lionel Robbins. Hayek, in his contributions to *Collectivist Economic Planning* (Hayek, 1935), later expanded in "The Competitive Solution" (1940) and his well-known papers "Economics and Knowledge" (1937) and "The Use of Knowledge in Society" (1945), and Robbins, in his *The Great Depression* (1934), had changed the terms of the debate by focusing not on the problem of calculation, but on the problem of knowledge. For Hayek and Robbins, the failure of socialist organization is due to a mechanism design problem, in that planners cannot allocate resources efficiently because they cannot obtain complete information on consumer preferences and resource availability. Furthermore, even if the planners were somehow able to acquire these data, it would take years to compute the millions of prices used by a modern economy. The Lange–Lerner–Taylor approach claimed to solve this preference-revelation problem by trial-and-error, so no actual computations would be necessary.[8]

---

[7] It would no doubt be gratuitous to point out that since the collapse of central planning in Eastern Europe the writer of that comment has changed his mind, writing that although fifty years ago, it was felt that Lange had decisively won the argument for socialist planning, "now it turns out, of course, that Mises was right" (Heilbroner, 1990, p. 92).

[8] Lange actually claimed years later that even market socialism would be made obsolete with the advent of high-speed computers, which could instantly solve the huge system of simultaneous equations for the central planner. "Were I to rewrite my [1936] essay today my task would be much simpler. My answer to Hayek and Robbins would be: So what's the trouble? Let us put the simultaneous equations on an electronic computer and we shall obtain the solution in less than a second. The market process with its cumbersome *tâtonnements* appears old-fashioned. Indeed, it may be considered as a computing device of the pre-electronic age" (Lange, 1965, pp. 401–02). Obviously, Lange did not have much

With the widespread acceptance of the theory of market socialism, there developed an "orthodox line" on the socialist calculation debate, neatly summarized in Abram Bergson's well-known survey of "Socialist Economics" (1948) and in Joseph Schumpeter's *Capitalism, Socialism and Democracy* (1942, pp. 172–86). According to this line, Mises first raised the problem of the possibility of economic calculation under socialism, only to be refuted by Pareto and Barone; Hayek and Robbins then "retreated" to the position that socialist planners could calculate in theory, but that in practice the information problem would make this too difficult; then the market socialists showed that trial and error would eliminate the need for complete information on the part of the planners. Therefore, the argument goes, economic theory *per se* can say nothing conclusive about the viability of central planning, and the choice between capitalism and socialism must be purely political.

Calculation versus Incentives

The orthodox line on socialist planning has been modified in recent years with the development of incentive and information theory. The differences between capitalism and socialism, it is now typically held, lie in the different incentive properties of the two systems. Centrally directed systems are thought to be subject to greater agency costs—managerial discretion, shirking, and so on—than market systems (see, for example Winiecki, 1990). After all, Lange himself warned that "*the real danger of socialism is that of a bureaucratization of economic life*" (Lange, 1936–37, p. 109; italics in original).

As has been pointed out elsewhere (Rothbard, 1991, pp. 51–52), however, the calculation debate was not primarily about agency or managerial incentives. The incentive problem had long been known[9] (if not fully developed) and was expressed in the famous question: "Under socialism, who will take out the garbage?" That is, if everyone is compensated "according to his needs," what will be the incentive to do the dirty and unpleasant

---

experience with a computer. Also, during his time as chairman of the Polish Economic Council in the 1950s, Lange never tried to put market socialism into practice (see Lange, 1958).

[9]We tend to forget just how old the idea of socialism is, that it is not a twentieth-century invention; the subtitle of Alexander Gray's famous book *The Socialist Tradition* (1946) is "Moses to Lenin."

tasks; or, for that matter, any tasks at all? The traditional socialist answer was that self-interest is a product of capitalism, and that socialism would bring about a change in human nature. In the worker's paradise would emerge a "New Socialist Man," eager to serve and motivated only by the needs of his fellows. These early theorists seem to have assumed, to borrow the expression used by Oliver Williamson (1991a, p. 18) in a critique of a more recent socialist proposal, "the abolition of opportunism by agencies of the state." Experience has exposed the charming naiveté of such notions.

But Mises's challenge to socialism is distinct from this well-known incentive problem.[10] Assume for the moment that everyone is willing to work just as hard under central direction as under a market system. There still remains the problem of exactly what directives the Central Planning Board will issue. The Board will have to decide what goods and services should be produced, how much of each to produce, what intermediate goods are needed to produce each final good, and so on. In a complex, modern economy with multiple stages of production, resource allocation requires the existence of money prices for capital goods, prices that under capitalism arise from an ongoing process of competitive bidding by entrepreneurs for the factors of production. This process cannot be replicated by input-output analysis, computer simulations, or any other form of artificial market. Mises's main point was that socialism fails because decision makers require meaningful prices for all of these factors to choose from the vast array of possible factor combinations. "Without recourse to calculating and comparing the benefits and costs of production using the structure of monetary prices determined at each moment on the market, the human mind is only capable of surveying, evaluating, and directing production processes whose scope is drastically reduced to the compass of the primitive household economy" (Salerno, 1990a, p. 52).

The distinction between calculation and incentives is important because the modern economics literature on organizational design—from transaction cost explanations of firm size, to public choice theories of bureaucracy, to recent work on market socialism and the "soft budget constraint" (Kornai, 1986)—focuses primarily on incentive problems (possi-

---

[10]Mises does devote a section of the 1920 paper to "Responsibility and Initiative in Communal Concerns," but he clearly considers this a secondary problem for socialist planners, not the primary one. In the book-length treatment, *Socialism* (1922), Mises discusses the incentive problem in greater detail (pp. 163–84).

bly encouraged by Lange's famous warning about bureaucracy). Incentive theory asks how, within a specified relationship, a principal can get an agent to do what he wants him to do. Mises's problem, however, was different: How does the principal know what to tell the agent to do? That is, just what activities ought to be undertaken? What investments should be made? Which product lines expanded and which ones contracted? The ideas developed in the calculation debate suggest that when organizations are large enough to conduct activities that are exclusively internal—so that no reference to the outside market is available—they will face a calculation problem as well as an incentive problem.

In this sense, market-socialist proposals are mostly irrelevant to the real problems of socialist organization. This is the case Mises himself sought to make in his critique of market socialism in *Human Action* (Mises, 1949, pp. 694–711). There he complained that the market socialists—and, for that matter, all general equilibrium theorists—misconceive the nature of "the economic problem." Lange, Lerner, and Taylor looked primarily at the problem of consumer goods pricing, while the crucial problem facing a modern economy concerns the capital structure: namely, in what way should capital be allocated to various activities? The market economy, Mises argued, is driven not by "management"—the performance of specified tasks, within a framework given to the manager—but by *entrepreneurship*, the speculation, arbitrage, and other risk-bearing activities that determine just what the managerial tasks are. It is not managers but entrepreneurs, acting in the capital and money markets, who establish and dissolve corporations, create and destroy product lines, and so on. These are precisely the activities that even market socialism seeks to abolish. In other words, to the extent that incentives are important, what socialism cannot preserve are high-powered incentives not in management, but in entrepreneurial forecasting and decision making.

Mises has been described as saying that it is unreasonable to expect managers of socialist enterprises to "play market," to act as if they were managers of private firms where their own direct interests were at stake. This may be true, but Mises's prime concern was that entrepreneurs cannot be asked to "play speculation and investment" (Mises, 1949, p. 705). The relevant incentive problem, he maintains, is not that of the subordinate manager (the agent), who takes the problem to be solved as given, but that of the speculator and investor (the principal), who decides just what is the problem to be solved. Lange, Lerner, and Taylor see the market through a strictly static, neoclassical lens, where all the parameters of the system are given and only a computational problem needs to be solved. In fact the market economy is a dynamic, creative, evolving process, in which entrepreneurs—using economic calculation—make industries grow and shrink, cause new and different production methods to be tried and others withdrawn, and constantly change the range of available products. It is these features of market capitalism, and not the incentives of agents to work hard, that are lost without private property ownership.

Indeed, traditional command-style economies, such as that of the former USSR, appear to be able only to mimic those tasks that market economies have performed before; they are unable to set up and execute original tasks.

> The [Soviet] system has been particularly effective when the central priorities involve catching up, for then the problems of knowing what to do, when and how to do it, and whether it was properly done, are solved by reference to a working model, by exploiting what Gerschenkron ... called the "advantage of backwardness." ... Accompanying these advantages are shortcomings, inherent in the nature of the system. When the system pursues a few priority objectives, regardless of sacrifices or losses in lower priority areas, those ultimately responsible cannot know whether the success was worth achieving. The central authorities lack the information and physical capability to monitor all important costs—in particular opportunity costs—yet they are the only ones, given the logic of the system, with a true interest in knowing such costs. (Ericson, 1991, p. 21).

Without economic calculation, there is no way to figure out if tasks have been performed efficiently. Hence without markets for physical and financial capital—which determine what tasks will be performed and whether they have been performed adequately—an economic system has difficulty generating anything *new*, and must rely on outside references to tell it what to do. Of course, the only reason the Soviet Union and the communist nations of Eastern Europe could exist at all is that they never fully succeeded in establishing socialism worldwide, so they could use world market prices to establish implicit prices for the goods they bought and sold internally (Rothbard, 1991, pp. 73–74). In Mises's words, these economies were not isolated social systems. They were operating in an environment in which the price system still worked. They could resort to economic calculation on the ground of the prices established abroad. Without the aid of these prices their actions would have been aimless and planless. Only because they were able to refer to these foreign prices were they able to calculate, to keep books, and to prepare their much talked about plans. (Mises, 1949, pp. 698–99).

As we will see below, the firm is in the same situation: it needs outside market prices to plan and evaluate its actions.

Rothbard and the Limits of Organization

Rothbard's main contribution to the theory of the firm was to generalize Mises's analysis of the problem of resource allocation under socialism to the context of vertical integration and the size of the organization. Rothbard writes in *Man, Economy, and State* that up to a point, the size of the firm is determined by costs, as in the textbook model. But "the ultimate limits are set on the relative size of the firm by the necessity for *markets* to exist in every factor, in order to make it possible for the firm to calculate its profits and losses" (Rothbard, 1962, p. 599). This argument hinges on the notion of "implicit costs." The market value of opportunity costs for factor services—what Rothbard calls "estimates of implicit incomes"—can be determined only if there are external markets for those factors (pp. 607–09). For example, if an entrepreneur hires himself to manage his business, the opportunity cost of his labor must be included in the firm's costs. But without an actual market for the entrepreneur's managerial services, he will be unable to figure out his opportunity cost; his balance sheets will therefore be less accurate than they would if he could measure his opportunity cost.

The same problem affects a firm owning multiple stages of production. A large, integrated firm is typically organized as groups of semi-autonomous business units or "profit centers," each unit or division specializing in a particular final or intermediate product. The central management of the firm uses the implicit incomes of the business units, as reflected in statements of divisional profit and loss, to allocate physical and financial capital across the divisions. More profitable divisions are expanded, while less profitable divisions are scaled back. Suppose the firm has an upstream division selling an intermediate component to a downstream division. To compute the divisional profits and losses, the firm needs an economically meaningful "transfer price" for the component. If there is an external market for the component, the firm can use that market price as the transfer price.[11] Without a market price, however, a transfer price must be estimated in another way.

In practice, this is typically done on a cost-plus basis; sometimes, the buying and selling divisions are left free to bargain over the price (Eccles and White, 1988; Shelanski, 1993; King, 1994). At the very least, any artificial or substitute transfer prices will contain less information than actual market prices; Rothbard (1962, p. 613) puts it more strongly, calling a substitute price "only an arbitrary symbol." In either case, firms relying on these prices will suffer. "Not being able to calculate a price, the firm could not rationally allocate factors and resources from one stage [or division] to another" (Rothbard, 1962, p. 613) The use of internally traded intermediate goods for which no external market reference is available introduces distortions that reduce organizational efficiency. This gives us the element missing from contemporary theories of economic organization, an upper bound: the firm is constrained by the need for external markets for all internally traded goods. In other words, no firm can become so large that it is both the unique producer and user of an intermediate product; for then no market-based transfer prices will be available, and the firm will be unable to calculate divisional profit and loss and therefore unable to allocate resources correctly between divisions. As Rothbard puts it:

> Since the free market always tends to establish the most efficient
> and profitable type of production (whether for type of good,

---

[11] Rothbard (1962, pp. 612, n. 56) notes that the implicit transfer price may be somewhat more or less than the existing market price, since the entry of either the buying or the selling division into the external market may bid the price up or down slightly. Unlike Hirshleifer (1956), then, Rothbard does not require the external market to be perfectly competitive for a market-based transfer price to be economically meaningful. For Rothbard, "thin" markets are adequate: all that is necessary to have a genuine "external market" is the existence of at least one other producer (seller) of the intermediate good. (Of course, if external prices are perfectly competitive, then the economy must be in a competitive general equilibrium, in which information is perfect and all contracts are complete, and in which there is thus no need for firms.) Rothbard does not discuss the potential "holdup" problem that follows from relationship-specific investment under bilateral monopoly (Klein, Crawford, and Alchian, 1978), which should be considered a cost of reliance on an external market with a single supplier.

method of production, allocation of factors, or size of firm), we must conclude that complete vertical integration for a capital-good product can never be established on the free market (above the primitive level). *For every capital good, there must be a definite market in which firms buy and sell that good.* It is obvious that this economic law *sets a definite maximum to the relative size of any particular firm on the free market....* Economic calculation becomes ever more important as the market economy develops and progresses, as the stages and the complexities of type and variety of capital goods increase. Ever more important for the maintenance of an advanced economy, then, is the preservation of markets for all the capital and other producers' goods. (Rothbard, 1962, p. 613; italics in original)

Like the centrally planned economy, the firm needs market signals to guide its actions; without them the firm cannot survive. Note that in general, Rothbard is making a claim only about the upper bound of the firm, not the incremental cost of expanding the firm's activities (as long as external market references are available). As soon as the firm expands to the point where at least one external market has disappeared, however, the calculation problem exists. The difficulties become worse as more and more external markets disappear, as "islands of noncalculable chaos swell to the proportions of masses and continents. As the area of incalculability increases, the degrees of irrationality, misallocation, loss, impoverishment, etc., become greater" (p. 548). In other words, the firm is limited by the extent to which markets exist for the goods it allocates internally. Without market prices for these goods, the firm must rely on relatively costly and inefficient methods of generating its own accounting prices, to perform internal calculations.[12]

Significantly, it is at this point in the discussion in *Man, Economy, and State* (p. 548) that Rothbard launches into a discussion of the socialist calculation debate, making it obvious that the two issues are inextricably linked. The reason that a socialist economy cannot calculate is not that

---

[12]This does not mean that because external prices are necessary for large firms to function efficiently, firms will necessarily become larger where external markets are "thick" or better developed. On the contrary, large firms typically arise precisely where external markets are poorly developed or hampered by government intervention; these are the kinds of circumstances that give entrepreneurs an advantage in coordinating activities internally. However, such firms are still constrained by the need for some external market reference.

it is socialist, but because a single agent owns and directs all resources. Expanding on this point in his 1976 essay on "Ludwig von Mises and Economic Calculation Under Socialism," Rothbard explains:

> There is one vital but neglected area where the Mises analysis of economic calculation needs to be expanded. For in a profound sense, the theory is not about socialism at all! Instead, it applies to any situation where one group has acquired control of the means of production over a large area—or, in a strict sense, throughout the world. On this particular aspect of socialism, it doesn't matter whether this unitary control has come about through the coercive expropriation brought about by socialism or by voluntary processes on the free market. For what the Mises theory focuses on is not simply the numerous inefficiencies of the political as compared to the profit-making market process, but the fact that a market for capital goods has disappeared. This means that, just as socialist central planning could not calculate economically, no One Big Firm could own or control the entire economy. The Mises analysis applies to any situation where a market for capital goods has disappeared in a complex industrial economy, whether because of socialism or because of a giant merger into One Big Firm or One Big Cartel. (Rothbard, 1976, p. 75)

The Mises analysis thus applies to any situation where the market for a particular capital good disappears because a firm has become so large that it is the unique producer and user of that capital good. As we have seen, such a firm will not be viable.

It is surprising that Rothbard's extension of Mises's argument has received virtually no attention in the Austrian literature, even though the point appears four times in *Man, Economy, and State* (p. 536, p. 543, pp. 547–48, and p. 585) and again in the 1976 essay.[13] The argument needs further development and elaboration, which should prove a useful exercise because the contemporary literature on the size of the firm lacks an

---

[13]Lavoie briefly notes the Rothbard analysis in his *Rivalry and Central Planning* (1985, p. 62n). Fritz Machlup, in a comment on Rothbard's 1976 essay, says he is "intrigued" by the analogy between the central planner's problem and the firm's problem, calling it "an issue I have tried to sell in several of my publications ... but unfortunately not with sufficient success" (Machlup, 1976a, p. 114). He cites an early book (Machlup, 1934, esp. pp. 209–14) and a later article (Machlup, 1974, esp. pp. 42–45 and 52–54), both published in German, on the problem of "artificial" transfer prices. The argument is also foreshadowed by Hayek in *Prices and Production* (1931, p. 63) in a discussion on vertical integration.

adequate explanation for the limits to organization. The Rothbard analysis also suggests a line of research in business strategy: all else equal, firms able to use market-based transfer prices should outperform, in the long run, firms using administered or negotiated transfer prices.[14] As of yet, there is little empirical work on this topic, despite a growing interest in Austrian economics within the strategic management field (Jacobson, 1992; Lewin and Phelan, 1999; Foss and Mahnke, 2000; Langlois, 2001; Roberts and Eisenhardt, 2003; Yu, 2003; Ng, 2005; Mathews, 2006).

A related issue that has received considerable attention, however, is the difficulty of allocating overhead or fixed cost across divisions. If an input is essentially indivisible (or nonexcludable), then there is no way to compute the opportunity cost of just the portion of the input used by a particular division (see Rogerson, 1992, for a discussion of these problems).[15] Firms with high overhead costs should thus be at a disadvantage relative to firms able to allocate costs more precisely between business units. Indeed, in the literature on cost accounting there has been some recent interest in "market simulation accounting" (Staubus, 1986), by which firms try to assess the price at which an asset would trade in an active market, based on observed market prices and related information. The Rothbardian position on the limits to firm size suggests that the market simulation approach may prove a useful accounting technique.

By the time of the 1976 paper, Rothbard had adopted an explicitly Coasian framework in his discussion of the limits to firm size. His own treatment, Rothbard says,

> serves to extend the notable analysis of Professor Coase on the market determinants of the size of the firm, or the relative extent of corporate planning within the firm as against the use of exchange and the price mechanism. Coase pointed out that there are diminishing benefits and increasing costs to each of these two alternatives, resulting, as he put it, in an " 'optimum' amount of planning" in

---

[14]This line of reasoning has interesting implications for the study of innovation. Since the innovating firm is more likely to be using unique intermediate goods, particularly in industries where few of the relevant manufacturing capabilities exist in the market (Langlois and Robertson, 1995), innovation carries with its benefits the cost of more severe internal distortions. Economic calculation is then another obstacle the innovator must overcome.

[15]Mises (1944, p. 32) recognized the problem of allocating overhead costs, mentioning this as a possible exception to the notion that divisional accounting costs can reflect "true" costs.

the free market system. Our thesis adds that the costs of internal corporate planning become prohibitive as soon as markets for capital goods begin to disappear, so that the free-market optimum will always stop well short not only of One Big Firm throughout the world market but also of any disappearance of specific markets and hence of economic calculation in that product or resource. (Rothbard, 1976, p. 76)

This is noteworthy because even as late as 1972, Coase was describing his 1937 paper as "much cited and little used" (Coase, 1972, p. 62). Alchian and Demsetz's "Production, Information Costs, and Economic Organization" came out only in 1972, and Williamson's *Markets and Hierarchies* in 1975. Rothbard was thus among the earliest writers to develop and extend the Coasian perspective.

Alternative Austrian Approaches

There is some debate within the Austrian literature about whether the basic Coasian approach is compatible with Austrian economics. O'Driscoll and Rizzo (1985, p. 124), while acknowledging Coase's approach as an "excellent static conceptualization of the problem," argue that a more evolutionary framework is needed to understand how firms respond to change. Some Austrian economists have suggested that the Coasian framework may be too narrow, too squarely in the general-equilibrium tradition to deal adequately with Austrian concerns (Boudreaux and Holcombe, 1989; Langlois, 1994a). They contend that the contemporary theory of the firm, following Coase, retains the perspective of static equilibrium analysis and profit maximization over a fixed set of outcomes with known probabilities. As an alternative, some writers propose the framework in Frank Knight's *Risk, Uncertainty, and Profit* (1921). The Knightian framework, they argue, offers genuine uncertainty, disequilibrium and process analysis, and thus a scope for real entrepreneurship—aspects purportedly more congenial to Austrians. "The Coasian and Knightian theories of the firm deal with the issue [of the existence of firms] from two different vantage points. The Coasian theory takes the inputs and outputs in the firm's production process as given, and models the firm as an organization that acts to minimize the costs of transforming these inputs into outputs.... However, in Knight's model, entrepreneurship is the primary role of the firm (Boudreaux and Holcombe, 1989, p. 152). Williamson's transaction cost economics, as characterized by Langlois (1994a, p. 175), does broaden the notion of cost minimization to include transaction costs as well as production costs, but it remains essentially a static exercise with a limited role for expectations: "Seldom does the theory give thought to the possibility that organizational forms may be influenced as much by environments that exist only as future possibilities, imagined or feared."

To be sure, the Knightian concept of the profit-seeking entrepreneur, investing resources under uncertainty, is one of the great contributions to the theory of the firm. As discussed in chapters 4, 5, and 6 below, it is close to Mises's concept of the entrepreneur (closer, in my view, than Israel Kirzner's understanding of entrepreneurship). Still, these critiques of the Coasian framework paint with too broad a brush; as Foss (1993c) points out, there are "two Coasian traditions." One tradition, the nexus-of-contracts branch associated with Alchian and Demsetz (1972), studies the design of *ex ante* mechanisms to limit shirking when supervision is costly. Here the emphasis is on monitoring and incentives in an (exogenously determined) moral-hazard relationship. The aforementioned criticisms may apply to this branch of the modern literature, but they do not apply to the other tradition, the governance or asset-specificity branch, especially in Williamson's more heterodox formulation. Williamson's transaction cost framework incorporates non-maximizing behavior (bounded rationality); true, "structural" uncertainty or genuine surprise (complete contracts are held not to be feasible, meaning that all *ex post* contingencies cannot be contracted upon *ex ante*); and process or adaptation over time (trading relationships develop over time, typically undergoing a "fundamental transformation" that changes the terms of trade). In short, "at least some modern theories of the firm do not at all presuppose the 'closed' economic universe—with all relevant inputs and outputs being given, human action conceptualized as maximization, etc., that [some critics] claim are underneath the contemporary theory of the firm" (Foss, 1993a, p. 274). Stated differently, one can adopt an essentially Coasian perspective without abandoning the Knightian or Austrian view of the entrepreneur as an uncertainty-bearing, innovating decision-maker.[16]

---

[16]Nor do all Coasian perspectives deny the importance of specialized knowledge lines in determining a firm's capabilities or "core competence." Transaction cost economics, for example, simply holds that the need for *ex post* governance of contracts in the presence

Similarly, the approach described in this chapter differs from that advanced in the literature on "market-based management" (Ellig, 1993; Ellig and Gable, 1993; Koch, 2007). Market-based management is the philosophy that firm success depends critically on the ability to replicate market-like features within the organization. One of these is "internal markets" for intermediate goods (and services such as financial, legal, accounting, and R&D support) along with the establishment of strict profit-center divisions. Like market prices, these internal prices convey information about local circumstances. Other features include an explicit "mission" or recognition of the firm's core competence, clearly defined roles and responsibilities for lower-level employees (analogous to property rights in a market economy), employee rewards based on performance (a profit-and-loss system), a well-defined "corporate culture" (customs, behavioral norms), and decentralized decision making.

Underlying market-based management is the team-production or nexus-of-contracts model of the firm advanced by Alchian and Demsetz (1972), supplemented with the "capabilities" theory of Edith Penrose (1959), G. B. Richardson (1972), David Teece (1980; 1982), and others. But the market-based management literature, like other writings in the nexus-of-contracts tradition, appears to mischaracterize the nature of "planning" within the firm. For example, it attributes to the Coase–Williamson tradition the view that "internal markets are doomed to failure, because the business firm is by nature a command hierarchy" (Ellig, 1993, p. 9). The Coasian tradition, however, does not imply that firms do or should adopt a command-and-control structure; on the contrary, as we have already seen, the modern firm will tend to be significantly decentralized, so that managers and workers at all levels of operations can make use of local knowledge. All decisions are not made from above, by executive fiat; the "M-form" corporation described by Williamson and Chandler is a blend of market and hierarchy, of centralization and decentralization.

In other words, the entrepreneur does make some decisions by "fiat"; the firm is definitely a *taxis*, rather than a *cosmos* (to use Hayek's esoteric

of relationship-specific investments, and not "tacit knowledge" *per se*, is the most useful way to think about the boundaries of the firm. For the case that Austrian economics is more compatible with the capabilities literature (for substantive, not only methodological, reasons), see Minkler (1993b) and Langlois (1994a).

terminology).[17] This does not imply, however, that all decisions must be made from the top; we can agree with the market-based management literature that "neither central planning nor command-and-control are the defining characteristics of a business firm" (Ellig, 1993, p. 11). Indeed, given competition in the product and factor markets, firms will always tend to select the optimum amount of "market-like" features. The firm's problem, then, is not too much "conscious" planning; the crucial issue is whether these plans are made, and tested, from within a larger market setting. The entrepreneur's plans can be carried out, as we saw above, only when there are definite markets for all internally traded goods or activities. What firms need is not necessarily internal markets, but the information generated by market prices.

Conclusion

This chapter has highlighted some Austrian contributions to the theory of the firm and suggested directions for future research along the same lines. In particular, Rothbard's argument about the need for markets in intermediate goods, and how that places limits on the scale and scope of the organization, deserves further development. The chapter also points the way toward an Austrian approach that makes the entrepreneur, and his acts of resource allocation using monetary calculation, central to the theory of the firm.

---

[17] See also Tullock (1969).

CHAPTER 2

Entrepreneurship and Corporate Governance[†]

In his "closing salvo" in the socialist calculation debate, Mises (1949, pp. 694–711) argued that the market socialists failed to understand the role of financial markets in an industrial economy. Even with markets for consumer goods, he explained, socialism would fail because it substituted collective ownership of the means of production for private capital markets. Through these markets, owners of financial capital decide which firms, and which industries, receive resources to make consumer goods. In a modern economy, most production takes place in publicly held corporations. Of prime importance, then, is the problem of corporate governance: How do owners of financial capital structure their agreements with those who receive that capital, to prevent its misuse? Unfortunately, there exists little research in this area from an Austrian perspective.

In this chapter, I focus on the financial-market entrepreneur—what Rothbard (1962, 1985) calls the capitalist-entrepreneur—to outline some features of an Austrian theory of corporate governance. I begin by reviewing the traditional, production-function theory of the firm and suggesting two alternative perspectives: that of the entrepreneur and that of the

[†]Published originally in *Quarterly Journal of Austrian Economics* 2, no. 2 (Summer 1999): 19–42. A Spanish translation, "Función empresarial y control de la dirección de le empresa," appeared in *Libertas* 16, no. 31 (October 1999): 3–49.

capitalist. I next discuss the Coasian, or "contractual" approach to the firm and argue that it provides a useful organizing framework for Austrian research on the firm. The subsequent section proposes entrepreneurship and economic calculation as building blocks for an Austrian theory of the firm. Finally, after a brief review of capital-market behavior and the disciplinary role of takeovers, I outline four areas for Austrian research in corporate governance: firms as investments, internal capital markets, comparative corporate governance, and financiers as entrepreneurs.

Limits of the Standard Approach to the Firm

As we saw in chapter 1, the "firm" of economics textbooks is not really a firm at all. The firm is treated as a production function or production possibilities set, a "black box" that transforms inputs into outputs. While descriptively vacuous, the production-function approach has the appeal of analytical tractability along with its elegant parallel to neoclassical consumer theory (profit maximization is like utility maximization, isoquants are indifference curves, and so on). Nonetheless, many economists now see it as increasingly unsatisfactory, as unable to account for a variety of real-world business practices: vertical and lateral integration, mergers, geographic and product-line diversification, franchising, long-term commercial contracting, transfer pricing, research joint ventures, and many others. The inadequacy of the traditional theory of the firm explains much of the recent interest in agency theory, transaction cost economics, the capabilities approach, and other facets of the "new institutional economics."[1] A more serious problem with the traditional theory, however, has received less attention. The theory of profit maximization is nearly always told from the perspective of the manager, the agent who operates the plant, not that of the owner, who supplies the capital to fund the plant. Yet owners control how much authority to delegate to operational managers, so capitalists are the ultimate decision makers. To understand the firm, then, we must focus on the actions and plans of the suppliers of financial capital.

Focusing on capital markets and the corporate governance problem highlights a fundamental analytical problem with the traditional approach

---

[1] The new institutional economics is reviewed and critiqued in Furubotn and Richter (1997), Klein (2000), Williamson (2000), Ménard and Shirley (2005) and Brousseau and Glachant (2008).

to the theory of the firm. In the production-function approach, money capital is treated as a factor of production. The manager's objective is to maximize the difference between total revenues and total costs, with the cost of capital treated simply as another cost (and typically assumed to be exogenous). The residual, "profit," is retained by the manager. Hence financial capital receives scant attention. As discussed below, this can be a serious flaw.

Two Alternative Perspectives

What, then, is the proper way to understand the business firm? Two alternative perspectives deserve consideration. The first perspective, which has received substantial attention in the Austrian literature, is that of the entrepreneur, or what Mises (1949, p. 256) calls the "entrepreneur-promoter." Entrepreneurship, in the Misesian sense, is the act of bearing uncertainty. Production unfolds through time, and thus the entrepreneur must purchase factors of production in the present (paying today's prices, which are known), in anticipation of revenues from the future sale of the product (at tomorrow's prices, which are uncertain). Entrepreneurial profit or loss is the difference between these revenues and the initial outlays, less the general rate of interest. As such, profit is the reward for successfully bearing uncertainty. Successful promoters make accurate forecasts of future prices and receive returns greater than their outlays. Those whose forecasts are less accurate earn losses. Promoters who systematically make poor forecasts quickly find themselves unable to secure any further resources for investment and eventually exit the market.[2]

The second perspective is that of the capitalist, the owner of the firm. Ownership can also be thought of as a factor of production—what Rothbard (1962, pp. 601–05) calls the "decision making factor"—but it is

---

[2]Mises (1949, p. 254) defines the entrepreneurial function broadly, referring to "the aspect of uncertainty inherent in every action." He quotes the English idiom: "There's many a slip 'twixt cup and lip" (p. 254). He defines entrepreneur-promoters more narrowly, as uncertainty-bearers "who are especially eager to profit from adjusting production to the expected changes in conditions, those who have more initiative, more venturesomeness, and a quicker eye than the crowd, the pushing and promoting pioneers of economic improvement." He laments that the same word, "entrepreneurship," has been used both for the general concept of uncertainty-bearing and the narrower role of the bold, active, creative, business person.

different from the other factors. In an ownership approach, money capital is treated as a unique factor of production, the "controlling factor"; the investor is both ultimate decision-maker and residual claimant. The firm's objective is to maximize the return on the owner's investment. Because the owner delegates certain functions to managers, a central focus of the theory of the firm becomes the problem of corporate governance: how do suppliers of capital structure their arrangements with managers in a way that maximizes their returns?

This chapter argues that the most interesting problems in the theory of the firm relate to the intersection between the entrepreneurial function and the capitalist function. Indeed, as Mises argued, the driving force behind the market economy is a particular type of entrepreneur, the capitalist-entrepreneur, who risks his money capital in anticipation of future, uncertain, returns. Moreover, as discussed below, the entrepreneur is nearly always also a capitalist, and the capitalist is also an entrepreneur.

Economists now increasingly recognize the importance of the capitalist in the direction of the firm's affairs. In the introduction to his influential book *Strong Managers, Weak Owners*, Mark Roe (1994, p. vii) makes the point succinctly:

> Economic theory once treated the firm as a collection of machinery, technology, inventory, workers, and capital. Dump these inputs into a black box, stir them up, and one got outputs of products and profits. Today, theory sees the firm as more, as a management structure. The firm succeeds if managers can successfully coordinate the firm's activities; it fails if managers cannot effectively coordinate and match people and inputs to current technologies and markets. At the very top of the firm are the relationships among the firm's shareholders, its directors, and its senior managers. If those relationships are dysfunctional, the firm is more likely to stumble.

As Roe suggests, the relationships between the firm's owners (shareholders) and its top managers are centrally important in determining firm performance.[3]

---

[3]For surveys of the literature on corporate governance see Gilson (1996); Shleifer and Vishny (1997) and Zingales (1998).

The Contractual Approach

Both the entrepreneurial perspective and the ownership perspective can be understood from within the "contractual" framework associated with Coase (1937). In the Coasian framework, as developed and expanded by Williamson (1975, 1985, 1996), Klein, et al. (1978), Grossman and Hart (1986), Hart and Moore (1990), and others, the boundary of the firm is determined by the tradeoff, at the margin, between the relative transaction costs of external and internal exchange. In this sense, firm boundaries depend not only on technology, but on organizational considerations; that is, on the costs and benefits of various contracting alternatives.

Moreover, economic organization, both internal and external, imposes costs because complex contracts are usually incomplete. The transaction-cost literature makes much of the distinction between complete and incomplete contracts. A complete contract specifies a course of action, a decision, or terms of trade contingent on every possible future state of affairs. In textbook models of competitive general equilibrium, all contracts are assumed to be complete. The future is not known with certainty, but the probability distributions of all possible future events are known.[4] In an important sense, the model is "timeless": all relevant future contingencies are considered in the *ex ante* contracting stage, so there are no decisions to be made as the future unfolds.

The Coasian approach relaxes this assumption and holds that complete, contingent contracts are not always feasible. In a world of "true" (structural, rather than parametric) uncertainty, the future holds genuine surprises (Foss, 1993a), and this limits the available contracting options. In simple transactions—for instance, procurement of an off-the-shelf component—uncertainty may be relatively unimportant, and spot-market contracting works well. For more complex transactions, such as the purchase and installation of specialized equipment, the underlying agreements will typically be incomplete—the contract will provide remedies for only some possible future contingencies.[5] One example is a relational contract,

---

[4]What Knight (1921) would describe as "risk," rather than "uncertainty."

[5]Williamson (1975, 1985, 1996) attributes contractual incompleteness to cognitive limits or "bounded rationality," following Simon's (1961, p. xxiv) interpretation of human action as "intendedly rational, but only limitedly so." Other economists are more agnostic, assuming only that some quantities or outcomes are unobservable (or not verifiable to third

an agreement that describes shared goals and a set of general principles that govern the relationship (Goldberg, 1980). Another is implicit contract—an agreement that while unstated, is presumably understood by all sides.[6] Regardless, contractual incompleteness exposes the contracting parties to certain risks. In particular, investment in relationship-specific assets exposes agents to a potential "holdup" problem: if circumstances change, their trading partners may try to expropriate the rents accruing to the specific assets. Suppose an upstream supplier tailors its equipment to service a particular customer. After the equipment is in place, the customer may demand a lower price, knowing that the salvage value of the specialized equipment is lower than the net payment it offers. Anticipating this possibility, the supplier will be unwilling to install the custom machinery without protection for such a contingency, even if the specialized technology would make the relationship more profitable for both sides.

One way to safeguard rents accruing to specific assets is vertical (or lateral) integration, where a merger eliminates any adversarial interests. Less extreme options include long-term contracts (Joskow, 1985, 1987, 1988, 1990), partial ownership agreements (Pisano, Russo, and Teece, 1988; Pisano, 1990), or agreements for both parties to invest in offsetting relationship-specific investments (Heide and John, 1988). Overall, parties may employ several governance structures. The Coasian literature tries to match the appropriate governance structure with the particular characteristics of the transaction.[7]

Building Blocks of an Austrian Theory of the Firm

Beginning with the basic Coasian or contractual framework, we can add two elements as building blocks to an Austrian theory of the firm: entrepreneurship and economic calculation. Entrepreneurship represents the bearing of uncertainty. Economic calculation is the tool entrepreneurs use to assess costs and expected future benefits. Consider each in turn.

---

parties, such as the courts), in which case contracts cannot be made contingent on these variables or outcomes.

[6] This is the sense in which Kreps (1990a) understands "corporate culture."

[7] As noted in chapter 1 above (pp. 18–21), some Austrians have questioned the Coasian, contractual approach as an appropriate basis for an Austrian theory of the firm. I do not share these concerns, however, seeing Coase's framework as a general heuristic that can accommodate various notions of the *origins* of internal and external transaction costs, including those emphasized in the Austrian literature.

Entrepreneurship

Entrepreneurship, in the Misesian sense, is the act of bearing uncertainty. In an ever-changing world, decisions must be made based on expectations of future events. Because production takes time, resources must be invested before the returns on those investments are realized. If the forecast of future returns is inaccurate, the expected profits will turn out to be losses. This is, of course, true not only of financial investors, but of all human actors. If the future were known with certainty, man would not act, since his action would not change the future. Thus, all purposeful human action carries some risk that the means chosen will not bring about the desired end. In this sense, all human actors are entrepreneurs.

Austrians tend to focus on this kind of pure entrepreneurship, the entrepreneurial aspect of all human behavior. In doing so, however, they often overlook a particular case of entrepreneurship, the driving force behind the structure of production: the capitalist-entrepreneur, who risks his money capital in anticipation of future events. Kirzner's (1973; 1979) influential interpretation of Mises identifies "alertness" or "discovery," rather than uncertainty bearing, as the defining property of entrepreneurship. In Kirzner's framework, entrepreneurial profit is the reward to superior alertness to profit opportunities. The simplest case is that of the arbitrageur, who discovers a discrepancy in present prices that can be exploited for financial gain. In a more typical case, the entrepreneur is alert to a new product or a superior production process and steps in to fill this market gap before others.

Kirzner's formulation has been criticized, however, for a lack of attention to uncertainty. According to this criticism, mere alertness to a profit opportunity is not sufficient for earning profits. To reap financial gain, the entrepreneur must invest resources to realize the discovered profit opportunity. "Entrepreneurial ideas without money are mere parlor games until the money is obtained and committed to the projects" (Rothbard, 1985, p. 283). Moreover, excepting the few cases where buying low and selling high are nearly instantaneous (say, electronic trading of currencies or commodity futures), even arbitrage transactions require some time to complete. The selling price may fall before the arbitrageur has made his sale, and thus even the pure arbitrageur faces some probability of loss. In Kirzner's formulation, the worst that can happen to an entrepreneur is the failure to discover an existing profit opportunity. Entrepreneurs either earn profits or break even, but it is unclear how they suffer losses.[8]

Mises, by contrast, consistently identifies entrepreneurship with both profit and loss. "There is a simple rule of thumb to tell entrepreneurs from non-entrepreneurs. The entrepreneurs are those on whom the incidence of losses on the capital employed falls" (Mises, 1951, p. 112). Moreover, while Mises indeed acknowledges the element of entrepreneurship in all human action, it is clear that the potential losses of the capitalist-entrepreneurs are particularly important:

> Mises applies the concept of the entrepreneur to all cases of uncertainty-bearing, and since laborers face uncertainty in deciding where to move or what occupation to go into, laborers are also entrepreneurs. But the most important case of entrepreneurship, the driving force in shaping the actual structure and patterns of production in the market economy, are the capitalist-entrepreneurs, the ones who commit and risk their capital in deciding when, what, and how much to produce. The capitalists, too, are far more subject to actual monetary losses than are the laborers. (Rothbard, 1985, p. 282)[9]

Mises is careful to distinguish entrepreneurship from management, the carrying out of those tasks specified by the capitalist-entrepreneur. "[T]hose who confuse entrepreneurship and management close their eyes to the economic problem" (Mises, 1949, p. 704). It is the capitalist-entrepreneurs who control the allocation of capital to the various branches of industry.

It is clear from this formulation that the capitalist-entrepreneur must own property. He cannot invest without prior ownership of financial capital. (1871, pp. 159–61) treatment of production includes as entrepreneurial functions economic calculation, the "act of will," and "supervision of the execution of the production plan." These functions "entail property ownership and, therefore, mark the Mengerian entrepreneur as a capitalist-entrepreneur" (Salerno, 1999a, p. 30). Menger describes "command of the services of capital" as a "necessary prerequisite" for economic activity. Even in large firms, although he may employ "several helpers," the entrepreneur himself continues to bear uncertainty, perform economic calculation, and

---

[8]See chapter 5 below for further discussion of this point.

[9]Of course, bondholders, as well as equity holders, are partly entrepreneurs, since even bondholders bear some default risk.

supervise production, even if these functions "are ultimately confined ... to determining the allocation of portions of wealth to particular productive purposes only by general categories, and to selection and control of persons" (Menger, 1871, pp. 160–61; quoted in Salerno 1999a, p. 30).[10] An Austrian theory of the firm, then, is essentially a theory about the ownership and use of capital. As Yu (1999, p. 7) puts it, "the Austrian firm is a collection of capital resources."

Unfortunately, the Austrian literature on the firm often confuses entrepreneurship with innovation, strategic planning, leadership, and other functions more properly associated with management than ownership. Witt (1998), for example, describes entrepreneurship as a form of "cognitive leadership." Witt outlines a potential Austrian theory of the firm by combining recent literature on cognitive psychology with Kirzner's concept of entrepreneurship. Entrepreneurs require complementary factors of production, he argues, which are coordinated within the firm. For the firm to be successful, the entrepreneur must establish a tacit, shared framework of goals—what the management literature terms "leadership." A proper Austrian theory of the firm, then, must take account of the ways in which entrepreneurs communicate their business conceptions within the organization.

The problem with this argument is that while organizational leadership is undoubtedly important, it is not particularly "entrepreneurial." Entrepreneurship has little necessarily to do with having a business plan, communicating a "corporate culture," or other dimensions of business leadership; these are attributes of the successful manager, who may or may not be an entrepreneur.[11] Moreover, even if top-level managerial skill were the same as entrepreneurship, it is unclear why "cognitive leadership"—tacit communication of shared modes of thought, core capabilities, and the like—should be more entrepreneurial than other, comparatively mundane managerial tasks such as structuring incentives, limiting opportunism, administering rewards, and so on.

---

[10] For more on Misesian entrepreneurship and its various interpretations, see chapter 5 below.

[11] One distinction between entrepreneurship (as uncertainty bearing) and management is that managerial functions can be purchased on the market: innovation can be outsourced to R&D labs; strategic planning can be contracted out to consultants; corporate identities, both internal and external, can be developed and communicated by outside specialists; and so on.

Economic Calculation

All entrepreneurs, particularly capitalist-entrepreneurs, use economic calculation as their primary decision-making tool. By economic calculation we simply mean the use of present prices and anticipated future prices to compare present costs with expected future benefits. In this way, the entrepreneur decides what goods and services should be produced, and what methods of production should be used to produce them. "The business of the entrepreneur is not merely to experiment with new technological methods, but to select from the multitude of technologically feasible methods those which are best fit to supply the public in the cheapest way with the things they are asking for most urgently" (Mises, 1951, p. 110). To make this selection, the entrepreneur must be able to weigh the costs and expected benefits of various courses of action.

As discussed in the previous chapter, the need for economic calculation places ultimate limits on the size of the organization. Indeed, many writers have recognized the connections between the socialist calculation debate and the problems of internal organization (Montias, 1976; Williamson, 1991c). Kirzner, for example, interprets the costs of internal organization in terms of Hayek's knowledge problem:

> In a free market, any advantages that may be derived from "central planning" ... are purchased at the price of an enhanced knowledge problem. We may expect firms to spontaneously expand to the point where additional advantages of "central" planning are just offset by the incremental knowledge difficulties that stem from dispersed information. (Kirzner, 1992, p. 162)

What, precisely, drives this knowledge problem? The mainstream literature on the firm focuses mostly on the costs of market exchange, and much less on the costs of governing internal exchange. The new research has yet to produce a fully satisfactory explanation of the limits to firm size (Williamson, 1985, chap. 6). In Coase's words, "Why does the entrepreneur not organize one less transaction or one more?" Or, more generally, "Why is not all production carried on in one big firm?" (Coase, 1937, pp. 393–94). Existing contractual explanations rely on problems of authority and responsibility (Arrow, 1974); incentive distortions caused by residual ownership rights (Grossman and Hart, 1986; Hart and Moore, 1990; Hart, 1995); and the costs of attempting to reproduce market governance features within the firm (Williamson, 1985, chap. 6). Rothbard (1962, pp. 609–16) offered an explanation for the firm's vertical boundaries based on Mises's claim that economic calculation under socialism is impossible. Rothbard argued that the need for monetary calculation in terms of actual prices not only explains the failures of central planning under socialism, but places an upper bound on firm size.

Rothbard's account begins with the recognition that Mises's position on socialist economic calculation is not exclusively, or even primarily, about socialism, but about the role of prices for capital goods. Entrepreneurs allocate resources based on their expectations about future prices, and the information contained in present prices. To make profits, they need information about all prices, not only the prices of consumer goods but the prices of factors of production. Without markets for capital goods, these goods can have no prices, and hence entrepreneurs cannot make judgments about the relative scarcities of these factors. In any environment, then—socialist or not—where a factor of production has no market price, a potential user of that factor will be unable to make rational decisions about its use. Stated this way, Mises's claim is simply that efficient resource allocation in a market economy requires well-functioning asset markets. To have such markets, factors of production must be privately owned.

Rothbard's contribution, described more fully in chapter 1 above, was to generalize Mises's analysis of this problem under socialism to the context of vertical integration and the size of the organization. Rothbard writes in *Man, Economy, and State* that up to a point, the size of the firm is determined by costs, as in the textbook model. However, "the ultimate limits are set on the relative size of the firm by the necessity for markets to exist in every factor, in order to make it possible for the firm to calculate its profits and losses" (Rothbard, 1962, p. 599).

Consider, for example, a large, integrated firm organized into semi-autonomous profit centers, each specializing in a particular final or intermediate product. The central management of the firm uses the implicit incomes of the business units, as reflected in statements of divisional profit and loss, to allocate physical and financial capital across the divisions. To compute divisional profits and losses, the firm needs an economically meaningful transfer price for all internally transferred goods and services. If there is an external market for the component, the firm can use that market price as the transfer price. Without a market price, however, the transfer price must be estimated, either on a cost-plus basis or by bargaining between the buying and selling divisions (Gabor, 1984; Eccles and White, 1988; King, 1994). Such estimated transfer prices contain less information than actual market prices.

The use of internally traded intermediate goods for which no external market reference is available thus introduces distortions that reduce organizational efficiency. This gives us the element missing from contemporary theories of economic organization, an upper bound: the firm is constrained by the need for external markets for all internally traded goods. In other words, no firm can become so large that it is both the unique producer and user of an intermediate product; for then no market-based transfer prices will be available, and the firm will be unable to calculate divisional profit and loss and therefore unable to allocate resources correctly between divisions. Of course, internal organization does avoid the holdup problem, which the firm would face if there were a unique outside supplier; conceivably, this benefit could outweigh the increase in "incalculability" (Rothbard, 1962, p. 614). Usually, however, the costs from the loss of calculation will likely exceed the costs of external governance.[12]

Like Kirzner (1992), Rothbard viewed his contribution as consistent with the basic Coasian framework, noting that his treatment of the limits of the firm "serves to extend the notable analysis of Professor Coase on the market determinants of the size of the firm, or the relative extent of corporate planning within the firm as against the use of exchange and the price mechanism. . . . The costs of internal corporate planning become prohibitive as soon as markets for capital goods begin to disappear, so that the free-market optimum will always stop well short not only of One Big Firm throughout the world market but also of any disappearance of specific markets and hence of economic calculation in that product or resource" (Rothbard, 1976, p. 76). "Central planning" within the firm, then, is

---

[12]Similarly, Rothbard's claim is not that because external prices are necessary for large firms to function efficiently, firms will tend to become large where external markets are "thick" or better developed. On the contrary, large firms typically arise precisely where external markets are poorly developed or hampered by government intervention; these are the kinds of circumstances that give entrepreneurs an advantage in coordinating activities internally (Chandler, 1977). However, such firms are still constrained by the need for some external market reference.

possible only when the firm exists within a larger market setting.

Capital Markets

If the capitalist-entrepreneur is the driving force behind the industrialized, market economy, then economists should focus their attention on the financial markets, the capitalist-entrepreneur's main venue. It is here that this most important form of entrepreneurship takes place. Of course, in the traditional, production-function theory of the firm, capital markets do little but supply financial capital to managers, who can get as much capital as they wish at the going market price. In a more sophisticated understanding, managers do not decide how much capital they want; capitalists decide where capital should be allocated. In doing so, they provide essential discipline to the plant-level manager, whom Mises (1949, p. 301) calls the entrepreneur's "junior partner."

When capitalists supply resources to firms, they usually delegate to managers the day-to-day responsibility for use of those resources. Managers may thus be able to use those resources to benefit themselves, rather than the capitalist. The problem of managerial discretion—what we now call the principal-agent problem—occupies much current research in the theory of the firm. Under what conditions can managers exercise discretionary behavior? What kinds of rules, or mechanisms, can be designed to align the manager's interest with the owner's? Without effective rules, what actions will managers choose? An early application was the proposed "separation of ownership and control" in the modern corporation. Berle and Means (1932) argued that the modern firm is run not by its owners, the shareholders, but by salaried managers, whose interests are different from those of shareholders and include executive perks, prestige, and similar rewards. If the corporation is diffusely held, no individual shareholder has sufficient motivation to engage in (costly) monitoring managerial decisions, and therefore discretion will flourish at the expense of the market value of the firm. However, Berle and Means did not consider how owners might limit this discretion *ex ante*, without the need for detailed *ex post* monitoring.

Agency theory—now the standard language of corporate finance—addresses these problems. As developed by Jensen and Meckling (1976); Fama (1980); Fama and Jensen (1983), and Jensen (1986), agency theory studies the design of *ex ante* incentive-compatible mechanisms to reduce agency costs in the face of potential moral hazard (malfeasance) by agents. Agency costs are defined by Jensen and Meckling (1976, p. 308) as the sum of "(1) the monitoring expenditures of the principal, (2) the bonding expenditures by the agent, and (3) the residual loss." The residual loss represents the potential gains from trade that fail to be realized because perfect incentives for agents cannot be provided when the agent's actions are unobservable. In a typical agency model, a principal assigns an agent to do some task (producing output, for instance), but has only an imperfect signal of the agent's performance (for example, effort). The agency problem is analogous to the signal-extraction problem popularized in macroeconomics by Lucas (1972): how much of the observable outcome is due to the agent's effort, and how much is due to factors beyond the agent's control? The optimal incentive contract balances the principal's desire to provide incentives to increase the agent's effort (for example, by basing compensation on the outcome) with the agent's desire to be insured from the fluctuations in compensation that come from these random factors.

Owners of corporations (shareholders) use a variety of control or governance mechanisms to limit the managerial discretion described by Berle and Means. Both "internal" and "external" governance may be employed. Internally, owners may establish a board of directors to oversee the actions of managers. They can use performance-based compensation to motivate managers to act in the owners' interest (for instance, giving managers stock options instead of cash bonuses). They can adopt a particular organizational form, such as the "M-form" structure, in which managerial discretion is more easily kept in check (Williamson, 1975). Finally, they can rely on competition within the firm for top-level management positions—what Fama (1980) calls the internal market for managers—to limit the discretionary behavior of top-level management.

Even more important are external forces that help align managers' interests with those of shareholders. Competition in the product market, for example, assures that firms whose managers engage in too much discretionary behavior will fail, costing the managers their jobs. In countries where universal banking is permitted, large equity holders such as banks can exercise considerable influence over managerial behavior. The external governance mechanism that has received the most attention, however, is the market for ownership itself, the "market for corporate control."

Henry Manne's essay, "Mergers and the Market for Corporate Control" (1965), responded to Berle and Means by noting that managerial discretion will be limited if there is an active market for control of corporations. When managers engage in discretionary behavior, the share price of the firm falls, and this invites takeover and subsequent replacement of incumbent management. Therefore, while managers may hold considerable autonomy over the day-to-day operations of the firm, the stock market places strict limits on their behavior.

The central insight of Manne's paper is also found in Mises's *Human Action* (1949), in the passage distinguishing what Mises calls "profit management" from "bureaucratic management" (pp. 300–07). It is true, Mises acknowledges, that the salaried managers of a corporation hold considerable autonomy over the day-to-day operations of the firm. Nonetheless, the shareholders make the ultimate decisions about allocating resources to the firm, in their decisions to buy and sell stock:

> [The Berle–Means] doctrine disregards entirely the role that the capital and money market, the stock and bond exchange, which a pertinent idiom simply calls the "market," plays in the direction of corporate business.... [T]he changes in the prices of common and preferred stock and of corporate bonds are the means applied by the capitalists for the supreme control of the flow of capital. The price structure as determined by the speculations on the capital and money markets and on the big commodity exchanges not only decides how much capital is available for the conduct of each corporation's business; it creates a state of affairs to which the managers must adjust their operations in detail. (Mises, 1949, p. 303)

Mises does not identify the takeover mechanism *per se* as a means for capitalists to exercise control—takeovers were much less popular before the late 1950s, when the tender offer began to replace the proxy contest as the acquisition method of choice—but the main point is clear: the true basis of the market system is not the product market, the labor market, or the managerial market, but the capital market, where entrepreneurial judgments are exercised and decisions carried out.

Toward an Austrian Theory of Corporate Governance

Given that financial-market entrepreneurship is the defining feature of a market economy, that economic calculation is the capitalist-entrepreneur's primary tool, and that economic calculation requires well-functioning capital markets, what can capitalist-entrepreneurs do to govern their relationships with operational managers? What should be the basis of an Austrian theory of corporate governance? This section suggests four areas that Austrians should address: (1) the concept of the firm as an investment; (2) the relationship between internal and external capital markets; (3) comparative corporate governance; and (4) financiers as entrepreneurs. Consider each in turn.

Firms as Investments

Because the owner, and not the manager, is the ultimate decision-maker, the Austrian theory of the firm should comprise two elements: a theory of investment (corporate finance), and a theory of how investors provide incentives for managers to use these resources efficiently (corporate governance). In microeconomics textbooks, by contrast, what the capital investors give to the firm is treated as just another factor of production. Its price, the "rental price of capital" or interest, is simply another cost to the producer. Any excess of revenues over costs, including the cost of capital, goes to the manager (sometimes confusingly called the "entrepreneur"). This residual is called "profit," though it is not profit in the Misesian sense.

In the ownership perspective, as developed by Gabor and Pearce (1952, 1958), Vickers (1970, 1987), Moroney (1972), and others, the firm is viewed as an investment. The firm's goal is to maximize the return on invested capital. This money capital may be regarded as a factor of production, but it is a unique factor, the "controlling" factor that receives the net proceeds of the operation. Other factors, such as labor (including management) and physical capital, are regarded as "contracting" factors that receive a fixed payment. The services of the top-level manager are thus treated as a cost, while the investor is considered the residual claimant. Also note that because the capitalist bears the risk that the investment will fail, upon investing the capitalist has become an entrepreneur. Furthermore, to the extent that the entrepreneur (as Kirznerian discoverer) hires himself out to the capitalist as a salaried manager, his compensation is not entrepreneurial profit; it is a cost to the owner of the firm (Rothbard, 1985, p. 283). This has significant implications for firm behavior. First, the firm will not always expand output to the point where marginal revenue equals marginal cost. For if the firm is earning positive net returns at its current level of output, instead of increasing output until marginal net returns fall to zero, the firm could simply take those returns and employ them elsewhere, either to set up a new firm in the same industry or to diversify into a new industry (Gabor and Pearce, 1952, p. 253). The efficient scale of production is determined by outside investment opportunities, not simply the marginal returns from producing a single output.

Indeed, it is easy to show that under fairly weak assumptions, the output level that maximizes the profit rate is less than the output level that maximizes the level of profit. Consider a standard, concave profit function; add a "money capital requirement," the amount of capital required to finance a given level of output. As long as the money capital requirement is increasing in output, the output level that maximizes the profit rate—profit divided by the money capital required to finance that output level—is less than the output level that maximizes profit. From the capitalist's perspective, output should be expanded to the point where the return on the last dollar of money capital is just equal to the opportunity cost of that last dollar of money capital. But as long as the plant manager is not free to invest his financial capital elsewhere, the manager's cost curves do not reflect this opportunity cost. Hence, the manager chooses a higher output level than that which maximizes the capitalist's return.

Significantly, for internal accounting purposes, firms are typically structured such that the goal of any operating unit is to maximize the return on its invested capital. In fact, not only do firms set up divisions as profit centers, as discussed above, but groups of profit centers are frequently grouped together as "investment centers" within the firm itself. Reece and Cool (1978) studied 620 of the largest US firms in 1978 and found that seventy-four percent had investment centers. These subunits are commonly evaluated according to a return on investment (ROI) criterion, such as the ratio of accounting net income generated by the investment center divided by total assets invested in the investment center. More recently, measures such as residual income and "economic value added" (EVA) have become popular as an alternative to ROI (Stern, Stewart, and Chew, 1995). The point is that individual divisions are being evaluated on the same basis as the corporation itself—namely, what kind of return is being generated on the financial resources invested.

Second, the firm-as-investment concept relates closely to an emerging literature on merger as a form of firm-level investment (Bittlingmayer, 1996; Andrade and Stafford, 2004). Once managers have acquired financial resources from capitalists, these managers have some discretion over how to invest those resources. To supplement the "normal" forms of firm-level investment—capital expenditures and R&D—managers may choose to purchase assets of existing firms through merger. Merger may be a different form of investment; Andrade and Stafford (2004) find, for example, that mergers in particular industries tend to be clustered over time, while rankings of non-merger forms of investment by industry tend to remain constant. This suggests that merger activity is encouraged by specific industry or policy shocks, like deregulation, the emergence of junk-bond financing, and increased foreign competition (Mitchell and Mulherin, 1996). Nonetheless, mergers will be evaluated by the returns they generate, just like any other investment.

Internal Capital Markets

In his extension of the Coasian framework, Williamson (1975, 1981) describes the modern multidivisional or "M-form" corporation as a means of intra-firm capital allocation. Capital markets allocate resources between stand-alone, single-product firms. In the diversified, multidivisional firm, by contrast, resources are allocated internally, as the entrepreneur distributes funds among profit-center divisions. This "internal capital market" replicates the allocative and disciplinary roles of the financial markets, shifting resources toward more profitable lines of production.[13] Coase claimed that firms "supplant" markets when the transaction costs

---

[13] Such a process is described explicitly in the 1977 *Annual Report* of Fuqua Industries, a diversified firm with interests in lawn and garden equipment, sports and recreation, entertainment, photofinishing, transportation, housing, and food and beverages:

> Fuqua's strategy is to allocate resources into business segments having prospects of the highest return on investment and to extract resources from areas where the future return on investment does not meet our ongoing requirements.... The same principle of expanding areas of high return and shrinking areas of low return is constantly extended to product lines and markets within individual Fuqua operations. Only with a diversified business structure is the application of this modern fundamental business investment policy practical.

of market exchange exceed those of internal production. Williamson adds that diversified, multidivisional firms "supplant" capital markets when the costs of external finance exceed those of internal resource allocation.

According to the internal capital markets theory, diversified firms arise when limits in the capital market permit internal management to allocate and manage funds more efficiently than the external capital market. These efficiencies may come from several sources. First, the central headquarters of the firm (HQ) typically has access to information unavailable to external parties, which it extracts through its own internal auditing and reporting procedures (Williamson, 1975, pp. 145–47).[14] Second, managers inside the firm may also be more willing to reveal information to HQ than to outsiders, since revealing the same information to the capital market would also reveal it to rival firms, potentially hurting the firm's competitive position. Third, HQ can also intervene selectively, making marginal changes to divisional operating procedures, whereas the external market can discipline a division only by raising or lowering the share price of the entire firm. Fourth, HQ has residual rights of control that providers of outside finance do not have, making it easier to redeploy the assets of poorly performing divisions (Gertner, Scharfstein, and Stein, 1994). More generally, these control rights allow HQ to add value by engaging in "winner picking" among competing projects when credit to the firm as a whole is constrained (Stein, 1997). Fifth, the internal capital market may react more "rationally" to new information: those who dispense the funds need only take into account their own expectations about the returns to a particular investment, and not their expectations about other investors' expectations. Hence there would be no speculative bubbles or waves.

Bhidé (1990) uses the internal capital markets framework to explain both the conglomerate merger wave of the 1960s and the divestitures of the 1980s, regarding these developments as responses to changes in the relative efficiencies of internal and external finance. For instance, corporate refocusing can be explained as a consequence of the rise of takeover by

---

Another highly diversified firm, Bangor Punta Corporation, explains that the role of its corporate headquarters is "to act as a central bank supplying operating units with working capital and capital funds" (1966 *Annual Report*).

[14] Myers and Majluf (1984) show that if the information asymmetry between a stand-alone firm and potential outside investors is large enough, the firm may forego investments with positive net present value rather than issue risky securities to finance them.

tender offer rather than proxy contest, the emergence of new financial techniques and instruments like leveraged buyouts and high-yield bonds, and the appearance of takeover and breakup specialists, like Kohlberg Kravis Roberts, which themselves performed many functions of the conglomerate HQ (Williamson, 1992). Furthermore, the emergence of the conglomerate in the 1960s can itself be traced to the emergence of the M-form corporation. Because the multidivisional structure treats business units as semi-independent profit or investment centers, it is much easier for an M-form corporation to expand via acquisition than it is for the older unitary structure. New acquisitions can be integrated smoothly when they can preserve much of their internal structure and retain control over day-to-day operations. In this sense, the conglomerate could emerge only after the multidivisional structure had been diffused widely throughout the corporate sector.

Internal capital market advantages, then, explain why diversification can increase the value of the firm. During the 1960s, entrepreneurs took advantage of financial-market imperfections (many due to regulatory interference) to form large, highly diversified firms (Hubbard and Palia, 1999; Klein, 2001). They also benefited from government spending in high-technology and other defense-related businesses, which were particularly suited for acquisition. In the two subsequent decades, financial-market performance improved, reducing the internal capital market advantages of conglomerate firms.

If entrepreneurs have a special ability to manage information and allocate financial resources within the firm—if diversified firms "supplant" external capital markets—then why are capital markets necessary at all? Why not, to paraphrase Coase's (1937, pp. 393–94) second question, organize the entire economy as one giant conglomerate? The answer is that the argument for internal capital market advantages does not "scale up"; it applies only to firms that are themselves engaged in rivalrous competition. This situation, in turn, implies strict limits to firm size, even for large conglomerates.

The argument for the efficiency of internal capital markets is that compared with outside investors, the entrepreneur can extract additional information about divisional requirements and performance. It is not that the entrepreneur's knowledge substitutes for the knowledge embodied in market prices. To evaluate the merit of a proposed investment, the central management of a diversified conglomerate still relies on market prices to calculate expected (money) benefits and cost. Internal accounting does not substitute for money prices; it merely uses the information contained in prices in a particular way. When capital-goods prices are distorted—for example, because of financial market regulation—then the entrepreneur's additional knowledge is that much more valuable. So under those conditions we would expect an increase in M-form corporations, allocating resources via internal capital markets. During the 1960s, that is exactly what we observed.

Correctly understood, the internal capital markets hypothesis does not state that internal capital markets supplant financial markets. It states that internal capital markets supplement financial markets. Even ITT's Harold Geneen, LTV's James Ling, Litton's "Tex" Thornton, and the other conglomerators of the 1960s were constrained by the need for economic calculation in terms of money prices. Thornton's "Whiz Kids" have been criticized for their advocacy of "scientific management" or "management by the numbers." Yet Thornton's techniques were quite successful at Litton. It was only when his disciple Robert McNamara tried to apply the same techniques to a nonmarket setting—the Vietnam War—that the limitations of "scientific management" were revealed.[15]

Comparative Corporate Governance

How well do various systems of corporate governance function? The last few years have seen the growth of a new literature on "comparative corporate governance," the study of alternative means of governing relations between firm owners and managers. The typical comparison is between stock-market systems like those in the US and UK, and bank-centered systems like those in Germany and Japan (Roe, 1994; Gilson and Black, 1998; Milhaupt, 1997). According to Roe, the phenomenon he calls "strong managers, weak owners" is an outgrowth not of the market process, but of legal restrictions on firm ownership and control. In the US, for example, banks and other institutions are forbidden from owning firms; antitrust laws prohibit industrial combinations like the Japanese keiretsu; and anti-takeover restrictions dilute the effects of the takeover mechanism. Laws that require diffuse ownership create what Roe terms the "Berle–Means

---

[15] For more on the relationship between Thornton and McNamara, see Shapley (1993), and Byrne (1993).

corporation," in which "fragmented ownership shifts power in the firm to managers" (p. 93).

Mises makes a very similar argument in *Human Action*. There he notes that "the emergence of an omnipotent managerial class is not a phenomenon of the unhampered market economy," but a result of government policy (Mises, 1949, p. 304). Here he expands upon his earlier analysis in *Bureaucracy* (1944, p. 12), where he attacks the claim that bureaucracy follows naturally from firm size. Mises conceives of bureaucracy as rule-following, as opposed to profit-seeking, behavior. He reserves the term "bureaucratic management" for the governing of activities that have no cash value on the market. As long as a firm's inputs and outputs are bought and sold, the central management of the firm will have the information provided by market prices to evaluate the efficiency of the various branches and divisions within the firm. Then subordinate managers can be given wide discretion to make daily operational decisions without the pursuit of profit.[16] If an organization produces a good or service that has no market price—the output of a government agency, for example—then subordinate managers must be given specific instructions for how to perform their tasks.

The fact that managers in a private firm have latitude to make day-to-day decisions, Mises argues, does not make the firm "bureaucratic." "No profit-seeking enterprise, no matter how large, is liable to become bureaucratic provided the hands of its management are not tied by government interference. The trend toward bureaucratic rigidity is not inherent in the evolution of business. It is an outcome of government meddling with business" (Mises, 1944, p. 12). By this Mises means that government interference impedes the entrepreneur's use of economic calculation and the attempt to use prices to impose managerial discipline. Mises gives three examples (pp. 64–73): taxes and price regulations that interfere with corporate profits (distorting an important signal of managerial performance);

---

[16]Chapter 1 of *Bureaucracy*, on profit management and the sources of entrepreneurial profit, contains a remarkably lucid account of economic calculation under capitalism and its impossibility under socialism. "To the entrepreneur of capitalist society a factor of production through its price sends out a warning: Don't touch me, I am earmarked for another, more urgent need. But under socialism these factors of production are mute" (Mises, 1944, p. 29). Mises also provides a very Coase-like discussion of the make-or-buy decision, though without citation (p. 33).

laws that interfere with hiring and promotion (including the need to hire public relations staffs and legal and accounting personnel to comply with government reporting requirements); and the omnipresent threat of arbitrary antitrust or regulatory activity, in response to which entrepreneurs must become adept at "diplomacy and bribery" (p. 72). Absent such legal restrictions, Mises would argue, managerial autonomy is no inefficiency; it's an essential tool for operating a large, decentralized organization. But the firm must have accurate divisional accounting statements to evaluate managerial performance, and for this it needs the information contained in market prices.

Financiers as Entrepreneurs

As mentioned above, much current research in the theory of the firm focuses on the agency problem. Under what conditions can managers exercise discretionary behavior? What kinds of rules, or mechanisms, can be designed to align the manager's interest with the owner's? Without effective rules, what actions will managers choose? Mises was well aware of the agency problems, or conflicts of interest, that emerge in organizations (e.g., Mises, 1944, pp. 42–47). But, as we have seen, he saw the firm's owner or owners as playing the primary entrepreneurial role, and paid special attention to the mechanisms available to owners to limit this discretion. Financiers, acting in stock and bond markets—writing today, Mises would probably have discussed private-equity markets as well—are the large firm's ultimate decision-makers. Rothbard (1962, p. 602) puts it this way:

> Hired managers may successfully direct production or choose production processes. But the ultimate responsibility and control of production rests inevitably with the owner, with the businessman whose property the product is until it is sold. It is the owners who make the decision concerning how much capital to invest and in what particular processes. And particularly, it is the owners who must choose the managers. The ultimate decisions concerning the use of their property and the choice of the men to manage it must therefore be made by the owners and by no one else.

Kirzner (1973, p. 68) makes a similar point about alertness: it can never be fully delegated. "It is true that 'alertness' ... may be hired; but one who hires an employee alert to possibilities of discovering knowledge has himself displayed alertness of a still higher order.... The entrepreneurial decision to hire is thus the ultimate hiring decision, responsible in the last resort for all factors that are directly or indirectly hired for his project." Kirzner goes on to quote Knight (1921, p. 291): "What we call 'control' consists mainly of selecting someone else to do the 'controlling.'"

Significantly, Mises's treatment of the importance of financial markets is key to his final rebuttal in *Human Action* to Lange, Lerner, and the other market-socialist critics of his calculation argument (Mises, 1949, pp. 694–711). The market socialists, he argued, fail to understand that the main task performed by a market system is not the pricing of consumer goods, but the allocation of capital among various branches of industry. By focusing on production and pricing decisions within a given structure of capital, the socialists ignore the vital role of capital markets. Rothbard (1993) notes that the same criticism can be applied to the textbook, production-function model of the firm, where capital is also taken for granted. "Neoclassical microtheory talks about 'managers' producing up to the point where $MR = MC$, without ever talking about who or what is allocating capital to them. In short, neoclassical firms are implicitly assumed to have a fixed amount of capital allocated to them ... and they can only use that capital to invest in their own firm and nowhere else. Hence, the nonsensical conclusion that each firm's manager will try to squeeze out the last cent of profit, pushing production until $MR = MC$." Fortunately, the new literature on transaction-cost determinants of contractual relations has begun to bring capital back into the received microtheory.

Failure to understand the entrepreneurial role of capital providers plagues the mainstream literature in corporate finance and corporate control. For example, there is considerable debate about the effectiveness of the takeover mechanism in providing managerial discipline. If managers desire acquisitions to increase their own prestige or span of control—to engage in "empire building"—then an unregulated market will generate too many takeovers. Merger critics such as Ravenscraft and Scherer (1987), discussed in chapter 3 below, support increased restrictions on takeover activity. Jensen (1986, 1993) suggests changes in the tax code to favor dividends and share repurchases over direct reinvestment, thus limiting managers' ability to channel free cash flow into unproductive acquisitions.

However, the fact that some mergers—indeed, many mergers, take-overs, and reorganizations—turn out to be unprofitable does not imply market failure or necessarily prescribe any policy response. Errors will always be made in a world of uncertainty. Even the financial markets, which aggregate the collective wisdom of the capitalist-entrepreneurs, will sometimes make the wrong judgment on a particular business transaction. Sometimes the market will reward, *ex ante*, a proposed restructuring that has no efficiency rationale. But this is due not to capital market failure, but to imperfect knowledge. Final judgments about success and failure can be made only *ex post*, as the market process plays itself out. Moreover, there is no reason to believe that courts or regulatory authorities can make better judgments than the financial markets. The decisions of courts and government agencies will, in fact, tend to be far worse: unlike market participants, judges and bureaucrats pursue a variety of private agendas, unrelated to economic efficiency. Furthermore, the market is quick to penalize error as it is discovered; no hearings, committees, or fact-finding commissions are required. In short, that firms often fail is surprising only to those committed to textbook models of competition in which the very notion of "failure" is defined away.

Another criticism of the market for corporate control is that unregulated financial markets engage in too few takeovers, due to a free-rider problem associated with tender offers (see, for example, Scharfstein 1988). Critics point out that if the difference between the current (undervalued) price of the firm and its after-takeover market value is common knowledge, then the target firm's shareholders will refuse to tender their shares until the current price is bid up, appropriating a share of the returns to the acquiring firm. These critics conclude that regulation, not the takeover market, should be used to discipline managers.

The flaw in this argument is that it assumes perfect knowledge on the part of investors. The typical shareholder will not usually have the same information as incumbent managers, outside "raiders," and other specialists. It is not in the small shareholder's interest to learn these details; that is why he delegates such responsibilities to the managers in the first place. As Hayek (1945) described it, there is a "division of knowledge" in society. The raider who perceives and exploits a difference between a firm's current market value and its potential value under new management has an opportunity for an entrepreneurial profit (less the transaction costs of takeover). Because shareholders have delegated these responsibilities, they will not usually earn a share of this profit. Nonetheless, as explained above, because shareholders (owners) choose to delegate operational responsibility to managers—contracting out for the managerial function—they themselves retain the ultimate rights of control.

Moreover, the post-takeover market value of the firm is uncertain; the raider's profit, if he is successful, is the reward for bearing this uncertainty. In this sense, the takeover artist is a Misesian capitalist-entrepreneur. This account, however, could use further elaboration. For example, how is the bearing of uncertainty distributed among participants in various forms of restructuring? How do regulatory barriers hamper the capitalist-entrepreneur's ability to exercise the entrepreneurial function in this context?

Conclusions

The main message of this chapter is that Austrians can continue to work within the contractual, or Coasian, approach to the firm in elaborating the insights discussed above. In particular, the problem of corporate governance, and the corollary view that firms are investments, belongs at the forefront of Austrian research on the theory of the firm. Emphasis should thus be placed on the plans and actions of the capitalist-entrepreneur.

A particularly undeveloped area concerns the provision of capital to small, "entrepreneurial" ventures. Most of the literature on governance focuses on the large corporation, and the use of stock and bond markets to govern these organizations. Equally important, however, are smaller, privately held firms, financed with venture capital or other forms of investment. So far, the firm-as-investment literature has said little about these organizations, despite their growing importance, particularly in high-growth, technologically-advanced industries like software and biotechnology. Further research in this area is sorely needed.

CHAPTER 3

Do Entrepreneurs Make Predictable Mistakes? Evidence From Corporate Divestitures[†]

With Sandra K. Klein

After a brief lull in the early 1990s, the market for corporate control became increasingly active toward the end of the decade. Both 1996 and 1997 set new records for the number of US merger filings, and 1998, 1999, and 2000 brought high-profile "mega-mergers" in financial services, energy, telecommunications, pharmaceuticals, and automobiles. In banking alone, for example, a wave of mergers over the last decade has led to widespread industry restructuring and consolidation. While total industry activity continues to expand, the number of US banks and banking organizations both fell by almost 30 percent between 1988 and 1997 (Berger, Demsetz, and Strahan, 1999).

Like other business practices that do not conform to textbook models of competition, mergers, acquisitions, and financial restructurings have long been viewed with suspicion by some commentators and regulatory

[†]Published originally in *Quarterly Journal of Austrian Economics* 4, no. 2 (Summer 2001): 3–25. Reprinted in Nicolai J. Foss and Peter G. Klein, eds., *Entrepreneurship and the Firm: Austrian Perspectives on Economic Organization* (Aldershot, UK: Edward Elgar, 2002).

authorities. However, the academic literature clearly suggests that corporate restructurings do, on average, create value. Event studies of acquisitions consistently find positive average combined returns to acquirer and target shareholders. As summarized by Jensen (1991, p. 15), "the most careful academic research strongly suggests that takeovers—along with leveraged restructurings prompted by the threat of takeover—have generated large gains for shareholders and for the economy as a whole." These gains, historically about 8 percent of the combined value of the merging companies, "represent gains to economic efficiency, not redistribution between various parties" (Jensen, 1991, p. 23).[1]

At the same time, however, several studies have found a sharp divergence between market participants' pre-merger expectations about the post-merger performance of merging firms and the firms' actual performance rates. Ravenscraft and Scherer's (1987) large-scale study of manufacturing firms, for example, found that while the share prices of merging firms did on average rise with the announcement of the proposed restructuring, post-merger profit rates were unimpressive. Indeed, they find that nearly one-third of all acquisitions during the 1960s and 1970s were eventually divested. Ravenscraft and Scherer conclude that acquisitions, particularly diversifying acquisitions, typically promote managerial "empire building" rather than efficiency. While acknowledging that product and capital markets eventually discipline poorly performing firms, forcing divestitures and other restructurings, Ravenscraft and Scherer (p. 217) argue for tighter government restrictions on mergers, particularly diversifying acquisitions and acquisitions financed by stock: "When the roads are strewn with wrecks, government officials cannot rest content because the tow trucks, ambulances, and hearses are doing a good job removing the remnants and clearing the right-of-way."[2]

Implicit in this criticism is the idea that divestitures of previously ac-

---

[1] On the gains from mergers, acquisitions, and other restructurings, see also the surveys by Jensen and Ruback (1983), Jarrell, Brickley, and Netter (1988), Roll (1988), Romano (1992), and Andrade, Mitchell, and Stafford (2001).

[2] Jensen (1986, 1993) argues similarly that diversifying acquisitions resulted from widespread agency problems in corporations, though he does not recommend any regulatory response: "The legal/political/regulatory system is far too blunt an instrument to handle the problems of wasteful managerial behavior effectively" (1993, p. 850). Instead, he advocates alternative forms of organization such as leveraged buyout associations and venture capital funds (see especially Jensen, 1989).

quired assets expose past errors, and that these errors should have been foreseen (and perhaps prevented, if regulators had been sufficiently empowered). Certain types of acquisitions, it is claimed, are more likely to be later divested, so managers should generally avoid them. If such acquisitions occur, this is then cited as evidence for widespread agency problems. In this sense, the takeover wave of the 1980s is typically understood as an "undoing" of the earlier, conglomerate merger wave of the 1960s and early 1970s. According to conventional wisdom, the 1980s was a period of respecialization or "refocus," showing the failures of unrelated diversification. The three decades from 1960 to 1990 thus represent a "round trip of the American corporation" (Shleifer and Vishny, 1991, p. 54).

This view is based partly on evidence from studies of the conglomerate period by Rumelt (1974, 1982), Ravenscraft and Scherer (1987, 1991), Porter (1987), Kaplan and Weisbach (1992), and others who find no evidence that unrelated diversification brought long-term benefits to the firms that diversified.[3] Combined with evidence of negative stock-market returns to diversification during the 1980s (Bhagat, Shleifer, and Vishny, 1990; Lang and Stulz, 1994; Berger and Ofek, 1995; Comment and Jarrell, 1995), many observers conclude that unrelated diversification is *per se* inefficient, and that the conglomerate era is best understood as an agency phenomenon.

The conventional wisdom on conglomerate sell-offs can be challenged on at least four grounds. First, divestitures of previously acquired assets do not necessarily show that the original acquisitions were failures. Weston (1989) argues that divestitures occur for a variety of reasons, such as changes in corporate strategies and antitrust rules, and not necessarily poor performance. Kaplan and Weisbach (1992) studied 217 large acquisitions completed between 1971 and 1982 and found that while 43.9 percent had been divested by 1989, only about a third of those divestitures were responses to poor post-merger performance.[4] Thus the mere fact that

---

[3] Servaes (1996) also finds that conglomerate firms in the 1960s were valued at a discount relative to specialized firms. However, Matsusaka (1993) and Hubbard and Palia (1999) show that market participants rewarded conglomerate acquisitions during this period, and Klein (2001) offers valuation evidence consistent with the event-study results.

[4] Other empirical studies of asset sales and restructurings include Hite, Owens, and Rogers (1987); Lang, Poulsen, and Stulz (1994); John and Ofek (1995); and Schlingemann, Stulz, and Walkling (2002). These papers look at divestitures more generally, and not only at divestitures of previously acquired assets.

many acquisitions are later divested does not prove widespread managerial misconduct.

Second, the market for corporate control is already highly regulated, and it is difficult to draw from current and recent experience strong conclusions about how unhampered capital markets would work. For example, Ravenscraft and Scherer (1987, 1991), Porter (1987), and other critics propose particular sequences of inefficient and efficient restructurings: diversifying, empire-building acquisitions in the 1960s and early 1970s, and then efficient divestitures in the 1980s. But why did entrepreneurs make systematic mistakes during the conglomerate period, but not later? Can changes in the legal, political, and regulatory environments account for clusters of errors during specific periods?

Third, even if divestitures are seen as revealing prior mistakes, the failure of a particular acquisition does not necessarily indicate a failure of the acquisition *strategy*. Certain kinds of acquisitions—for example, acquisitions of firms in knowledge-intensive, high-technology industries—may be inherently riskier than others. If the returns from a successful integration of the target's activities with the firm's existing activities are sufficiently high, then the acquisition has positive expected value, even if it is more likely to fail than a safer acquisition. Matsusaka (2001) offers this kind of interpretation of corporate diversification. Diversifying acquisitions represent experiments, as firms try various combinations of businesses, seeking those that match their capabilities (in the sense of Penrose, 1959; Nelson and Winter, 1982; and Wernerfelt, 1984). After learning their capabilities, firms divest acquisitions that turn out to be poor matches. In this sense, divestitures reflect successful experiments—the acquirer has learned that the target's industry is not a good match for its capabilities. Such "match-seeking" firms will actively acquire and divest over time.[5]

---

[5] Sanchez, Heene, and Thomas (1996, p. 28) suggest that the same is true for networks and alliances.

> In a dynamic market context, longevity of interfirm alliances is not necessarily an indicator of successful collaboration. A succession of short-term alliances by a firm, for example, may suggest that the firm has a superior ability to learn from its partners, or that it may have superior ability to quickly reconfigure its chain of firm-addressable resources in response to changing competitive and market conditions.

Mosakowski (1997) also offers an experimentation theory of diversification (without looking at subsequent divestitures).

This chapter elaborates a fourth, "Austrian" interpretation of corporate divestitures, one that builds on the three just mentioned. Austrian writers view market competition as a dynamic, rivalrous process that unfolds gradually through time—a "discovery procedure," in Hayek's (1978) famous phrase. The future holds genuine surprises, not merely a closed set of events whose probabilities are unknown. From this perspective, the long-term success of an acquisition, like any entrepreneurial action, cannot be "predicted." Entrepreneurs rely on judgment, or what Mises (1949) calls understanding. Understanding is intuitive, subjective, and qualitative, and thus inherently imperfect. For this reason, divestitures of underperforming subunits may be seen as efficient responses to unforeseen changes in industry and regulatory conditions, or more generally, to poor judgments by profit-seeking entrepreneurs. *Ex post* viability is not a good indicator of *ex ante* efficiency.

We begin with the theory of entrepreneurship proposed by Mises (1949), posing it as a challenge to the agency view of divestitures. We then present empirical evidence that the long-term performance of corporate acquisitions cannot, in general, be predicted by measures of agency conflicts. Instead, divestitures of previously acquired assets are more likely when firms are experimenting, learning, and otherwise trying to deal with uncertainty about future conditions. We also show that mistaken acquisitions are more likely under certain circumstances, namely during periods of intense, industry-specific regulatory activity. Our own research on restructuring (Klein and Klein, 2008) shows that significantly higher rates of divestiture follow mergers that occur in a cluster of mergers in the same industry. As argued by Mitchell and Mulherin (1996), Andrade, et al. (2001), and Andrade and Stafford (2004), mergers frequently occur in industry clusters, suggesting that mergers are driven in part by industry-specific factors, such as regulatory shocks. When an industry is regulated, deregulated, or re-regulated, economic calculation becomes more difficult, and entrepreneurial activity is hampered. It should not be surprising that poor long-term performance is more likely under those conditions.

This last result is consistent with the view, expressed repeatedly in the Austrian literature, that entrepreneurial error is associated with government intervention in the marketplace—in particular, with government ownership of property and interference with the price system. Mises (1920) famously showed that economic calculation is not possible without private property in all markets, especially markets for factors of production. The Austrian business-cycle literature (Mises, 1912; Hayek, 1935; Garrison, 2000) suggests that entrepreneurial errors are more likely under government-sponsored credit expansion. This chapter makes a related argument: entrepreneurial decisions to make acquisitions that will later be regretted, and divested, are more likely in the wake of government intervention in particular industries.

The remainder of the chapter is organized as follows. The first section reviews the Austrian literature on entrepreneurship, uncertainty, and economic calculation, suggesting that the *ex post* success of entrepreneurial actions cannot be forecasted based on generally available information. The second section introduces recent theory and evidence on the reasons for mergers and divestitures, contrasting two opposing views of sell-offs: empire-building and experimentation. The third section reviews some empirical evidence on the pre-merger causes of divestiture, challenging the generally accepted, empire-building explanation. The final section concludes.

Entrepreneurship, Profit, and Loss

As discussed in chapter 2 above, Misesian entrepreneurship is a fundamentally dynamic phenomenon, unfolding in calendar time. Entrepreneurial profit or loss is the difference between eventual, uncertain revenues and initial outlays, less the general rate of interest. Of course, Mises's entrepreneur-promoter is absent from textbook models of competitive general equilibrium in which uncertainty is defined away, replaced by probabilistic risk. In these models, it is possible to anticipate which actions, on average, would be profitable. In a world of "true" (structural, rather than parametric) uncertainty, however, profit opportunities do not exist "out there," waiting to be realized by anyone willing to take a specified action. Instead, profit opportunities are created through entrepreneurial action. As I read Mises, entrepreneurial skill is not simply luck or "alertness," the ability to recognize profit opportunities that appear, *ex nihilo*, to the discoverer. Rather, entrepreneurship is judgment: "Alertness is the mental quality of being on the lookout for something new; judgment is the mental process of assigning relevance to those things we already know"

(High, 1982, p. 167). In this context,

> promoter-entrepreneurs are those who seek to profit by actively promoting adjustment to change. They are not content to passively adjust their ... activities to readily foreseeable changes or changes that have already occurred in their circumstances; rather, they regard change itself as an opportunity to meliorate their own conditions and aggressively attempt to anticipate and exploit it. (Salerno, 1993, p. 123; see also Hülsmann, 1997)

All entrepreneurs, particularly those who operate in financial markets, use economic calculation as their primary decision-making tool.[6] By economic calculation, Mises means simply the use of present prices and anticipated future prices to compare present costs with expected future benefits. In this way the entrepreneur decides what goods and services should be produced, and what methods of production should be used to produce them. "The business of the entrepreneur is not merely to experiment with new technological methods, but to select from the multitude of technologically feasible methods those which are best fit to supply the public in the cheapest way with the things they are asking for most urgently" (Mises, 1951, p. 110). To make this selection, the entrepreneur must weigh the costs and expected benefits of various courses of action, and for this he needs the cardinal numbers provided by money prices. Monetary calculation, then, requires private property and market prices.

As we saw in chapter 1, Mises's famous 1920 essay on economic calculation under socialism is not so much about socialism *per se*; it is an argument about the role of prices for capital goods (Rothbard, 1993, pp. 547–78). Entrepreneurs make decisions about resource allocation based on their expectations about future prices and the information contained in present prices. To make profits, they need information about all prices, not only the prices of consumer goods but the prices of factors of production. Without markets for capital goods, these goods can have no prices, and therefore entrepreneurs cannot make judgments about the relative scarcities of these factors. In short, resources cannot be allocated efficiently. In any environment, then—socialist or not—where a factor

---

[6] Chapter 2 above argues that financial-market entrepreneurship is a particularly important form of entrepreneurial activity, though it has received little attention in the Austrian literature.

of production has no market price, a potential user of that factor will be unable to make rational decisions about its use. Stated this way, Mises's claim is simply that efficient resource allocation in a market economy requires well-functioning asset markets.

Despite Mises's explicit focus on entrepreneurship, much of modern production theory—indeed, the entire neoclassical theory of the firm—focuses not on entrepreneurs, but managers. The traditional theory of profit maximization is nearly always told from the perspective of the manager, the agent who operates the plant, not that of the owner, who supplies the capital to fund the plant. Yet owners control how much authority to delegate to operational managers, so capitalists are, in an important sense, the ultimate decision-makers. To understand the firm, then, we must focus on the actions and plans of the suppliers of financial capital, the capitalist-entrepreneurs.

It is true, of course, that when capitalist-entrepreneurs supply resources to firms, they usually delegate to managers the day-to-day responsibility for use of those resources. The resulting possibility for managerial discretion is of course the focal problem of the modern literature on corporate finance and the theory of the firm. As discussed in chapter 2 above, the literature on corporate governance identifies a variety of mechanisms by which shareholders can limit this discretion, such as establishing boards of directors, using performance-based pay, adopting the "M-form" structure, and exploiting competition among managers and potential managers. Outside the firm, competition in product, labor, and capital markets helps align managers' interests with those of shareholders.[7]

We should therefore be cautious in attributing the eventual divestiture of many acquisitions, particularly during the 1960s and 1970s, to managerial motives. Moreover, the claim that the acquisitive conglomerates of the 1960s and 1970s were inefficient is inconsistent with recent evidence that during those years, diversifying acquisitions—particularly those that created internal capital markets—tended to increase the market values of the acquiring firms (Matsusaka, 1993; Hubbard and Palia, 1999; Klein, 2001). In light of this evidence, "[t]he simple view that the 1980s 'bust-ups' were a corrective to past managerial excesses is untenable" (Matsusaka,

---

[7]Jensen (1993) argues that internal control mechanisms are generally weak and in-effective, while external control mechanisms—where allowed to function—are typically superior.

1993, p. 376). In short, both theory and empirical evidence cast doubt on the conventional wisdom that corporate managers made systematic, predictable mistakes by acquiring (often unrelated) subunits during the 1960s and 1970s, and that financial-market participants made systematic mistakes by approving these acquisitions.

Mergers, Sell-offs, and Efficiency: Theory and Evidence

Why, in general, do firms expand and diversify through merger? Why do they sometimes retreat and "refocus" through divestiture? The theory of merger is a subset of the theory of the optimal size and shape of the firm, a relatively undeveloped area in the Austrian literature. Chapters 1 and 2 above argue for a modified Coasian, or contractual, view of firm boundaries, in which the limits to organization are given by the need to perform economic calculation using prices generated in external markets. Other writers see the Austrian approach as more congenial to the resource-based theory of the firm, defining firms' capabilities in terms of Hayekian tacit knowledge (Langlois, 1992, 1994a; Minkler, 1993a). In either case, we can think of merger or takeover as a response to a valuation discrepancy: acquisition occurs when the value of an existing firm's assets is greater to an outside party than to its current owners. Put differently, a merger can be a response to economies of scope, in that the value of the merging firms' assets combined exceeds their joint values separately.[8] As with any voluntary exchange, the transaction is (*ex ante*) advantageous to both parties, and should thus be welfare-enhancing.

New combinations of corporate assets can generate efficiencies by replacing poorly performing managers (Jensen and Ruback, 1983; Mitchell

---

[8]Two popular explanations for multiproduct economies of scope center on internal capital markets and strategic resources. According to the internal-capital-markets hypothesis, as expressed by Alchian (1969), Williamson (1975), Gertner, et al. (1994), and Stein (1997), internal capital markets have advantages where access to external funds is limited. The central office of the diversified firm can use informational advantages, residual control rights, and its ability to intervene selectively in divisional affairs to allocate resources within the firm better than the external capital markets would do if the divisions were stand-alone firms. In the resource-based view, the firm is regarded as a stock of knowledge, establishing a range of competence that may extend across multiple product lines. Excess profits or supranormal returns are seen as rents accruing to unique factors of production (Montgomery and Wernerfelt, 1988) and firms diversify because they have excess capacity in these unique factors.

and Lehn, 1990), creating operating synergies (Weston, Chung, and Hoag, 1990, pp. 194–95), or establishing internal capital markets (Alchian, 1969; Williamson, 1975; Gertner, et al., 1994; Stein, 1997). In particular, considerable evidence suggests that the market for corporate control disciplines incumbent management. For example, Morck, Shleifer, and Vishny (1988) found that firms with lower Tobin's q-ratios are more likely to be targets of takeovers. Tobin's q measures the ratio of the firm's market value to the replacement cost (or book value) of its assets. Because firms with low market-to-book ratios have low expected cash flows relative to the amount of invested capital, the market-to-book ratio can be interpreted as a measure of the firm's investment opportunities (Smith and Watts, 1992; Gaver and Gaver, 1993), or as a measure of managerial inefficiency or agency conflict within the firm (Lang, Stulz, and Walkling, 1991). Low-q firms are the most likely takeover targets.

Given the benefits of takeovers, why are many mergers later "reversed" in a divestiture or spin-off? Here we distinguish between two basic views. The first, which may be termed *empire-building*, holds that entrenched managers make acquisitions, often paying with the acquiring firm's (inflated) stock, primarily to increase their own power, prestige or control. These acquisitions produce negligible efficiency gains, and are thus more likely to be divested *ex post*. Most important, because the acquiring firm's motives are suspect, such acquisitions are *ex ante* inefficient; neutral observers can predict, based on pre-merger characteristics, that these mergers are unlikely to be viable over time. By permitting these acquisitions, capital-market participants are also guilty of systematic error. Admittedly, in the empire-building view, markets did eventually correct these mistakes with the restructurings of the 1980s.[9] Still, farsighted regulators could have reduced social costs by limiting such acquisitions in the first place.

A second view, which we term *entrepreneurial market process*, acknowledges that unprofitable acquisitions may be mistakes *ex post*, but argues

---

[9] This raises the question of why, if managers were sufficiently entrenched to make inefficient acquisitions in the first place, would they not remain sufficiently entrenched to hold on to poorly performing targets, rather than divest them and risk revealing their underlying objectives? Boot (1992, p. 1402) argues that an entrenched manager will not divest because the external market will take divestiture as an admission of failure and a bad signal of his ability. The argument that divestitures indicate agency problems thus assumes a change in corporate control between the original acquisitions and the later divestitures.

that poor long-term performance does not indicate *ex ante* inefficiency. In the market-process perspective, a divestiture of previously acquired assets may mean simply that profit-seeking entrepreneurs have updated their forecasts of future conditions or otherwise learned from experience. As Mises (1949, p. 582) puts it, "the outcome of action is always uncertain. Action is always speculation." Consequently, "the real entrepreneur is a *speculator*, a man eager to utilize his opinion about the future structure of the market for business operations promising profits. This specific antici- pative understanding of the conditions of the uncertain future defies any rules and systematization" (Mises, 1949, p. 582, emphasis in original).[10]

As discussed above, this notion of entrepreneurial decision making under uncertainty squares with recent theories of acquisitions as a form of experimentation (Mosakowski, 1997; Boot, Milbourn, and Thakor, 1999; Matsusaka, 2001). In these models, profit-seeking entrepreneurs can learn their own capabilities only by trying various combinations of activities, which could include diversifying into new industries. Firms may thus make diversifying acquisitions even if they know these acquisitions are likely to be reversed in a divestiture. This process generates information that is useful for revising entrepreneurial plans, and thus an acquisition strategy may be successful even if individual acquisitions are not. In these cases, the long-term viability of an acquisition may be systematically re- lated to publicly observable, pre-merger characteristics associated with ex- perimentation, but not characteristics associated with managerial discre- tion.

To explain the particular pattern of mergers and acquisitions observed over the last several decades, market-process explanations must appeal to changes in the legal, political, competitive, or regulatory environments that affect the ability of entrepreneurs to anticipate future conditions. Why, for instance, was it particularly difficult for entrepreneurs to forecast the success of acquisitions in the 1960s and 1970s? Why did entrepreneurs feel a greater need to experiment with various combinations of businesses during those years?

One possibility is that complex organizations with active internal cap- ital markets were necessary in the 1960s, but became less important after capital markets were deregulated in the 1970s. The investment community

---

[10]See chapter 6 below for details on Mises's approach to uncertainty.

in the 1960s has been described as a small, close-knit group where competition was minimal and peer influence strong Bernstein (1992). As Bhidé (1990, p. 76) puts it, "internal capital markets ... may well have possessed a significant edge because the external markets were not highly developed. In those days, one's success on Wall Street reportedly depended far more on personal connections than analytical prowess." During that period, the financial markets were relatively poor sources of capital. In 1975, the SEC deregulated brokerage houses and removed its rule on fixed-price commissions. The effect of deregulation, not surprisingly, was to increase competition among providers of investment services. "This competitive process has resulted in a significant increase in the ability of our external capital markets to monitor corporate performance and allocate resources" (p. 77). As the cost of external finance has fallen, firms have tended to rely less on internal finance, and thus the value added from internal-capital-market allocation has fallen. Consequently, firms have adopted simpler, more "focused" structures that rely more heavily on external capital markets and outsourcing, possibly explaining some of the divestitures observed in the last two decades.

Are Divestitures Predictable? Evidence from a Duration Study

This section summarizes some ongoing research on the causes of divestiture (Klein and Klein, 2008). If acquisitions are most often symptoms of managerial empire-building, as suggested by Ravenscraft and Scherer (1987), Porter (1987), and other critics, then pre-merger characteristics associated with high levels of managerial discretion should be systematically related to the long-term failure and reversal of these acquisitions. In the market-process view, by contrast, long-term performance should be correlated only with pre-merger characteristics associated with experimentation, rapidly changing environments, or knowledge-intensive industries. Our empirical research finds little support for the empire-building hypothesis, and much stronger support for the market-process view. Specifically, we find that most characteristics typically associated with empire-building are poor predictors of merger duration. The evidence also suggests that divestiture is more likely when the original acquisition is driven by industry-specific competitive or regulatory shocks.

Klein and Klein (2008) study 222 pairs of firms that merged during the 1977–1983 period. Of the 222 acquisitions, 64, or almost 30 percent, had been divested by July 1995. We used a duration or "hazard" model to study the effects of pre-merger characteristics on the time to divestiture. Duration models help explain how exogenous factors, unobserved factors, and time itself affect the average duration until some discrete event (in our case, divestiture) occurs. Duration analysis allows us to see, historically, how characteristics of the acquiring and acquired firms affect the likelihood that the acquired firm will later be divested.

To study the effects of pre-merger characteristics on average merger duration, we estimated a hazard regression of duration (measured as the natural logarithm of the number of days) on a constant and on a series of potentially exogenous factors. For assessing the empire-building hypothesis, we included three characteristics associated with high levels of managerial discretion: relatedness of target and acquirer, differences in price-earnings ratios, and the medium of payment. Relatedness addresses the common view that managers deliberately pursue unrelated targets to expand their control or make themselves more valuable to the firm. Following Kaplan and Weisbach (1992), we examined this claim by constructing a dummy variable equal to one if the acquiring and target firm share at least one two-digit SIC code and zero otherwise.

Differences in price-earnings ratios are commonly seen as another indicator of merger motives. Merger critics have often suggested that acquiring firms grow and prosper by "bootstrapping." This refers to the practice whereby bidding firms seek targets with low P/E ratios to boost their reported earnings per share. It is trivially mathematically true that when a firm with a high P/E multiple acquires a firm with a low P/E multiple and pays with its own stock, the acquirer's earnings per share will rise, simply because the combined earnings of the two firms will then be divided by a smaller number of total shares outstanding. Hence, it is argued, acquiring firms can expand rapidly, with market approval, as managers exploit this accounting opportunity.[11]

---

[11] This is Malkiel's (1990, p. 58) explanation for the conglomerate boom: "the major impetus for the conglomerate wave of the 1960s was that the acquisition process itself could be made to produce growth in earnings per share.... By an easy bit of legerdemain, [conglomerate managers] could put together a group of companies with no basic potential at all and produce steadily rising per-share earnings." For a more balanced discussion of

Of course, this argument assumes market participants could be systematically fooled by a simple algebraic trick. Admittedly, much more complicated financial and balance-sheet manipulations are often used in corporate-control transactions: bidders in the 1960s and 1970s sometimes financed acquisitions with convertible bonds, convertible preferred stocks, and other unique instruments. Although investors could (and eventually did) require that earnings be reported on a "fully diluted" basis, to take account of these manipulations, Malkiel (1990, p. 61) reports that "most investors in the middle 1960s ignored such niceties and were satisfied only to see steadily and rapidly rising earnings." However, there is no evidence that bootstrapping was either prevalent or successful (Barber, Palmer, and Wallace, 1995; Matsusaka, 1993).

Nonetheless, we included a measure of relative P/E ratios to see if acquirers that choose targets with lower P/E ratios are historically more likely to divest those same targets, implying that bootstrapping does tend to fool investors, as increases in reported earnings disguise inefficient acquisitions.

We also included a series of dummy variables to represent the medium of payment used in the merger. Several theories suggest that how an acquisition is financed can affect performance. First, the bootstrapping technique described above works only for mergers financed by stock swap. Second, Jensen (1986) holds that financing takeovers by issuing debt serves to discipline the acquiring firm's management by reducing post-merger discretion in the use of free cash flow. If true, we would expect entrenched managers to avoid making acquisitions using debt, opting for stock swaps instead.

In the market-process or experimentation view, by contrast, divestitures occur when the acquirer receives new information about the target after the merger has taken place. Plausibly, some relevant characteristics of potential target firms can be learned only by experience, forcing entrepreneurs to revise their plans accordingly. What kinds of targets are most likely to have unknown characteristics? Large firms engage in more activities than smaller firms, so potential acquirers have more to learn. On the other hand, smaller firms are less likely to have been written about in the business press, so one could plausibly argue that private information is a bigger problem for small targets.[12] We included target size in our

---

the bootstrapping practice see Lynch (1971, pp. 55–56).

[12] However, in our sample, all targets are themselves publicly traded corporations, so

regressions to see if either aspect is relevant. Firms in rapidly changing, knowledge-intensive industries are also likely to have characteristics hidden from potential acquirers. To capture this effect, we created a dummy variable based on two-digit SIC codes. The dummy takes a value of one if the target is in any of the following industries: computers (systems, software, and services), medical products, communications, aerospace, and miscellaneous high-tech industries. We also included target R&D because R&D is difficult to value, especially to outsiders, and thus firms in R&D-intensive industries are likely to have hidden characteristics. Potential acquirers would know potential targets' R&D expenditures (which is reported), but this may not give the acquirers much information on the quality of the research or even the content of the R&D.

Finally, unrelated acquisitions, as discussed above, may be a form of experimentation, as firms try new combinations of activities to find those that best fit their existing capabilities. Although match-seeking acquisitions are more likely to be divested, they can still be part of a value-maximizing acquisition strategy. Our relatedness variable, described above, can proxy for match-seeking behavior. However, the best way to identify match-seeking firms is to look directly at historical patterns of acquisitions and divestitures. A firm with a history of repeated acquisitions and divestitures, especially acquisitions into unrelated industries, is likely to be a match-seeker, and thus any current acquisition is more likely to be divested. Unfortunately, our merger sample is too small to compile detailed acquisition and divestiture histories on individual acquirers. As a first approximation, we searched our sample for acquiring firms with at least one previous acquisition that was later divested within a few years of the acquisition. We created a dummy variable equal to one if the acquirer in a particular merger met these criteria, and zero otherwise.[13]

As noted above, periods of intense merger activity in particular industries may be responses to industry-specific competitive or regulatory shocks. Mitchell and Mulherin (1996), Andrade, et al. (2001), and Andrade and Stafford (2004) argue that mergers tend to occur in industry clusters, suggesting that industry-specific factors are important. Mitchell

---

lack of media exposure is unlikely to be a problem.

[13] Mosakowski (1997) suggests that younger firms face greater uncertainty, or a higher level of "causal ambiguity," about the best use of their resources, which implies that firm age could also be a proxy for match-seeking behavior.

and Mulherin argue that corporate takeovers are often the most cost-effective way for industries to respond to these shocks. Moreover, they add, "because takeovers are driven in part by industry shocks, it is not surprising that many firms exhibit volatile performance following takeovers, with actual failures following some negative shocks" (Mitchell and Mulherin, 1996, p. 195).

To capture the effects of industry-specific shocks such as regulatory and tax changes, we included measures of industry clustering, both for acquirers and for targets, in our regressions. We did find substantial clustering in our sample. For example, slightly more than half of the mergers during the 1977–83 period occurred in only five of the thirty-seven (two-digit) SIC industries in our sample, both for acquirers and targets, with three-quarters occurring in ten industries. We constructed clustering variables by counting the number of mergers in each two-digit SIC category in each year and creating variables for each merger corresponding to the number of mergers occurring (a) within one year of the merger under observation (including the year before the merger, the year of the merger, and the year after the merger, to span a three-year window), (b) within two years of the merger (a five-year window), and (c) within the entire sample (a seven-year window). If risky acquisitions or increased levels of experimentation tend to appear during periods of industry-specific shocks, then these clustering variables will have negative and significant effects on the length of time to divestiture.

Our results challenge the empire-building hypothesis and offer evidence more consistent with the market-process view. Of the variables associated with agency problems, only relatedness has a statistically significant effect on merger duration. Neither P/E differences nor the medium of payment has a statistically significant coefficient in any of several specifications. The coefficient on relatedness is positive, meaning that related acquisitions are less likely, on average, to be divested (as in Kaplan and Weisbach, 1992). However, the coefficient on relatedness is also consistent with the market-process explanation. Of the five variables associated with this view, the coefficient on relatedness is positive and significant, the coefficient on target R&D is negative and significant, and the coefficient on the match-seeking indicator is negative and significant, all as expected. The coefficients on target size and the indicator for high-technology industries have the expected signs (positive and negative, respectively) but are not statistically significant.

Overall, our findings suggest that the divestitures in our sample are not, on average, the predictable result of unwise acquisitions. Rather, divestitures follow experimentation and learning, healthy characteristics of a market economy. Moreover, industry clustering appears to have a regular effect on average merger duration. The coefficients on our acquirer-clustering variables are consistently negative and statistically significant. (The coefficients on the target-clustering variables, by contrast, are not statistically significant.) This suggests that volatile performance does follow shocks, as suggested by Mitchell and Mulherin (1996).

This finding is consistent with the view that firms make acquisitions when faced with increased uncertainty (see Spulber, 1992, pp. 557–59). Regulatory interference could be a major cause of such uncertainty. As discussed above, government intervention makes economic calculation more difficult, and can ultimately render calculation impossible. When faced with increased regulatory interference, firms apparently respond by experimenting, making riskier acquisitions, and consequently making more mistakes, *ex post*.

Conclusions

Do entrepreneurs make predictable mistakes? Theory and evidence suggest otherwise. Contrary to the conventional wisdom on mergers and sell-offs, divestitures of previously acquired assets do not necessarily indicate that the original acquisitions were mistakes. Indeed, empire-building motives do not seem to be systematically related to long-term merger performance. Instead, divestitures are more likely to be associated with experimentation, learning, and other socially beneficial activities.

Acquisitions are uncertain endeavors, and the entrepreneur-promoter —along with the manager to whom he delegates authority—is a speculator. If the consequences of his actions were determinate, he would not be an entrepreneur, but rather, as some economic theories seem to treat him, "a soulless automaton" (Mises, 1949, p. 582). However, the future can never be known with certainty; long-term profit and loss cannot be predicted based on current information. As Mises explains:

> What distinguishes the successful entrepreneur and promoter from other people is precisely the fact that he does not let himself be

guided by what was and is, but arranges his affairs on the ground of his opinion about the future. He sees the past and the present as other people do; but he judges the future in a different way. (p. 585)

As discussed above, it is hardly surprising that these judgments are less than perfect. The relevant question for policy is whether there is a feasible alternative to market-based corporate governance. Our reading of the political-economy literature leaves us doubtful that such an alternative exists.

CHAPTER 4

The Entrepreneurial Organization of Heterogeneous Capital[†]

With Kirsten Foss, Nicolai J. Foss, and Sandra K. Klein

The theory of entrepreneurship comes in many guises. Management scholars and economists have made the entrepreneur an innovator, a leader, a creator, a discoverer, an equilibrator, and more. In only a few of these theories, however, is entrepreneurship explicitly linked to asset ownership (examples include Casson, 1982; Foss, 1993b; Foss and Klein, 2005; Knight, 1921; Langlois and Cosgel, 1993; Mises, 1949). Ownership theories of entrepreneurship start with the proposition that entrepreneurial judgment is costly to trade, an idea originally suggested by Knight (1921). When judgment is complementary to other assets, it makes sense for entrepreneurs to own these complementary assets. The entrepreneur's role, then, is to arrange or organize the capital goods he owns. Entrepreneurial judgment is ultimately judgment about the control of resources.

In a world of identical capital goods, entrepreneurial judgment plays a relatively minor role. Unfortunately, mainstream neoclassical economics,

[†]Published originally in *Journal of Management Studies* 44, no. 7 (November 2007): 1165–86.

upon which most economic theories of entrepreneurship are based, lacks a systematic theory of capital heterogeneity. Strongly influenced by Knight's (1936) concept of capital as a permanent, homogeneous fund of value, rather than a discrete stock of heterogeneous capital goods, neoclassical economists have devoted little attention to capital theory. For this reason, ownership theories of entrepreneurship, as well as contemporary theories of firm boundaries, ownership, and strategy, are not generally founded on a systematic theory of capital or asset attributes. This chapter outlines the capital theory associated with the Austrian school of economics and derives implications for entrepreneurship and economic organization.

The Austrian school of economics (Menger, 1871; Böhm-Bawerk, 1889; Mises, 1949; Hayek, 1948, 1968b; Kirzner, 1973; Lachmann, 1956; Rothbard, 1962) is well known in management studies for its contributions to the theory of entrepreneurship and the complementary "market process" account of economic activity (Chiles, 2003; Chiles and Choi, 2000; Hill and Deeds, 1996; Jacobson, 1992; Langlois, 2001; Roberts and Eisenhardt, 2003). Other characteristically Austrian ideas such as the time structure of capital and the "malinvestment" theory of the business-cycle theory have received much less attention. To several Austrians, the theory of entrepreneurship was closely related to the theory of capital. As Lachmann (1956, pp. 13, 16) argued: "We are living in a world of unexpected change; hence capital combinations ... will be ever changing, will be dissolved and reformed. In this activity, we find the real function of the entrepreneur." It is this "real function" that we elaborate in the following.

Management scholars will hardly be startled by the claim that entrepreneurs organize heterogeneous capital goods. The management literature abounds with notions of heterogeneous "resources," "competencies," "capabilities," "assets," and the like. Linking such work to entrepreneurship would seem to be a rather natural undertaking (see, e.g. Alvarez and Busenitz, 2001). However, modern theories of economic organization are not built on a unified theory of capital heterogeneity; instead, they simply invoke ad hoc specificities when necessary. The Austrian school offers a systematic, comprehensive theory of capital, and Austrian notions of capital heterogeneity can inform, synthesize, and improve the treatment of specificities in the theory of the firm. Adopting the Austrian view of capital also reveals new sources of transaction costs that influence economic organization.

The chapter proceeds as follows. We begin, building on Foss and Klein (2005), by linking the theory of entrepreneurship and the theory of the firm. The link involves first, defining entrepreneurship as the exercise of judgment over resource uses under uncertainty, and second, viewing the theory of economic organization as a subset of the theory of asset ownership. We then discuss "assets" in the specific context of capital theory, showing that the assumption of heterogeneous capital is necessary to the theory of the firm. We next summarize the Austrian theory of capital, elaborating and expanding on those parts of the theory most relevant for economic organization. The final section weaves these elements together to provide new insights into key questions of the emergence, boundaries, and internal organization of the firm. We conclude with some suggestions for testable implications that may be drawn from our theory.

Entrepreneurship, Judgment, and Asset Ownership

Entrepreneurs are the founders and developers of business firms. Indeed, the establishment of a new business venture is the quintessential manifestation of entrepreneurship. Yet, as Foss and Klein (2005) point out, the theory of entrepreneurship and the theory of the firm developed largely in isolation. The economic theory of the firm emerged and took shape as the entrepreneur was being banished from microeconomic analysis, first in the 1930s when the firm was subsumed into neoclassical price theory (O'Brien, 1984) and again in the 1980s as the theory of the firm was restated using game theory and information economics. Modern contributions to the theory of the firm (Hart, 1995; Milgrom and Roberts, 1992; Williamson, 1975, 1985, 1996) mention entrepreneurship only in passing, if at all.

Foss and Klein (2005) show how the theory of entrepreneurship and the theory of the firm can be linked using the concept of entrepreneurship as *judgment*.[1] This view traces its origins to the first systematic treatment of entrepreneurship in economics, Richard Cantillon's *Essai sur la nature de commerce en général* (1755). It conceives entrepreneurship as judgmental decision making under conditions of uncertainty. Judgment refers

---

[1] For related treatments along the same lines, see Casson (1982) and Langlois and Cosgel (1993).

primarily to business decision making when the range of possible future outcomes, let alone the likelihood of individual outcomes, is generally unknown (what Knight terms uncertainty, rather than mere probabilistic risk). More generally, judgment is required "when no obviously correct model or decision rule is available or when relevant data is unreliable or incomplete" (Casson, 1993).

As such, judgment is distinct from boldness, daring, or imagination (Aldrich and Wiedenmayer, 1993; Begley and Boyd, 1987; Chandler and Jansen, 1992; Hood and Young, 1993; Lumpkin and Dess, 1996), innovation (Schumpeter, 1911), alertness (Kirzner, 1973), leadership (Witt, 1998), and other concepts of entrepreneurship that appear in the economics and management literatures. Judgment must be exercised in mundane circumstances, as Knight (1921) emphasized, for ongoing operations as well as new ventures. Alertness is the ability to react to existing opportunities while judgment refers to the creation of new opportunities.[2] Those who specialize in judgmental decision making may be dynamic, charismatic leaders, but they need not possess these traits. In short, decision making under uncertainty is entrepreneurial, whether it involves imagination, creativity, leadership, and related factors or not.

Knight (1921) introduces judgment to link profit and the firm to uncertainty. Judgment primarily refers to the process of businessmen forming estimates of future events in situations in which the relevant probability distributions are themselves unknown. Entrepreneurship represents judgment that cannot be assessed in terms of its marginal product and which cannot, accordingly, be paid a wage (Knight, 1921, p. 311). In other words, there is no market for the judgment that entrepreneurs rely on, and therefore exercising judgment requires the person with judgment to start a firm. Of course, judgmental decision-makers can hire consultants, forecasters, technical experts, and so on. However, as we explain below, in doing so they are exercising their own entrepreneurial judgment. Judgment thus implies asset ownership, for judgmental decision making is ultimately decision making about the employment of resources. An

---

[2]In Kirzner's treatment, entrepreneurship is characterized as "a *responding* agency. I view the entrepreneur not as a source of innovative ideas *ex nihilo*, but as being *alert* to the opportunities that exist already and are waiting to be noticed" (Kirzner, 1973, p. 74, emphasis in original)

entrepreneur without capital goods is, in Knight's sense, no entrepreneur.[3]

The notion of entrepreneurship as judgment implies an obvious link with the theory of the firm, particularly those theories (transaction cost economics and the property-rights approach) that put asset ownership at the forefront of firm organization (Hart 1995; Williamson 1996; cf. also Langlois and Cosgel 1993). The firm is defined as the entrepreneur plus the alienable assets he owns and therefore ultimately controls. The theory of the firm then becomes a theory of how the entrepreneur arranges his heterogeneous capital assets, what combinations of assets will he seek to acquire, what (proximate) decisions will he delegate to subordinates, how will he provide incentives and use monitoring to see that his assets are used consistently with his judgments, and so on. Given this emphasis on entrepreneurship, one might expect the modern theory of the firm to be based on a coherent, systematic theory of capital. This is not the case, however.

Capital Theory and the Theory of the Firm

Shmoo Capital and Its Implications

Modern (neoclassical) economics focuses on a highly stylized model of the production process. The firm is a production function, a "black box" that transforms inputs (land, labor, capital) into output (consumer goods). We noted in chapters 1 and 2 that this model omits the critical organizational details of production, rarely looking inside the black box to see how hierarchies are structured, how incentives are provided, how teams are organized, and the like. An equally serious omission, perhaps, is that production is treated as a one-stage process, in which factors are instantly converted into final goods, rather than a complex, multi-stage process unfolding through time and employing rounds of intermediate goods. "Capital" is treated as a homogeneous factor of production, the K that appears in the production function along with L for labor. Following Solow (1957) models of economic growth typically model capital as what Paul Samuelson called "shmoo"—an infinitely elastic, fully moldable factor that can be

---

[3] This contrasts with Schumpeter's and Kirzner's conceptions of entrepreneurship, in which entrepreneurship can be exercised without the possession of any capital goods. On this contrast, see Foss and Klein (2005).

substituted costlessly from one production process to another.

In a world of shmoo capital, economic organization is relatively unimportant. All capital assets possess the same attributes, and thus the costs of inspecting, measuring, and monitoring the attributes of productive assets is trivial. Exchange markets for capital assets would be virtually devoid of transaction costs. A few basic contractual problems—in particular, principal–agent conflicts over the supply of labor services—may remain, though workers would all use identical capital assets, and this would greatly contribute to reducing the costs of measuring their productivity.

While transaction costs would not disappear entirely in such a world, asset ownership would be relatively unimportant. The possibility of specifying all possible uses of an asset significantly reduces the costs of writing complete, contingent contracts between resource owners and entrepreneurs governing the uses of the relevant assets.[4] Contracts would largely substitute for ownership, leaving the boundary of the firm indeterminate (Hart, 1995).

Capital in Modern Theories of the Firm

By contrast, all modern theories of the firm assume (often implicitly) that capital assets possess varying attributes, so that all assets are not equally valuable in all uses. Here we review how capital heterogeneity leads to non-trivial contracting problems, the solutions to which may require the creation of a firm.

ASSET SPECIFICITY APPROACHES. In transaction cost economics (TCE) (Williamson, 1975, 1985, 1996) and the "new" property-rights approach (Grossman and Hart, 1986; Hart and Moore, 1990), some assets are conceived as specific to particular users. If complete, contingent contracts specifying the most valuable uses of such assets in all possible states of the world cannot be written, then owners of productive assets face certain risks.

---

[4]Contracts might still be incomplete because contracting parties have different, subjective expectations about the likelihood of various contingencies affecting the value of the (homogeneous) capital asset. Agents may also differ in their ability to learn about possible uses of the capital good. In other words, Knightian uncertainty plus bounded rationality could drive contractual incompleteness even in a world without capital heterogeneity. However, the neoclassical world of shmoo capital is characterized by parametric uncertainty, common priors, and hyperrationality.

Primarily, if circumstances change unexpectedly, the original governing agreement may no longer be effective. The need to adapt to unforeseen contingencies constitutes an important cost of contracting. Failure to adapt imposes what Williamson (1991b) calls "maladaptation costs," the best known of which is the "holdup" problem associated with relationship-specific investments.

It is obvious that maladaptation costs largely disappear if all assets are equally valuable in all uses. Potential holdup would still be a concern for owners of relationship-specific human capital and raw materials, but disagreements over the efficient use of capital goods would become irrelevant.[5] The scope of entrepreneurial activity would also be severely reduced, since entrepreneurs would have no need to arrange particular combinations of capital assets.

RESOURCE- AND KNOWLEDGE-BASED APPROACHES. Resource-based (Barney, 1991; Lippman and Rumelt, 2003; Wernerfelt, 1984) and knowledge-based (Grant, 1996; Penrose, 1959) approaches also emphasize capital heterogeneity, but their focus is not generally economic organization, but rather competitive advantage.[6] The emphasis in these approaches is not economic organization, however, but competitive advantage. The latter is seen as emerging from bundles of resources (including knowledge). Different resource bundles are associated with different efficiencies translating into a theory of competitive advantage. Resource- and knowledge-based scholars often emphasize that heterogeneous assets do not give rise independently to competitive advantages. Rather, it is the interactions among these resources, their relations of specificity and co-specialization, that generate such advantages (e.g. Barney, 1991; Black and Boal, 1994; Dierickx and Cool, 1989). However, this notion is not developed from any comprehensive perspective on asset specificity and co-specialization (or complementarity) (as in Teece, 1982).

---

[5] Resources that are *initially* homogeneous could become heterogeneous over time, through learning by doing or co-specialization of human and physical capital. Here we refer to conditions of permanent homogeneity.

[6] Penrose's approach, unlike modern resource- and knowledge-based approaches, did emphasize one important element of economic organization, namely the rate of growth of the firm.

"Old" property rights theory. A sophisticated approach to capital heterogeneity can be drawn from the property-rights approach associated with economists such as Coase (1960), Alchian (1965), Demsetz (1964, 1967), and, particularly, Barzel (1997). These writers focus not on individual assets *per se*, but on bundles of asset attributes to which property rights may be held (Foss and Foss, 2001).

While it is common to view capital heterogeneity in terms of physical heterogeneity—beer barrels and blast furnaces are different because of their physical differences—the old property-rights approach emphasizes that capital goods are heterogeneous because they have different levels and kinds of valued attributes (in the terminology of Barzel, 1997).[7] Attributes are characteristics, functions, or possible uses of assets, as perceived by an entrepreneur. For example, a copying machine has multiple attributes because it can be used at different times, by different people, and for different types of copying work; that it can be purchased in different colors and sizes; and so on.[8] Property rights to the machine itself can be partitioned, in the sense that rights to its attributes can be defined and traded, depending on transaction costs (Foss and Foss, 2001).

Clearly, virtually all assets have multiple attributes. Assets are heterogeneous to the extent that they have different, and different levels of, valued attributes. Attributes may also vary over time, even for a particular asset. In a world of "true" uncertainty, entrepreneurs are unlikely to know all relevant attributes of all assets when production decisions are made. Nor can the future attributes of an asset, as it is used in production, be forecast with certainty. Future attributes must be discovered, over time, as assets are used in production. Or, to formulate the problem slightly differently, future attributes are *created* as entrepreneurs envision new ways of using assets to produce goods and services.[9]

---

[7]Foss and Foss (2005) link the property rights approach to the resource-based view, demonstrating how the more "micro" approach of the property rights approach provides additional insights into resource value. See also Kim and Mahoney (2002, 2005) for similar arguments.

[8]Clearly, this notion of subjectively perceived attributes of capital assets is related to Penrose's (1959) point that physically identical capital assets may yield different *services*, depending on, for example, the nature of the administrative framework in which they are embedded.

[9]In this chapter we do not distinguish between "discovery" and "creation" as alternative conceptions of the entrepreneurial act (Alvarez and Barney, 2007). Chapter 5 below discusses this distinction in detail.

SUMMING UP. While capital heterogeneity thus plays an important role in transaction cost, resource-based, and property-rights approaches to the firm, none of these approaches rests on a unified, systematic theory of capital. Instead, each invokes the needed specificities in an ad hoc fashion to rationalize particular trading problems for transaction cost economics, asset specificity; for capabilities theories, tacit knowledge; and so on. Some writers (Demsetz, 1991; Langlois and Foss, 1999; Winter, 1988) argue that the economics of organization has shown a tendency (albeit an imperfect one) to respect an implicit dichotomy between production and exchange. Thus, as Langlois and Foss (1999) argue, there is an implicit agreement, that the production function approach with its attendant assumptions (e.g. blueprint, knowledge) tells us what we need to know about production, so theories of the firm can focus on transacting and how transactional hazards can be mitigated by organization. Production issues, including capital theory, never really take center stage. This is problematic if production itself reveals *new* problems of transacting that may influence economic organization.

The Attributes Approach to Capital Heterogeneity

An alternative tradition in economics, the Austrian school, does have a systematic, comprehensive theory of capital, though it has not generally been applied to the business firm.[10] Instead, most of the substantial literature on Austrian capital theory focuses on the economy's overall capital structure and how money and credit markets affect the allocation of resources across different stages of the production process.[11]

Austrian Capital Theory

The concept of heterogeneous capital has a long and distinguished place in Austrian economics.[12] Early Austrian writers argued that capital has

---

[10]Of the several dozen papers on Austrian economics and the theory of the firm (including, for instance, the papers collected in Foss and Klein, 2002), only a few deal with Austrian capital theory (see Chiles, Meyer, and Hench, 2004; Lewin, 2005; Yu, 1999; and various papers by the present authors)

[11]Hayek's 1974 Nobel Prize in economics was awarded for his technical work on the business cycle and not, as is commonly believed, for his later work on knowledge and "spontaneous order." For a modern restatement of Austrian business cycle theory, see Garrison (2000).

[12]For overviews see Strigl (1934), Kirzner (1966), and Lewin (1999).

a time dimension as well as a value dimension. Carl Menger (1871), founder of the Austrian school, characterized goods in terms of "orders": goods of lowest order are those consumed directly. Tools and machines used to produce those consumption goods are of a higher order, and the capital goods used to produce the tools and machines are of an even higher order. Building on his theory that the value of all goods is determined by their ability to satisfy consumer wants (i.e. their marginal utility), Menger showed that the value of the higher-order goods is given or "imputed" by the value of the lower-order goods they produce. Moreover, because certain capital goods are themselves produced by other, higher-order capital goods, it follows that capital goods are not identical, at least by the time they are employed in the production process. The claim is not that there is no substitution among capital goods, but that: the degree of substitution is limited; as Lachmann (1956) put it, capital goods are characterized by "multiple specificity." Some substitution is possible, but only at a cost.[13]

Kirzner (1966) added an important refinement to the Austrian theory of capital by emphasizing the role of the entrepreneur (the theme that dominates Kirzner's later, better known, work). Earlier Austrian writers, particularly Böhm-Bawerk, tried to characterize the economy's capital structure in terms of its physical attributes, Böhm-Bawerk attempted to describe the temporal "length" of the structure of production by a single number, the "average period of production." Kirzner's approach avoids these difficulties by defining capital assets in terms of subjective, individual *production plans*, plans that are formulated and continually revised by profit-seeking entrepreneurs. Capital goods should thus be characterized, not by their physical properties, but by their place in the structure of

---

[13] Hayek's *Prices and Production* (1931) emphasized the relationship between the value of capital goods and their place in the temporal sequence of production. Because production takes time, factors of production must be committed in the present for making final goods that will have value only in the future after they are sold. However, capital is heterogeneous. As capital goods are used in production, they are transformed from general-purpose materials and components to intermediate products specific to particular final goods. Consequently, these assets cannot be easily redeployed to alternative uses if demands for final goods change. The central macroeconomic problem in a modern capital-using economy is thus one of *intertemporal* coordination: how can the allocation of resources between capital and consumer goods be aligned with consumers' preferences between present and future consumption? In *The Pure Theory of Capital* (1941) Hayek describes how the economy's structure of production depends on the characteristics of capital goods durability, complementarity, substitutability, specificity, and so on.

production as *conceived by entrepreneurs*. The actual place of any capital good in the time sequence of production is given by the market for capital goods, in which entrepreneurs bid for factors of production in anticipation of future consumer demands. This subjectivist, entrepreneurial approach to capital assets is particularly congenial to theories of the firm that focus on entrepreneurship and the ownership of assets.[14]

Understanding Capital Heterogeneity

The Austrian approach to capital generated considerable controversy, both within the school itself and between the Austrians and rival schools of economic thought. Given the attention devoted to the problem of measuring a heterogeneous capital stock, it is surprising that relatively little analytical effort has been devoted to the concept of heterogeneity itself. The notion of heterogeneous capital is crucial not just for Austrian capital theory, but for (Austrian) economics in general. For example, the Austrian position in the socialist calculation debate of the 1930s (Hayek, 1933a; Mises, 1920) is based on an entrepreneurial concept of the market process, one in which the entrepreneur's primary function is to choose among the various combinations of factors suitable for producing particular goods (and to decide whether these goods should be produced at all), based on current prices for the factors and expected future prices of the final goods. If capital is shmoo with one price, then entrepreneurship is reduced to choosing between shmoo-intensive and labor-intensive production methods (or among types of labor), a problem a central planner could potentially solve. The failure of socialism, in Mises's (1920) formulation, follows precisely from the complexity of the economy's capital structure, and the subsequent need for entrepreneurial judgment. As Lachmann (1956, p. 16) points out, real-world entrepreneurship consists primarily of choosing among combinations of capital assets:

> [T]he entrepreneur's function ... is to specify and make decisions

---

[14] Penrose (1959) also emphasizes the subjectivity of the firm's perceived opportunity set (Kor and Mahoney, 2000). In her approach, entrepreneurs must learn how best to deploy their productive resources; because learning is idiosyncratic, firms with similar stocks of physical resources may differ in their strategic opportunities. Our emphasis on subjectively perceived attributes of capital assets may be seen as an example of a Penrosian perceived 'opportunity' set. Kirzner's concept of entrepreneurial "alertness," by contrast, is not a learned skill, but a talent or ability that is not subject to further explanation.

> on the concrete form the capital resources shall have. He specifies
> and modifies the layout of his plant.... As long as we disregard the
> heterogeneity of capital, the true function of the entrepreneur must
> also remain hidden.

Kirzner's argument that capital goods are heterogeneous not because of
their objective characteristics, but because they play particular roles within
the entrepreneur's overall production plan, further developed the link between entrepreneurship and capital heterogeneity.

In our interpretation, as discussed above and in Foss and Foss (2001),
capital goods are distinguished by their *attributes*, using Barzel's (1997)
terminology. As Alchian and Demsetz (1972, p. 793) note, "[e]fficient
production with heterogeneous resources is a result not of having *better* resources but in *knowing more accurately* the relative productive performances
of those resources." *Contra* the production function view in basic neoclassical economics, such knowledge is not *given*, but has to be created or discovered. Even in the literature on opportunity creation and exploitation,
in which entrepreneurial objectives are seen as emerging endogenously
from project champions' creative imaginations, entrepreneurial means (resources) are typically taken as given (see, for example Sarasvathy, 2001).

Heterogeneous Assets, Property Rights, and Ownership

Focusing on attributes not only helps conceptualize heterogeneous capital,
but also illuminates the vast literature on property rights and ownership.
Barzel (1997) stresses that property rights are held over attributes; in his
work, property rights to known attributes of assets are the relevant units
of analysis. In contrast, he dismisses the notion of asset ownership as
essentially legal and extra-economic. Similarly, Demsetz (1988a, p. 19)
argues that the notion of "full private ownership" over assets is "vague," and
"must always remain so" because "there is an infinity of potential rights of
actions that can be owned.... It is impossible to describe the complete set
of rights that are potentially ownable."

However, as we noted above, most assets have unspecified, unknown
future attributes, and an important function of entrepreneurship is to create or discover these attributes. Contrary to Demsetz, it is exactly this
feature that creates a distinct role for asset ownership, the acquisition of
legal title to a bundle of existing and future attributes. Specifically, own-

ership is a low-cost means of allocating the rights to attributes of assets that are created or discovered by the entrepreneur-owner. For instance, those who create or discover new knowledge have an incentive to use it directly because it is costly to transfer knowledge to others. In a well-functioning legal system, ownership of an asset normally implies that the courts will not interfere when an entrepreneur-owner captures the value of newly created or discovered attributes of an asset he owns. Consequently, the entrepreneur-owner can usually avoid costly negotiation with those who are affected by his creation or discovery. Moreover, asset ownership itself provides a powerful incentive to create or discover new attributes, as ownership conveys the legally recognized (and at least partly enforced) right to the income of an asset, including the right to income from new attributes.

Heterogeneous Capital and Experimental Entrepreneurship

The Austrian idea of heterogeneous capital is thus a natural complement to the theory of entrepreneurship.[15] Entrepreneurs who seek to create or discover new attributes of capital assets will want ownership titles to the relevant assets, both for speculative reasons and for reasons of economizing on transaction costs. These arguments provide room for entrepreneurship that goes beyond deploying a superior combination of capital assets with "given" attributes, acquiring the relevant assets, and deploying these to producing for a market; entrepreneurship may also be a matter of *experimenting* with capital assets in an attempt to discover new valued attributes.

Such experimental activity may take place in the context of trying out new combinations through the acquisition of or merger with other firms, or in the form of trying out new combinations of assets already under the control of the entrepreneur. The entrepreneur's success in experimenting with assets in this manner depends not only on his ability to anticipate future prices and market conditions, but also on internal and external transaction costs, the entrepreneur's control over the relevant assets, how much of the expected return from experimental activity he can hope to

---

[15]We note in passing that the understanding of management may also be furthered by beginning from heterogeneous capital assets and the need for coordination they imply. From a resource-based view, Mahoney (1995) argues that an important function of management is the coordination of such assets.

appropriate, and so on. Moreover, these latter factors are key determinants of economic organization in modern theories of the firm, which suggests that there may be fruitful complementarities between the theory of economic organization and Austrian theories of capital heterogeneity and entrepreneurship.

Organizing Heterogeneous Capital

Here we show how Austrian notions of capital heterogeneity give additional insights into the theory of the firm. The key questions are why firms emerge and what explains their boundaries (scope) and internal organization. In the following, we relate these issues to our emphasis on entrepreneurship as judgment about organizing and using heterogeneous capital assets.

The Emergence of the Firm

Coase (1937) explained the firm as a means for economizing on transaction costs, a theme elaborated by Williamson (1975, 1985, 1996). Alchian and Demsetz (1972) viewed the firm as an (albeit imperfect) solution to the free-rider problem in team production. Resource-based theories emphasize the need to generate and internalize tacit knowledge. It is not obvious where the entrepreneur fits into these approaches, however. Our framework suggests a slightly different approach.

INCOMPLETE MARKETS FOR JUDGMENT. Agents may realize rents from their human capital through three means: (1) selling labor services on market conditions; (2) entering into employment contracts; or (3) starting a firm. As Barzel (1987) argues, moral hazard implies that options (1) and (2) are often inefficient means of realizing rents. In other words, entrepreneurs know themselves to be good risks but are unable to communicate this to the market. For this reason, firms may emerge because the person whose services are the most difficult to measure (and therefore are most susceptible to moral hazard and adverse selection) becomes an entrepreneur, employing and supervising other agents, and committing capital of his own to the venture, thus contributing a bond.

However, there are other reasons why the market may not be able to evaluate entrepreneurial services. For example, Kirzner (1979, p. 181) argues that "entrepreneurship reveals to the market what the market did not realize was available, or indeed, needed at all." Casson (1982, p. 14) takes a more Schumpeterian position, arguing that "[t]he entrepreneur believes he is right, while everyone else is wrong. Thus the essence of entrepreneurship is being different because one has a different perception of the situation" (see also Casson, 1997). In this situation, non-contractibility arises because "[t]he decisive factors ... are so largely on the inside of the person making the decision that the 'instances' are not amenable to objective description and external control" (Knight, 1921, p. 251). Hence moral hazard is not the only important factor underlying non-contractibility. An agent may be unable to communicate his "vision" of a commercial experiment as a specific way of combining heterogeneous capital assets to serve future consumer wants in such a way that other agents can assess its economic implications. In such a case, he cannot be an employee, but will instead start his own firm. The existence of the firm can thus be explained by a specific category of transaction costs, namely, those that close the market for entrepreneurial judgment.

Note that in a world of uncertainty and change, these factors explain not only the emergence of new firms, but also the ongoing operations of existing firms. The entrepreneurial process of combining and recombining heterogeneous resources plays out continually, through time, as new attributes are created or discovered (and as consumer preferences and technological capabilities change). In our framework, the entrepreneurial act is not restricted to new venture formation; entrepreneurial judgment is necessarily exercised on an ongoing basis. Our approach is thus inconsistent with what we perceive as an undue emphasis on new venture creation in the applied entrepreneurship literature.

Finally, there is an important sense in which judgment can never be fully delegated. Resource owners, by possessing residual rights of control, are the decision-makers of last resort, no matter how many day-to-day decision rights they delegate to hired managers. Jensen (1989) famously distinguished "active" from "passive" investors. Active investors are those "who hold large equity or debt positions, sit on boards of directors, monitor and sometimes dismiss management, are involved with the long-term strategic direction of the companies they invest in, and sometimes manage the companies themselves" Jensen (1989, p. 65). While not denying the importance of this distinction, we argue that residual control rights make all resource owners "active," in the sense that they *must* exercise judgment over the use of their resources. In our approach, investors choose how "Jensen-active" they wish to be, which makes them "active" by definition.[16]

FIRMS AS CONTROLLED EXPERIMENTS. The idea of incomplete markets for judgment helps us understand the one-person firm. However, similar ideas may also be useful for understanding the multi-person firm. For instance, as discussed above, when capital is homogenous it is easy to conceive, coordinate, and implement plans for producing, marketing, and selling goods and services. The decision problem is one of choosing the intensities with which shmoo is applied to various activities. In the real world of heterogeneous capital assets, by contrast, production plans are much more difficult to conceive, coordinate, and implement. It is not necessarily obvious to which activities capital goods are most profitably applied and account has to be taken of complex relations between capital goods.

Given that the optimal relationships among assets are generally unknown *ex ante*, and often so complex that resorting to analytical methods is not possible (Galloway, 1996), some experimentation is necessary. First, one must isolate the system boundaries, that is, where the relevant relationships among assets are most likely to be. Second, the experimental process must be like a controlled experiment (or a sequence of such experiments) to isolate the system from outside disturbances. Third, there must be some sort of guidance for the experiment. This may take many forms, ranging from centrally provided instructions to negotiated agreements to shared understandings of where to begin experimenting, how to avoid overlapping experiments, how to revise the experiment in light of past results, and so on. The central problem is how this experimental process is best organized. Does the need for experimentation help explain the existence of the firm, or can such experimentation be organized efficiently through markets?

In a world of complete knowledge and zero transaction costs, all rights to all uses of all assets could be specified in contracts. By contrast, in a world of heterogeneous assets with attributes that are costly to measure and partly unforeseen, complete contracts cannot be drafted. The resulting set of incomplete contracts may constitute a firm, a process of coordination

---

[16]See the discussion in chapter 2 above on "Firms as Investments" and "Financiers as Entrepreneurs."

managed by the entrepreneur's central direction. If relationship-specific assets are involved, the holdup problem described above becomes a serious concern.

Thus, asset specificity may itself be an outcome of an experimental process. To be sure, Williamson (e.g., 1985, 1996) clearly allows for intertemporal considerations relating to what he calls the "fundamental transformation" (i.e., the transformation of large numbers to small numbers situation, and therefore the emergence of asset specificity). However, he doesn't describe this process in much detail. In the present approach, as experimental activity provides information about how to organize the system, assets will be increasingly specific in time and location. Temporal and site specificity will tend to increase as assets become more efficiently coordinated. This provides one rationale for organizing the experiments inside firms. Firms may also be justified by problems associated with the dispersion of knowledge across agents. Production systems may exhibit multiple equilibria, and it may not be obvious how to coordinate on a particular equilibrium or even which equilibria are preferred.

In principle, an experimenting team could hire an outside consultant who guides the experimental activity, giving advice on the sequence of actions and asset uses, initiating the experiments, drawing the appropriate conclusions from each experiment, determining how these conclusions should influence further experimentation, and so on. However, such an arrangement is likely to run into serious bargaining costs. Under market contracting any team member can veto the advice provided by the consultant, and submitting to authority may be the least costly way to organize the experimental activity. "Authority" here means that the entrepreneur has the right to redefine and reallocate decision rights among team members and to sanction team members who do not use their decision rights efficiently. By possessing these rights, entrepreneur-managers can conduct experiments without continuously having to renegotiate contracts, saving bargaining and drafting costs. Such an arrangement then provides a setting for carrying out "controlled" experiments in which the entrepreneur-manager changes only some aspects of the relevant tasks to trace the effects of specific rearrangements of rights. Establishing these property rights is tantamount to forming a firm.

The Boundaries of the Firm

In the approach developed in this chapter, the theory of firm boundaries is closely related to the theory of entrepreneurship. Mergers, acquisitions, divestitures, and other reorganizations can generate efficiencies by replacing poorly performing managers, creating operating synergies, or establishing internal capital markets. Like other business practices that do not conform to textbook models of competition, mergers, acquisitions, and financial restructurings have long been viewed with suspicion by some commentators and regulatory authorities. However, the academic literature clearly suggests that corporate restructurings do, on average, increase shareholder value (Jarrell, et al., 1988; Andrade, et al., 2001). Given such benefits, why are many mergers later "reversed" in a divestiture, spin-off, or carve-out? Chapter 3 above distinguishes between two basic views. The first, a kind of empire building, holds that entrenched managers make acquisitions primarily to increase their own power, prestige, or control, producing negligible efficiency gains, and that acquisitions by manager-controlled firms are likely to be divested *ex post*. An alternative view acknowledges that unprofitable acquisitions may be "mistakes" *ex post*, but argues that poor long-term performance does not indicate *ex ante* inefficiency. A divestiture of previously acquired assets may mean simply that profit-seeking entrepreneurs have updated their forecasts of future conditions or otherwise learned from experience. They are adjusting structure of heterogeneous capital assets specific to their firms.

Chapter 3 discusses empirical evidence that the long-term success or failure of corporate acquisitions cannot, in general, be predicted by measures of manager control or principal–agent problems. However, significantly higher rates of divestiture tend to follow mergers that occur in a cluster of mergers in the same industry. As argued by Mitchell and Mulherin (1996), Andrade, et al. (2001), and Andrade and Stafford (2004), mergers frequently occur in industry clusters, suggesting that mergers are driven in part by industry-specific factors, such as regulatory shocks. When an industry is regulated, deregulated, or re-regulated, economic calculation becomes more difficult, and entrepreneurial activity is hampered. It should not be surprising that poor long-term performance is more likely under those conditions.

Internal Organization

As Foss and Klein (2005) point out, most existing approaches to entrepreneurship, even if linked to the existence of firms, say little about the key questions of internal organization: How should decision rights be assigned? How should employees be motivated and evaluated? How should firms be divided into divisions and departments? The notion of judgment-based entrepreneurship offers insight into these questions as well.

PRODUCTIVE AND DESTRUCTIVE ENTREPRENEURSHIP. Consider first the way firm structure affects the exercise of entrepreneurial judgment—or a proxy version of such judgment—within the organization. In much of the entrepreneurship literature, there is a general, though usually implicit claim that all entrepreneurial activity is socially beneficial (Kirzner, 1973; Mises, 1949). However, as Baumol (1990) and Holcombe (2002) point out, entrepreneurship may be socially harmful if it takes the form of rent-seeking, attempts to influence governments (or management) to redistribute income in a way that consumes resources and brings about a social loss. It is therefore necessary to introduce a distinction between productive and destructive entrepreneurship.

In the context of firm organization, "destructive entrepreneurship" can refer to agents' effort to create or discover new attributes and take control over these in such a way that firm value is reduced. Thus, discovering new forms of moral hazard (Holmström, 1982), creating holdups (Williamson, 1996), and inventing new ways of engaging in rent-seeking activities (Baumol, 1990; Holcombe, 2002) are examples of destructive entrepreneurship. "Productive entrepreneurship" refers to the creation or discovery of new attributes leading to an increase in firm value. For example, a franchisee may discover new local tastes that in turn may form the basis for new products for the entire chain; an employee may figure out better uses of production assets and communicate this to the TQM team of which he is a member; a CEO may formulate a new business concept; etc. In the following, we use this distinction to sketch an entrepreneurial approach to internal organization. Note that we here use the term "entrepreneurship" more broadly than before, referring not only to decisions made by resource owners (entrepreneurship in the strict sense), but also to decisions made by employees, acting as proxy decision makers for the resource owners. Foss, Foss, and Klein (2007) refer to employee exercise of this discretion as *derived judgment*, meaning judgment that is derived from the owner's *original judgment*.

FUNDAMENTAL TRADEOFFS IN INTERNAL ORGANIZATION. The first such problem concerns the control of destructive entrepreneurial activities. For example, firms may delimit employees' use of telephone and Internet services by closely specifying their use rights over the relevant assets, instructing them to act in a proper manner towards customers and to exercise care when operating the firm's equipment, and the like. However, firms are unlikely to succeed entirely in their attempt to curb such activities. Monitoring employees may be costly; moreover, employees may creatively circumvent constraints, for example by inventing ways to hide their behavior. Although firms may know that such destructive entrepreneurship takes place, they may prefer not to try to constrain it further. This is because the various constraints that firms impose on employees (or, more generally, that contracting partners impose on each other) to curb destructive entrepreneurship may have the unwanted side effect that productive entrepreneurship is stifled (see Kirzner, 1985a).

More generally, imposing (too many) constraints on employees may reduce their propensity to create or discover new attributes of productive assets. At any rate, many firms increasingly appear to operate on the presumption that beneficial effects may be produced by reducing constraints on employees in various dimensions. For example, firms such as 3M give research employees time to use however they wish, in the hope of stimulating serendipitous discoveries. Many consulting firms do something similar. More generally, industrial firms have long known that employees with many decision rights—researchers, for example—must be monitored and constrained in different, and typically much looser, ways than those employees charged only with routine tasks. More broadly, the increasing emphasis on "empowerment" during recent decades reflects a realization that employees derive a benefit from controlling aspects of their job situation. Moreover, the total quality movement emphasizes that delegating various rights to employees motivates them to find new ways to increase the mean and reduce the variance of quality (Jensen and Wruck, 1994). To the extent that such activities increase firm value, they represent productive entrepreneurship.

Stimulating the productive creation and discovery of new attributes by relaxing constraints on employees results in principal–agent relationships that are less completely specified. This is not simply a matter of delegation, or co-locating decision rights and specific knowledge (Jensen and Meckling, 1992), but also giving agents opportunities to exercise their own, often far-reaching, judgments. However, as we have seen, this also permits potentially destructive entrepreneurship. Managing the tradeoff between productive and destructive entrepreneurship thus becomes a critical management task.

CHOOSING EFFICIENT TRADEOFFS. In this context, asset ownership is important because it gives entrepreneurs the right to define contractual constraints, that is, to choose their own preferred tradeoffs. Briefly stated, ownership allows the employer-entrepreneur's preferred degree of contractual incompleteness and therefore a certain combination of productive and destructive entrepreneurship to be implemented at low cost. This function of ownership is particularly important in a dynamic market process, the kind stressed by Knight (in the later chapters of Knight, 1921) and the Austrians. In such a context, an ongoing process of judgmental decision making requires contractual constraints to address the changing tradeoffs between productive and destructive entrepreneurship inside the firm. The power conferred by ownership allows the employer-entrepreneur to do this at low cost.[17]

Concluding Discussion

This chapter emphasizes the importance of capital heterogeneity for theories of entrepreneurship and the firm. If capital were homogeneous, the entrepreneurial act would be trivial. Many, if not most, of the interesting problems of economic organization would disappear. This implies that the theory of capital should be an integral part of theories of entrepreneurship and economic organization. It also suggests extending the Austrian emphasis on entrepreneurship in markets to entrepreneurship in firms.[18]

---

[17] For a fuller analysis of this point see Foss and Foss (2002).

[18] The alert reader will notice that while we enthusiastically endorse Kirzner's contributions to the Austrian theory of capital, our own conception of entrepreneurship differs substantially from his. Chapter 5 below explores this distinction in greater detail.

However, the concept of capital heterogeneity does more than simply establish the necessary conditions for entrepreneurship and the typical problems of economic organization. Taking fuller account of heterogeneous capital, as developed by the Austrian school, reveals exchange problems (i.e. transaction costs) that are relevant to economic organization but neglected in mainstream theories of the firm.[19] In a setting with heterogeneous capital and uncertainty, the process of entrepreneurial experimentation has distinct implications for economic organization. As we have argued, the process of experimenting with heterogeneous capital may be best organized within a firm, helping to explain why firms emerge. Similarly, experiments with heterogeneous capital assets may underlie much of the observed dynamics of the boundaries of firms. Thus, it is not *a priori* known whether capital assets controlled by potential takeover target will be a good fit with the firm's assets; this has to be tried out in an experimental fashion. Finally, we have argued that internal organization is also illuminated by a focus on judgment, heterogeneous capital, and experimentation.

To be sure, our analysis so far is preliminary and incomplete. We have concentrated on exploring the links between Austrian economics and conventional approaches to economic organization.[20] Because we offer here an exploratory, suggestive treatment, we have not described specific causal mechanisms and have not put any explicit, testable propositions on the table.

However, our approach is potentially rich in explanatory power. For example, because entrepreneurial judgment requires resource ownership, the theory of employment—the contractual relations between the entrepreneurs and those they hire to help them execute their plans—is ultimately a theory of *delegation*. Judgment, as the ultimate decision-making factor of production (in Grossman and Hart's terminology, the residual rights of control) cannot be delegated, by definition. But many other proximate decision rights can, and frequently are, delegated to employees. Operationalizing this insight, and deriving testable implications from it, can be done by identifying the circumstances under which particular

---

[19] In contrast, our emphasis on understanding economic organization in a dynamic context has obvious parallels to Langlois's (1992) notion of "dynamic transaction costs."

[20] See Shook, Priem, and McGee (2003) for ideas on empirical research on the behavioral aspects of entrepreneurial judgment.

decision rights (what we may call *derived judgment*) can be delegated to particular individuals. These circumstances can be described by characteristics of the business environment (technology, markets, regulation), employees' human capital (what Schultz, 1975, calls "the ability to deal with disequilibria"), and aspects of firm strategy. Consider the following applications.

DECENTRALIZATION. One approach to delegation is to build on the literature on optimal decentralization, such as Jensen and Meckling's (1992) important (and, in our judgment, under-appreciated) application of Hayek's and Polanyi's theory of knowledge to internal organization. Jensen and Meckling identify some benefits and costs of decentralizing decision rights to lower levels of an organization. The primary benefit is more effective use of specific (local, tacit) knowledge, while costs include potential agency problems and less effective use of central information. Decentralization, in Jensen and Meckling's terminology, achieves the co-location of knowledge and decision rights. Employees who are not owners, however, exercise only derived judgment, no matter how many decision rights they hold. Optimal decentralization can thus be interpreted in terms of the tradeoff between knowledge and judgment. Assigning decision rights to employees co-locates specific knowledge and derived judgment, while judgment itself remains in the hands of owners. The decision to decentralize therefore depends not only on the importance of specific knowledge, but on the "wedge" between ultimate and derived judgment. Where environmental uncertainty is high, this wedge may be sufficiently large that decentralization reduces firm value, even controlling for the importance of specific knowledge.

OCCUPATIONAL CHOICE. Another application relates to the literature on occupational choice. Many studies of entrepreneurship treat entrepreneurship as an *occupation* (i.e. self-employment), rather than a *function*, as we treat it here (see, for example, Hamilton, 2000). What is the correlation between self-employment and judgment? Self-employed individuals who finance their ventures with debt or personal savings are surely acting as Knightian entrepreneurs. If a new venture is financed with equity, then in our framework it is the financier—the venture capitalist or angel investor, for example—who is bearing the relevant uncertainty and therefore performing the entrepreneurial function, not the firm founder (except to the extent that the founder's compensation is a function of the outcome of the venture). We are unaware of existing empirical work relating self-employment to the entrepreneurial function, though such work should be important in understanding the role of self-employment in generating economic growth.

CONTRACT DESIGN. Moreover, our approach to the entrepreneurial function has implications for contract design. If we think of judgment as filling in the gaps of incomplete contracts, then the more complete the contract, the fewer circumstances in which "ultimate judgment" must be exercised, and hence the more decision rights that can be delegated. This implies an inverse relationship between contractual completeness and monitoring costs. While several TCE papers examine the determinants of completeness (Crocker and Masten, 1991; Crocker and Reynolds, 1993; Saussier, 2000), they generally focus on asset specificity, not monitoring costs, as the independent variable.

ORGANIZATIONAL LEARNING. Our approach also has implications for organizational learning. If entrepreneurship, and hence economic organization, is the act of arranging heterogeneous capital resources, then it is important to understand how individuals and teams learn to do this successfully. Mayer and Argyres (2004) show that contracting parties do not necessarily anticipate contractual hazards, and design arrangements to mitigate them, as TCE predicts; rather, contracting parties must often experience maladaptation to adjust to it. It is thus important to understand not only efficient contracting, but the process of learning to contract efficiently. In our framework, contracting—an exchange of legal rights and responsibilities governing the exchange of property titles—is part of the process of entrepreneurial experimentation. Just as asset attributes must be created or discovered over time, the efficient contractual arrangements governing asset uses must be created or discovered over time, through experimentation. Conceiving the problem this way calls for a theory of learning to organize heterogeneous capital.

More generally, we hope the analysis here inspires researchers to investigate the Austrian approach to capital and to explore its applications not only to the theory of entrepreneurship, but also to other aspects of economic organization and management. Management scholars are beginning to recognize the value of Austrian economics beyond generalities about the "market process" or "alertness." (Lachmann's capital theory, for example, features prominently in Chiles and Zarankin 2005; Chiles, Bluedorn, and Gupta 2007; Lewin 2005; Lewin and Phelan 2002.) We hope that researchers seeking to incorporate the concept of entrepreneurship into organization, strategy, and the theory of the firm will consider the Austrian notion of capital heterogeneity as a possible link between entrepreneurship and economic organization.

CHAPTER 5

Opportunity Discovery and Entrepreneurial Action[†]

Entrepreneurship is one of the fastest growing fields within economics, management, finance, and even law. Surprisingly, however, while the entrepreneur is fundamentally an economic agent—the driving force of the market, in Mises's (1949, p. 249) phrase—modern theories of economic organization and strategy maintain an ambivalent relationship with entrepreneurship. It is widely recognized that entrepreneurship is somehow important, but there is little consensus about how the entrepreneurial role should be modeled and incorporated into economics and strategy. Indeed, the most important works in the economic literature on entrepreneurship—Schumpeter's account of innovation, Knight's theory of profit, and Kirzner's analysis of entrepreneurial discovery—are viewed as interesting, but idiosyncratic, insights that do not easily generalize to other contexts and problems.

The awkward relationship between mainstream economics and entrepreneurship makes sense in the context of the development of the neoclassical theory of production and the firm. The increasingly formalized treatment of markets, notably in the form of general equilibrium theory,

[†]Published originally as "Opportunity Discovery, Entrepreneurial Action, and Economic Organization" in *Strategic Entrepreneurship Journal* 2, no. 3 (2008): 175–90.

not only made firms increasingly passive, it also made the model of the firm increasingly stylized and anonymous, doing away with those dynamic aspects of markets that are most closely related to entrepreneurship (O'Brien, 1984). In particular, the development of what came to be known as the production-function view (Williamson, 1985; Langlois and Foss, 1999)—roughly, the firm as it is presented in intermediate microeconomics textbooks with its fully transparent production possibility sets—was a deathblow to the economic theory of entrepreneurship. If any firm can do what any other firm does (Demsetz, 1988b), if all firms are always on their production possibility frontiers, and if firms always make optimal choices of input combinations and output levels, then there is nothing for the entrepreneur to do. Even in more advanced models of asymmetric production functions, hidden characteristics, and strategic interaction, firms or agents are modeled as behaving according to fixed rules subject to formalization by the analyst. The entrepreneur makes an occasional appearance in business history and in Schumpeterian models of innovation and technical change, but is largely absent from contemporary economic theory.

One exception is the Austrian School, which has given the entrepreneur a central role in the economy, at least since the proto-Austrian contribution of Richard Cantillon (1755). Key figures in the Austrian School, such as Carl Menger (1871), Eugen von Böhm-Bawerk (1889), Ludwig von Mises (1949), and Murray Rothbard (1962) all emphasized the entrepreneur in their causal-realistic analysis of economic organization and economic change. More recently, the Austrian economist Israel Kirzner has popularized the notion of entrepreneurship as discovery or alertness to profit opportunities. Kirzner's interpretation of Mises has been highly influential, not only within the Austrian School, but also in the opportunity-discovery or opportunity-recognition branch of entrepreneurship literature (Shane and Venkataraman, 2000; Gaglio and Katz, 2001; Shane, 2003).

However, as described below, the opportunity-discovery framework is problematic as a foundation for applied entrepreneurship research. Its central concept, the *opportunity*, was intended by theorists such as Kirzner to be used instrumentally, or metaphorically, as a means of explaining the tendency of markets to equilibrate, and not meant to be treated literally as the object of analysis. I argue that entrepreneurship can be more thoroughly grounded and more closely linked to theories of economic organization and strategy by adopting the Cantillon–Knight–Mises understanding of entrepreneurship as *judgment*, along with the Austrian School's subjectivist account of capital heterogeneity. The judgment approach emphasizes that profit opportunities do not exist, objectively, when decisions are made, because the result of action cannot be known with certainty. Opportunities are essentially subjective phenomena (Foss, Klein, Kor, and Mahoney, 2008). As such, opportunities are neither discovered nor created (Alvarez and Barney, 2007), but *imagined*. They exist, in other words, only in the minds of decision-makers. Moreover, the essentially subjective character of profit opportunities poses special challenges for applied research on the cognitive psychological aspects of discovery. Rather, I argue, opportunities can be treated as a latent concept underlying the real phenomenon of interest, namely entrepreneurial action.

I begin by distinguishing among occupational, structural, and functional approaches to entrepreneurship and explaining two influential interpretations of the entrepreneurial function—discovery and judgment. I turn next to the contemporary literature on opportunity identification, arguing that this literature misinterprets Kirzner's instrumental use of the discovery metaphor and mistakenly makes opportunities the unit of analysis. Instead, I describe an alternative approach in which investment is the unit of analysis, and link this approach to the theory of heterogeneous capital theory. I close with some applications to organizational form and entrepreneurial teams.

Entrepreneurship: Occupational, Structural, and Functional Perspectives

To organize the various strands of entrepreneurship literature, it is useful to distinguish among occupational, structural, and functional perspectives. *Occupational* theories define entrepreneurship as self-employment and treat the individual as the unit of analysis, describing the characteristics of individuals who start their own businesses and explaining the choice between employment and self-employment (Kihlstrom and Laffont, 1979; Shaver and Scott, 1991; Hamilton, 2000; Parker, 2004; Lazear, 2004, 2005). The labor economics literature on occupational choice, along with psychological literature on the personal characteristics of self-employed individuals, fits in this category. For example, McGrath and MacMillan

(2000) argue that particular individuals have an "entrepreneurial mindset" that enables and encourages them to find opportunities overlooked or ignored by others (and that this mindset is developed through experience, rather than formal instruction). *Structural* approaches treat the firm or industry as the unit of analysis, defining the "entrepreneurial firm" as a new or small firm. The literatures on industry dynamics, firm growth, clusters, and networks have a structural concept of entrepreneurship in mind (Aldrich, 1990; Acs and Audretsch, 1990; Audretsch, Keilbach, and Lehmann, 2005). Indeed, the idea that one firm, industry, or economy can be more "entrepreneurial" than another suggests that entrepreneurship is associated with a particular market structure (i.e., lots of small or young firms).

By contrast, the classic contributions to the economic theory of entrepreneurship from Schumpeter, Knight, Mises, Kirzner, and others model entrepreneurship as a *function*, activity, or process, not an employment category or market structure. The entrepreneurial function has been characterized in various ways: judgment (Cantillon, 1755; Knight, 1921; Casson, 1982; Langlois and Cosgel, 1993; Foss and Klein, 2005), innovation (Schumpeter, 1911), adaptation (Schultz, 1975, 1980), alertness (Kirzner, 1973, 1979, 1992), and coordination (Witt, 1998, 2003). In each case, these functional concepts of entrepreneurship are largely independent of occupational and structural concepts. The entrepreneurial function can be manifested in large and small firms, in old and new firms, by individuals or teams, across a variety of occupational categories, and so on. By focusing too narrowly on self-employment and start-up companies, the contemporary literature may be understating the role of entrepreneurship in the economy and business organizations.

Kirzner's (1973; 1979; 1992) concept of entrepreneurship as "alertness" to profit opportunities is one of the most influential functional approaches. The simplest case of alertness is that of the arbitrageur who discovers a discrepancy in present prices that can be exploited for financial gain. In a more typical case, the entrepreneur is alert to a new product or a superior production process and steps in to fill this market gap before others. Success, in this view, comes not from following a well-specified maximization problem, but from having some insight that no one else has, a process that cannot be modeled as an optimization problem.[1] As

---

[1] Kirzner is careful to distinguish alertness from systematic search, as in Stigler's (1961; 1962) analysis of searching for bargains or for jobs. A nice example is provided by Ricketts

discussed in chapter 2 above, because Kirzner's entrepreneurs perform only a discovery function, rather than an investment function, they do not own capital; they need only be alert to profit opportunities. They own no assets, they bear no uncertainty and, hence, they cannot earn losses. The worst that can happen to an entrepreneur is the failure to discover an existing profit opportunity. For these reasons, the link between Kirznerian entrepreneurship and other branches of economic analysis, such as industrial organization, innovation, and the theory of the firm, is weak. Hence, Kirzner's concept has not generated a large body of applications.[2]

An alternative account treats entrepreneurship as judgmental decision making under conditions of uncertainty. Judgment refers primarily to business when the range of possible future outcomes, let alone the likelihood of individual outcomes, is generally unknown (what Knight terms *uncertainty*, rather than mere probabilistic risk). This view finds expression in the earliest known discussion of entrepreneurship—that found in Richard Cantillon's *Essai sur la nature de commerce en general* (1755). Cantillon argues that all market participants, with the exception of landowners and the nobility, can be classified as either entrepreneurs or wage earners:

> Entrepreneurs work for uncertain wages, so to speak, and all others for certain wages until they have them, although their functions and their rank are very disproportionate. The General who has a salary, the Courtier who has a pension, and the Domestic who has wages, are in the latter class. All the others are Entrepreneurs, whether they establish themselves with a capital to carry on their enterprise, or are Entrepreneurs of their own work without any capital, and they may be considered as living subject to uncertainty; even Beggars and Robbers are Entrepreneurs of this class (Cantillon, 1755, p. 54).

(1987, p. 58): "Stigler's searcher decides how much time it is worth spending rummaging through dusty attics and untidy drawers looking for a sketch which (the family recalls) Aunt Enid thought might be by Lautrec. Kirzner's entrepreneur enters a house and glances lazily at the pictures which have been hanging in the same place for years. 'Isn't that a Lautrec on the wall?' "

[2]Exceptions include Ekelund and Saurman (1988), Harper (1995), Sautet (2001) and Holcombe (2002). Kirzner (1973, pp. 39–40) concedes that in a world of uncertainty, resource owners exercise entrepreneurial judgment in allocating their resources to particular uses. But he goes on (1973, pp. 40–43) to introduce the analytical device of "pure entrepreneurship," the act of discovery or alertness to profit opportunities by those with no resources under their control, and claims that this function, rather than uncertainty-bearing, is the "driving force" behind the market economy.

Judgment is distinct from boldness, innovation, alertness, and leadership. Judgment must be exercised in mundane circumstances, for ongoing operations as well as new ventures. Alertness is the ability to react to *existing* opportunities, while judgment refers to beliefs about *new* opportunities.[3] Those who specialize in judgmental decision making may be dynamic, charismatic leaders, but they need not possess these traits. In short, in this view, decision making under uncertainty is entrepreneurial, whether it involves imagination, creativity, leadership, and related factors or not.

Knight introduces judgment to link profit and the firm to uncertainty. Entrepreneurship represents judgment that cannot be assessed in terms of its marginal product and which cannot, accordingly, be paid a wage (Knight, 1921, p. 311). In other words, there is no market for the judgment that entrepreneurs rely on and, therefore, exercising judgment requires the person with judgment to start a firm. Judgment, thus, implies asset ownership, for judgmental decision making is ultimately decision making about the employment of resources. An entrepreneur without capital goods is, in Knight's sense, no entrepreneur (Foss and Klein, 2005).[4]

Entrepreneurship as uncertainty bearing is also important for Mises's

---

[3] In Kirzner's treatment, entrepreneurship is characterized as "a responding agency. I view the entrepreneur not as a source of innovative ideas *ex nihilo*, but as being alert to the opportunities that exist *already* and are waiting to be noticed" (Kirzner, 1973, p. 74). Of course, as Kirzner (1985b, pp. 54–59) himself emphasizes, the actions of entrepreneurs in the present affect the constellation of possible profit opportunities in the future. "[Alertness] does not consist merely in *seeing* the unfolding of the tapestry of the future in the sense of seeing a preordained flow of events. Alertness must, importantly, embrace the awareness of the ways the human agent can, by imaginative, bold leaps of faith, and determination, in fact *create* the future for which his present acts are created" (Kirzner, 1985b, p. 56). However, Kirzner (1985b, p. 57) continues, the only opportunities that *matter* for equilibration are those that do, in fact, "bear some realistic resemblance to the future as it will be realized."

[4] It is useful here to distinguish between broad and narrow notions of (Knightian) entrepreneurship. All human action involves judgment, and in an uncertain world, all action places some assets at risk (at minimum, the opportunity cost of the actor's time). In Mises's terminology, human action is the purposeful employment of means to bring about desired ends, which may or may not be realized. In this sense, we are all entrepreneurs, every day. Of course, this broad concept of entrepreneurship is not particularly operational, or empirically important. Economics and organization theorists, therefore, tend to focus on a narrower concept of entrepreneurship, namely the actions of the businessperson—the investment of tangible resources in pursuit of commercial gain. In the discussion that follows, I focus on this narrower, commercial notion of entrepreneurship.

theory of profit and loss—a cornerstone of his well-known critique of economic planning under socialism. Mises begins with the marginal productivity theory of distribution developed by his Austrian predecessors. In the marginal productivity theory, laborers earn wages, capitalists earn interest, and owners of specific factors earn rents. Any excess (deficit) of a firm's realized receipts over these factor payments constitutes profit (loss). Profit and loss, therefore, are returns to entrepreneurship. In a hypothetical equilibrium without uncertainty (what Mises calls the evenly rotating economy), capitalists would still earn interest as a reward for lending, but there would be no profit or loss.

Entrepreneurs, in Mises's understanding of the market, make their production plans based on the current prices of factors of production and the anticipated future prices of consumer goods. What Mises calls "economic calculation" is the comparison of these anticipated future receipts with present outlays, all expressed in common monetary units. Under socialism, the absence of factor markets and the consequent lack of factor prices renders economic calculation—and hence rational economic planning—impossible. Mises's point is that a socialist economy may assign individuals to be workers, managers, technicians, inventors, and the like, but it cannot, by definition, have entrepreneurs, because there are no money profits and losses. Entrepreneurship, and not labor, management or technological expertise, is the crucial element of the market economy. As Mises puts it, directors of socialist enterprises may be allowed to *play market*—to make capital investment decisions as if they were allocating scarce capital across activities in an economizing way. But entrepreneurs cannot be asked to "play speculation and investment" (Mises, 1949, p. 705). Without entrepreneurship, a complex, dynamic economy cannot allocate resources to their highest value use.

Entrepreneurship as Opportunity Identification

While Schumpeter, Kirzner, Cantillon, Knight, and Mises are frequently cited in the contemporary entrepreneurship literature in economics and management (Schultz, by contrast, is rarely cited), much of this literature takes, implicitly, an occupational or structural approach to entrepreneurship. Any relationship to the classic functional contributions is inspirational, not substantive.

The most important exception is the literature in management and organization theory on opportunity discovery or opportunity identification, or what Shane (2003) calls the "individual–opportunity nexus." Opportunity identification involves not only technical skills like financial analysis and market research, but also less tangible forms of creativity, team building, problem solving, and leadership (Long and McMullan, 1984; Hills, Lumpkin, and Singh, 1997; Hindle, 2004). While value can, of course, be created not only by starting new activities, but also by improving the operation of existing activities, research in opportunity identification tends to emphasize new activities. These could include creating a new firm or starting a new business arrangement, introducing a new product or service, or developing a new method of production. As summarized by Shane (2003, pp. 4–5):

> Entrepreneurship is an activity that involves the discovery, evaluation, and exploitation of opportunities to introduce new goods and services, ways of organizing, markets, process, and raw materials through organizing efforts that previously had not existed (Venkataraman, 1997; Shane and Venkataraman, 2000). Given this definition, the academic field of entrepreneurship incorporates, in its domain, explanations for why, when, and how entrepreneurial opportunities exist; the sources of those opportunities and the forms that they take; the processes of opportunity discovery and evaluation; the acquisition of resources for the exploitation of these opportunities; the act of opportunity exploitation; why, when, and how some individuals and not others discover, evaluate, gather resources for, and exploit opportunities; the strategies used to pursue opportunities; and the organizing efforts to exploit them (Shane and Venkataraman, 2000).

This conception is admirably broad, incorporating not only opportunity discovery, but also the processes by which opportunities are pursued and exploited. What unifies these varied aspects of the entrepreneurial function is the concept of the opportunity. The discovery and (potential) exploitation of opportunities is proposed as the unit of analysis for entrepreneurship research. But what exactly are opportunities? How are they best characterized? How much explicit characterization is necessary for applied research in entrepreneurial organization and strategy?

Opportunities: Objective or Subjective?

Shane and Venkataraman (2000, p. 220) define entrepreneurial opportunities as "those situations in which new goods, services, raw materials, and organizing methods can be introduced and sold at greater than their cost of production." These opportunities are treated as objective phenomena, though their existence is not known by all agents. Shane and Venkataraman also distinguish entrepreneurial opportunities from profit opportunities more generally. While the latter reflect opportunities to create value by enhancing the efficiency of producing existing goods, services, and processes, the former includes value creation through "the very perception of the means-ends framework" itself (Kirzner, 1973, p. 33). Shane and Venkataraman seem to have in mind the distinction between activities that can be modeled as solutions to well-specified optimization problems—what Kirzner (1973) calls "Robbinsian maximizing"—and those for which no existing model, or decision rule, is available.

However, Shane and Venkataraman appear to misunderstand Kirzner (and the Austrians more generally) on this point. In a world of Knightian uncertainty, *all* profit opportunities involve decisions for which no well-specified maximization problem is available. Kirzner does not mean that some economic decisions really *are* the result of Robbinsian maximizing, while others reflect discovery. Instead, Kirzner is simply contrasting two methodological constructions for the analysis of human action.

More generally, the opportunity identification literature seeks to build a positive research program by operationalizing the concept of alertness. How is alertness manifested in action? How do we recognize it empirically? Can we distinguish discovery from systematic search? As summarized by Gaglio and Katz (2001, p. 96):

> Almost all of the initial empirical investigations of alertness have focused on the means by which an individual might literally *notice without search*. For example, Kaish and Gilad (1991) interpret this as having an aptitude to position oneself in the flow of information so that the probability of encountering opportunities without a deliberate search for a specific opportunity is maximized. Therefore, in their operational measures of alertness, they asked founders to recall: (a) the amount of time and effort exerted in generating an information flow; (b) the selection of information sources for

generating an information flow; and (c) the cues inherent in information that signal the presence of an opportunity. From this data the authors deduced: (d) the quantity of information in the flow and (e) the breadth and diversity of information in the flow.

Their results conform to expectations in some ways but also reveal some unexpected patterns. Compared to the sample of corporate executives, the sample of new venture founders do appear to spend more time generating an information flow and do seem more likely to use unconventional sources of information. Interestingly, the founders do seem more attentive to risk cues rather than to market potential cues. However, the data also reveal that only inexperienced or unsuccessful founders engage in such intense information collection efforts. Successful founders actually behave more like the sample of corporate executives. Cooper *et al.* (1995) found a similar pattern of results in their survey of 1100 firms although Busenitz (1996), in an altered replication of Kaish and Gilad's survey, did not. Indeed Busenitz found few significant differences between corporate managers and new venture founders. In addition, validity checks of the survey measures yielded low reliability scores, which led the author to conclude that future research in alertness required improved theoretical and operational precision.

This positive research program misses, however, the point of Kirzner's metaphor of entrepreneurial alertness: namely, that it is only a metaphor. Kirzner's aim is not to characterize entrepreneurship *per se*, but to explain the tendency for markets to clear. In the Kirznerian system, opportunities are (exogenous) arbitrage opportunities *and nothing more*. Entrepreneurship itself serves a purely instrumental function; it is the means by which Kirzner explains market clearing. Of course, arbitrage opportunities cannot exist in a perfectly competitive general-equilibrium model, so Kirzner's framework assumes the presence of competitive imperfections, to use the language of strategic factor markets (Barney, 1986; Alvarez and Barney, 2004). Beyond specifying general disequilibrium conditions, however, Kirzner offers no theory of how opportunities come to be identified, who identifies them, and so on; identification itself is a black box. The claim is simply that outside the Arrow–Debreu world, in which all knowledge is effectively parameterized, opportunities for disequilibrium profit exist and tend to be discovered and exploited. In short, what Kirzner calls "entrepreneurial discovery" is simply that which causes markets to equilibrate.[5]

---

[5] The foregoing description applies primarily to what Kirzner calls the "pure entre

Contemporary entrepreneurship scholars, considering whether opportunities are objective or subjective (McMullen and Shepherd, 2006; Companys and McMullen, 2007), note that Kirzner tends to treat them as objective. Again, this is true, but misses the point. Kirzner is not making an ontological claim about the nature of profit opportunities *per se*—not claiming, in other words, that opportunities are, in some fundamental sense, objective—but merely using the concept of objective, exogenously given, but not yet discovered opportunities as a device for explaining the tendency of markets to clear.[6]

The Knightian perspective also treats entrepreneurship as an instrumental construct, used here to decompose business income into two constituent elements—interest and profit. Interest is a reward for forgoing present consumption, is determined by the relative time preferences of borrowers and lenders, and would exist even in a world of certainty. Profit, by contrast, is a reward for anticipating the uncertain future more accurately than others (e.g., purchasing factors of production at market prices below the eventual selling price of the product), and exists only in a world of true uncertainty. In such a world, given that production takes time, entrepreneurs will earn either profits or losses based on the differences between factor prices paid and product prices received.

For Knight, in other words, opportunities do not exist, just waiting to be discovered (and hence, by definition, exploited). Rather, entrepreneurs invest resources based on their expectations of future consumer demands and market conditions, investments that may or may not yield positive returns. Here the focus is not on opportunities, but on investment and uncertainty. Expectations about the future are inherently subjective and, under conditions of uncertainty rather than risk, constitute judgments that are not themselves modelable. Put differently, subjectivism implies

---

preneur" (see footnote 2 above). As he explains, flesh and blood entrepreneurs do not correspond exactly to this ideal type (they can simultaneously be laborers, capitalists, consumers, etc.)—and they do more than simply discover costless profit opportunities. However, in Kirzner's framework, the attributes of real-world entrepreneurs defy systematic categorization.

[6]Incidentally, the occupational choice literature cited above treats opportunities, implicitly or explicitly, as objective. Agents are assumed to compare the expected benefits of employment and self-employment, meaning that the set of possible entrepreneurial outcomes must be fixed, and the probability weights assigned to individual outcomes known in advance.

that opportunities do not exist in an objective sense. Hence, a research program based on formalizing and studying empirically the cognitive or psychological processes leading individuals to discover opportunities captures only a limited aspect of the entrepreneurial process. Opportunities for entrepreneurial gain are, thus, inherently subjective—they do not exist until profits are realized. Entrepreneurship research may be able to realize higher marginal returns by focusing on entrepreneurial action, rather than its presumed antecedents.[7]

Alvarez and Barney (2007) argue that entrepreneurial objectives, characteristics, and decision making differ systematically, depending on whether opportunities are modeled as discovered or created. In the "discovery approach," for example, entrepreneurial actions are responses to exogenous shocks, while in the "creation approach," such actions are endogenous. Discovery entrepreneurs focus on predicting systematic risks, formulating complete and stable strategies, and procuring capital from external sources. Creation entrepreneurs, by contrast, appreciate iterative, inductive, incremental decision making, are comfortable with emergent and flexible strategies, and tend to rely on internal finance.[8]

The approach proposed here is close to Alvarez and Barney's creation approach, but differs in that it places greater emphasis on the *ex post* processes of resource assembly and personnel management rather than the *ex ante* processes of cognition, expectations formation, and business planning. Moreover, Alvarez and Barney write as if "discovery settings" and "creation settings" are actual business environments within which entrepreneurs operate. Some entrepreneurs really do discover exogenously created profit opportunities, while others have to work creatively to establish them. As I read Knight and Kirzner, by contrast, both the discovery and creation perspectives are purely metaphorical concepts (useful for the economist or management theorist), not frameworks for entrepreneurial

---

[7]Here I follow Gul and Pesendorfer's (2005, p. 1) more general critique of neuroeconomics, namely that cognitive psychology and economics "address different questions, utilize different abstractions, and address different types of empirical evidence," meaning that the two disciplines are in essentially different, though potentially complementary, domains. In other words, understanding the cognitive processes underlying entrepreneurial behavior may be interesting and important, but not necessary for the economic analysis of the behavior itself.

[8]Miller (2007) distinguishes further between opportunity recognition, opportunity discovery, and opportunity creation.

decision making itself. This suggests that opportunities are best characterized neither as discovered nor created, but *imagined*. The creation metaphor implies that profit opportunities, once the entrepreneur has conceived or established them, come into being objectively, like a work of art. Creation implies that something is created. There is no uncertainty about its existence or characteristics (though, of course, its market value may not be known until later). By contrast, the concept of opportunity imagination emphasizes that gains (and losses) do not come into being objectively until entrepreneurial action is complete (i.e., until final goods and services have been produced and sold).[9]

Moreover, explaining entrepreneurial loss is awkward using both discovery and creation language. In Kirzner's formulation, for example, the worst that can happen to an entrepreneur is the failure to discover an existing profit opportunity. Entrepreneurs either earn profits or break even, but it is unclear how they suffer losses. Kirzner (1997) claims that entrepreneurs can earn losses when they misread market conditions. "Entrepreneurial boldness and imagination can lead to pure entrepreneurial losses as well as to pure profit. Mistaken actions by entrepreneurs mean that they have misread the market, possibly pushing price and output constellations in directions not equilibrative" Kirzner (1997, p. 72). But even this formulation makes it clear that it is mistaken *actions*—not mistaken discoveries—that lead to loss. Misreading market conditions leads to losses only if the entrepreneur has invested resources in a project based on this misreading. It is the failure to anticipate future market conditions correctly that causes the loss. It seems obscure to describe this as erroneous discovery, rather than unsuccessful uncertainty bearing.[10]

Likewise, realized entrepreneurial losses do not fit naturally within a

---

[9]The concept of "opportunity imagination" calls to mind Boulding's (1956, p. 15) notion of "image," defined as "the sum of what we think we know and what makes us behave the way we do." Human action, in Boulding's framework, is a response to the actor's (subjective) image of reality. This does not mean that images are completely detached from reality, but that reality is altered, or interpreted, by the actor's subjective beliefs. Penrose's (1959) concept, of the firm's subjective opportunity set also reflects entrepreneurial imagination in this sense (Kor, Mahoney, and Michael, 2007).

[10]In his defense, Kirzner's (1997) remarks appear in the context of defending the equilibrating tendency of the market, against the Walrasian picture of instantaneous market adjustment. Still, the defense could perhaps be made equally well without reference to the discovery metaphor.

creation framework. Alvarez and Barney (2007) emphasize that "creation entrepreneurs" do take into account potential losses, the "acceptable losses" described by Sarasvathy (2001). "[A]n entrepreneur engages in entrepreneurial actions when the total losses that can be created by such activities are not too large" (Alvarez and Barney, 2007, p. 19). However, when those losses are realized, it seems more straightforward to think in terms of mistaken beliefs about the future—expected prices and sales revenues that did not, in fact, materialize—than the "disappearance" of an opportunity that was previously created. Entrepreneurs do not, in other words, create the future, they imagine it, and their imagination can be wrong as often as it is right.[11]

Opportunities as a black box

Confusion over the nature of opportunities is increasingly recognized. As noted by McMullen, Plummer, and Acs (2007, p. 273),

> a good portion of the research to date has focused on the discovery, exploitation, and consequences thereof without much attention to the nature and source of opportunity itself. Although some researchers argue that the subjective or socially constructed nature of opportunity makes it impossible to separate opportunity from the individual, others contend that opportunity is as an objective construct visible to or created by the knowledgeable or attuned entrepreneur. Either way, a set of weakly held assumptions about the nature and sources of opportunity appear to dominate much of the discussion in the literature.

Do we need a precise definition of opportunities to move forward? Can one do entrepreneurship research without specifying what, exactly, entrepreneurial opportunities *are*? Can we treat opportunities as a black box, much as we treat other concepts in management, such as culture, leadership, routines, capabilities, and the like (Abell, Felin, and Foss, 2008)?

---

[11]To go from judgment to an explanation for market efficiency requires assumptions about the tendency of entrepreneurial judgments to be correct. Mises's (1951) explanation is based on a kind of natural selection, namely that market competition rewards those entrepreneurs whose judgments tend to be better than the judgments of their fellow entrepreneurs. Of course, one needn't go as far as Friedman (1953) in assuming that the result is "optimal" behavior, in the neoclassical economist's sense of optimality, to defend the effectiveness of this selection process.

One approach is to focus not on what opportunities are, but what opportunities do. Opportunities, in this sense, are treated as a latent construct that is manifested in entrepreneurial action—investment, creating new organizations, bringing products to market, and so on. A direct analogy can be drawn to the economist's notion of preferences. Economic theory (with the exception of behavioral economics, discussed later) takes agents' preferences as a given and derives implications for choice. The economist does not care what preferences "are," ontologically, but simply postulates their existence and draws inferences about their characteristics as needed to explain particular kinds of economic behavior. Empirically, this approach can be operationalized by treating entrepreneurship as a latent variable in a structural-equations framework (Xue and Klein, 2010).

By treating opportunities as a latent construct, this approach sidesteps the problem of defining opportunities as objective or subjective, real or imagined, and so on. The formation of entrepreneurial beliefs is treated as a potentially interesting psychological problem, but not part of the economic analysis of entrepreneurship. It also avoids thorny questions about whether alertness or judgment is simply luck (Demsetz, 1983), a kind of intuition (Dane and Pratt, 2007), or something else entirely.

The unit of analysis

As explained earlier, the opportunity-creation approach proposed by Alvarez and Barney (2007) differs in important ways from the opportunity-discovery approach. The creation approach treats opportunities as the result of entrepreneurial action. Opportunities do not exist objectively, *ex ante*, but are created, *ex nihilo*, as entrepreneurs act based on their subjective beliefs. "Creation opportunities are social constructions that do not exist independent of the entrepreneur's perceptions" (Alvarez and Barney, 2007, p. 15). In this sense, the creation approach sounds like the imagination approach described here. Still, like the discovery approach, the creation approach makes the opportunity the unit of analysis. How entrepreneurs create opportunities, and how they subsequently seek to exploit those opportunities, is the focus of the research program.

At one level, the distinction between opportunity creation and opportunity imagination seems semantic. Both hold that entrepreneurs act based on their beliefs about future gains and losses, rather than reacting to

objective, exogenously given opportunities for profit. There are some ontological and epistemological differences, however. The creation approach
is grounded in a social constructivist view of action (Alvarez and Barney,
2007). It holds that the market itself is a social construction, and that
realized gains and losses are, in part, subjective. The imagination approach
described here is, in this sense, less subjectivist than the creation approach.
It is tied closely to Mises's (1912; 1920) concept of monetary calculation,
in which realized gains and losses are objective and quantifiable, and used
to filter (or select) the quality of entrepreneurial expectations and beliefs.
It is compatible with a range of ontological positions, from evolutionary
realism to critical realism (Lawson, 1997; Mäki, 1996) to Misesian praxeology (Mises, 1949).

An alternative way to frame a subjectivist approach to entrepreneurship, emphasizing uncertainty and the passage of time, is to drop the
concept of "opportunity" altogether. If opportunities are inherently subjective and we treat them as a black box, then the unit of analysis should
not be opportunities, but rather some action—in Knightian terms, the assembly of resources in the present in anticipation of (uncertain) receipts in
the future. Again, the analogy with preferences in microeconomic theory
is clear: the unit of analysis in consumer theory is not preferences, but
consumption, while in neoclassical production theory, the unit of analysis
is not the production function, but some decision variable.

One could also view opportunities and actions as distinct—but complementary—aspects of the entrepreneurial process. To use Alvarez and
Barney's (2007) terminology, the discovery perspective treats actions as
responses to opportunities, while the creation perspective treats opportunities as the result of action. By contrast, the perspective outlined here
treats opportunities as a superfluous concept, once action is taken into
account. Opportunities exist only as manifested in action, and are neither
its cause nor consequence of action. Hence, we can dispense with the very
notion of opportunities itself and focus on the actions that entrepreneurs
take and the results of those actions.

One way to capture the Knightian concept of entrepreneurial action is
Casson and Wadeson's (2007) notion of "projects." A project is a stock of
resources committed to particular activities for a specified period of time.
Project benefits are uncertain, and are realized only after projects are completed. Casson and Wadeson (2007) model the set of potential projects as

a given, defining opportunities as potential projects that have not yet been chosen. As in the discovery-process perspective, the set of opportunities is fixed. However, as Casson and Wadeson point out, the assumption of fixed "project possibility sets" is a modeling convenience, made necessary by their particular theory of project selection. More generally, the use of projects as the unit of analysis is consistent with either the discovery or creation perspective. Focusing on projects, rather than opportunities, implies an emphasis on the actions that generate profits and losses. It suggests that entrepreneurship research should focus on the execution of business plans. In this sense, entrepreneurship is closely linked to finance—not simply "entrepreneurial finance" that studies venture funding and firm formation, but the more general problem of project finance under (true) uncertainty. Not only venture capital, but also public equity and debt, are entrepreneurial instruments in this perspective. Capital budgeting is also a form of entrepreneurial decision making. Of course contemporary finance theory focuses primarily on equilibrium models of resource allocation under conditions of risk, not Knightian uncertainty, so entrepreneurship theory cannot be simply a reframing of modern finance theory. Instead, a *financiers as entrepreneurs* approach treats investors not as passive suppliers of capital to decision-making firms, but as the locus of economic decision making itself, as economic agents who experiment with resource combinations (chapter 3 above), develop and exploit network ties (Meyer, 2000), manage and govern subordinates (Kaplan and Strömberg, 2003), and the like.

Entrepreneurial Action, Heterogeneous Capital, and Economic Organization

The close relationship between the Knightian concept of entrepreneurship as action under uncertainty and the ownership and control of resources suggests a bridge between entrepreneurship and the mundane activities of establishing and maintaining a business enterprise—what Witt (2003) calls the "organizational grind." Chapter 4 above offers an entrepreneurial theory of the economic organization that combines the Knightian concept of judgment and the Austrian approach to capital heterogeneity. In Knight's formulation, entrepreneurship represents judgment that cannot be assessed in terms of its marginal product and which cannot, accordingly, be paid a wage (Knight, 1921). In other words, there is no market for the judgment that entrepreneurs rely on and, therefore, exercising judgment requires the person with judgment to start a firm. Of course, judgmental decision-makers can hire consultants, forecasters, technical experts, and so on. However, in doing so they are exercising their own entrepreneurial judgment.[12] Thus, judgment implies asset ownership, for judgmental decision making is ultimately decision making about the employment of resources. The entrepreneur's role, then, is to arrange or organize the capital goods he/she owns. As Lachmann (1956, p. 16) puts it, "We are living in a world of unexpected change; hence capital combinations . . . will be ever changing, will be dissolved and reformed. In this activity, we find the real function of the entrepreneur."[13]

---

[12] In Foss, Foss, and Klein's (2007) terminology, the entrepreneur-owner exercises "original" judgment, while hired employees, to whom the owner delegates particular decision rights, exercise "derived" judgment as agents of the owner. This implies that top corporate managers, whose day-to-day decisions drive the organization of corporate resources, are acting only as "proxy-entrepreneurs," except to the extent that they themselves are part owners through equity holdings.

[13] Lachmann (1956) does not require the entrepreneur to own the assets he recombines; see chapter 4 above for a more detailed argument that ownership, as residual rights of control, is a necessary part of this entrepreneurial function. Consider also Marchal's (1951, pp. 550–51) explanation of the economic return to the entrepreneurial function:

> [E]ntrepreneurs obtain remuneration for their activity in a very different manner than do laborers or lenders of capital. The latter provide factors of production which they sell to the entrepreneur at prices which they naturally try to make as high as possible. The entrepreneur proceeds quite otherwise; instead of selling something to the enterprise, he identifies himself with the enterprise. Some people doubtless will say that he provides the function of enterprise and receives as remuneration a sum which varies according to the results. But this is a tortured way of presenting the thing, inspired by an unhealthy desire to establish arbitrarily asymmetry with the other factors. In reality, the entrepreneur and the firm are one and the same. His function is to negotiate, or to pay people for negotiating under his responsibility and in the name of the firm, with two groups: on the one hand, with those who provide the factors of production, in which case his problem is to pay the lowest prices possible; on the other hand, with the buyers of the finished products, from which it is desirable to obtain as large a total revenue as possible. To say all this in a few words, the entrepreneur, although undeniably providing a factor of production, perhaps the most important one in a capitalist system, is not himself to be defined in those terms.

Marchal expresses, in strong terms, the view described in chapter 4 that entrepreneurship is embodied in asset ownership (i.e., in the creation and operation of the firm). The

Chapter 4 above argues that Austrian capital theory provides a unique foundation for an entrepreneurial theory of economic organization. Neo-classical production theory, with its notion of capital as a permanent, homogeneous fund of value, rather than a discrete stock of heterogeneous capital goods, is of little help here.[14] Transaction cost, resource-based, and property-rights approaches to the firm do incorporate notions of heterogeneous assets, but they tend to invoke the needed specificities in an *ad hoc* fashion to rationalize particular trading problems—for transaction cost economics, asset specificity; for capabilities theories, tacit knowledge; and so on. The Austrian approach—starting with Menger's (1871) concepts of higher- and lower-order goods and extending through Böhm-Bawerk's (1889) notion of roundaboutness, Lachmann's (1956) theory of multiple specificities, and Kirzner's (1966) formulation of capital structure in terms of subjective entrepreneurial plans—offers a solid foundation for a judgment-based theory of entrepreneurial action.

As we saw in chapter 4, Barzel's (1997) idea that capital goods are distinguished by their *attributes* is one way to operationalize the Austrian notion of heterogeneity. Attributes are characteristics, functions, or possible uses of assets, as perceived by an entrepreneur. Assets are heterogeneous to the extent that they have different, and different levels of, valued attributes. Attributes may also vary over time, even for a particular asset. Given Knightian uncertainty, attributes do not exist objectively, but subjectively, in the minds of profit-seeking entrepreneurs who put these assets to use in various lines of production. Entrepreneurship thus not only involves deploying superior combinations of capital assets with given attributes, but also a means of experimenting with capital assets in an attempt to create or discover new valued attributes. In short, firms exist not only to economize on transaction costs, but also as a means for the exercise of entrepreneurial judgment, and as a low-cost mechanism for entrepreneurs to experiment with various combinations of heterogeneous capital goods. The boundary changes discussed in chapter 3 can be understood as the result of processes

---

entrepreneur is not merely an idea man, but rather an owner, who exercises judgment over the capital assets he owns and manages. This contrasts with Kirzner's analytical device of the "pure entrepreneur" who owns no capital. (I thank John Matthews for the reference to Marchal.)

[14]Ironically, the notion of capital as a homogeneous fund owes its popularity to Knight (1936).

of entrepreneurial experimentation. And internal organization is a means of delegating particular decision rights to subordinates who exercise derived judgment (Foss, Foss, and Klein, 2007).

Witt (1998) offers another approach to combining an Austrian concept of entrepreneurship with the theory of the firm. Entrepreneurs require complementary factors of production, he argues, which are coordinated within the firm. For the firm to be successful the entrepreneur must establish a tacit, shared framework of goals—what Casson (2000) calls a "mental model" of reality—which governs the relationships among members of the entrepreneur's team. As Langlois (1998) points out, it is often easier (less costly) for individuals to commit to a specific individual—the leader—rather than an abstract set of complex rules governing the firm's operations. The appropriate exercise of charismatic authority, then, facilitates coordination within organizations (Witt, 2003). This approach combines insights from economics, psychology, and sociology, and leans heavily on Max Weber. Leaders coordinate through effective communication, not only of explicit information, but also of mental models as described above. The successful entrepreneur excels at communicating such models.[15]

Here, as in Coase (1937), the employment relationship is central to the theory of the firm. The entrepreneur's primary task is to coordinate the human resources that make up the firm. The analysis in chapter 4, by contrast, focuses on alienable assets, as in Knight (1921). It defines the firm as the entrepreneur plus the alienable resources the entrepreneur owns and, thus, controls. Each approach has strengths and weaknesses. The cognitive approach explains the dynamics among team members, but not necessarily their contractual relationships. Must charismatic leaders necessarily own physical capital, or can they be employees or independent contractors? Formulating a business plan, communicating a corporate culture, and the like are clearly important dimensions of business leadership. But are they attributes of the successful manager or the successful entrepreneur? Even if top-level managerial skill were the same as entrepreneurship, it is unclear why charismatic leadership should be regarded as more *entrepreneurial* than other, comparatively mundane managerial tasks, such as structuring

---

[15]Earl's (2003) "connectionist approach" to entrepreneurship also focuses on coordination, but here the emphasis is on coordination among market participants, not within organizations. See also Koppl and Langlois (2001) and Langlois (2002).

incentives, limiting opportunism, administering rewards, and so on. On the other hand, the judgment approach does not generalize easily from the one-person firm to the multi-person firm.

Applications of Entrepreneurial Action

Shifting the focus of entrepreneurship research from opportunity identification to entrepreneurial action suggests several new issues and directions for entrepreneurship research.

Opportunities and Organizational Form

Distinguishing between opportunity discovery and entrepreneurial action reminds us that the two do not always go hand in hand. Efforts to encourage the former do not necessarily encourage the latter. Generally, efficiency requires that entrepreneurs (and what Foss, Foss, and Klein, 2007 call "proxy-entrepreneurs") bear the full wealth effects of their actions. For this reason, efforts to promote experimentation, creativity, etc., within the firm can encourage moral hazard unless rewards and punishments are symmetric. Outside the firm, strong intellectual property protection, incentives for discovery (such as SBIR awards), and the like may encourage overspending on discovery. The potential waste of resources on "patent races" is a well-known example (Barzel, 1968; Loury, 1979; Dasgupta and Stiglitz, 1980; Judd, Schmedders, and Yeltekin, 2003).

By contrast, if the essence of entrepreneurship is the assembly of resources under uncertainty, then the locus of entrepreneurship is not the generation of creative ideas, but the funding of projects. Financiers—venture capitalists, angel investors, banks, family members, even corporate shareholders—are, in this sense, entrepreneurs. Resource owners possess fundamental judgment rights that, by the nature of ownership, cannot be delegated, no matter how many proximate decision rights are delegated to subordinates (Foss, Foss, and Klein, 2007). In this perspective, even corporate shareholders are treated not as passive suppliers of capital (as they are treated both in neoclassical production theory and contemporary entrepreneurship theory), but as critical decision-makers.[16]

---

[16]See the discussion in chapter 2 above on "firms as investments" and "financiers as entrepreneurs."

Some applications, such as the staging of venture finance (Gompers, 1995), are obvious. Another application is the inherent uncertainty of the gains from corporate takeovers. As discussed in chapter 2 above, the "raider's" return to a successful takeover is thus a form of pure entrepreneurial profit. More generally, note that in this perspective, finance is treated not as an input into the entrepreneurial process, but as the very essence of that process. Entrepreneurship is, in other words, manifested in investment. Of course, the terms "finance" and "investment" are used here in a broad sense, referring to the provision not only of financial capital, but also human capital, and tangible and intangible resources—anything that can be considered an input or factor of production. Entrepreneurship is conceived as the act of putting resources at risk, with profit as the reward for anticipating future market conditions correctly, or at least more correctly than other entrepreneurs.

Entrepreneurial Teams

Focusing on entrepreneurial action also responds to recent calls to link the theory of entrepreneurship more closely to the theory of group behavior (Stewart, 1989; Mosakowski, 1998; Cook and Plunkett, 2006). Some efforts to develop a theory of team entrepreneurship focus on shared mental models, team cognition, and other aspects of the process of identifying opportunities. Penrose's (1959) concept of the firm's "subjective opportunity" set is an obvious link to judgment-based theories of entrepreneurship (Kor, et al., 2007).[17] Entrepreneurs can also form networks to share expectations of the potential returns to projects (Greve and Salaff, 2003; Parker, 2008).

On the other hand, even if one views the perception of a (subjectively identified) opportunity as an inherently individual act, entrepreneurial action can be a team or group activity. Venture capital, later-stage private equity, and bank loans are often syndicated. Publicly traded equity is diffusely held. Professional services firms and closed-membership cooperatives represent jointly owned pools of risk capital. Moreover, the firm's top management team—to whom key decision rights are delegated—can

---

[17]Spender (2006, p. 2) argues that "Penrose's model of managerial learning [is] an accessible instance of the epistemological approach proposed by Austrian economists such as Hayek, Kirzner, and Schumpeter."

be regarded as a bundle of heterogeneous human resources, the interactions among which are critical to the firm's performance (Foss, et al., 2008).

This approach also suggests relationships between the theory of entrepreneurship and the theory of collective action (Olson, 1965; Hansmann, 1996). Once an entrepreneurial opportunity has been perceived, the entrepreneur may need to assemble a team of investors and/or a management team, raising problems of internal governance. Shared objectives must be formulated; different time horizons must be reconciled; free riding must be mitigated; and so on. Cook and Plunkett (2006) and Chambers (2007) discuss how these problems are addressed within closed-membership, or new-generation cooperatives. Traditionally organized, open-membership cooperatives suffer from what Cook (1995) calls *vaguely defined property rights*. Because their equity shares are not alienable assets that trade in secondary markets, traditional cooperatives suffer from a particular set of free-rider, horizon, portfolio, control, and influence costs problems.[18]

In response, a new type of cooperative began to emerge in the 1990s. These new-generation cooperatives required up-front equity investments (in traditional cooperatives, equity is generated *ex post*, through retained earnings), restricted patronage to member investors, and allowed for limited transferability of investment and delivery rights.[19] One of the key challenges in developing new-generation cooperatives is the establishment of a founding investment team with shared objectives and constraints and an effective governing board. According to project champions—those entrepreneurs who formulated the original vision of the organization—the biggest obstacle they faced was convincing other farmer investors, with whom they had close social ties, to invest (Chambers, 2007). In other words, the successful movement from opportunity identification to entrepreneurial action depended critically on transaction cost and collective action considerations, social capital, and reputation. Team entrepreneurship, in the Knightian sense described above, is a subset of the general theory of economic organization.

---

[18] See Cook and Iliopoulos (2000) and Cook and Chaddad (2004) for details.

[19] Cook, Burress, and Klein (2008) document the emergence of a cluster of new-generation cooperatives in the tiny community of Renville County, Minnesota.

Summary and Conclusions

The arguments presented here suggest that the entrepreneurship literature may have over-emphasized the origins and characteristics of entrepreneurial opportunities. Instead, opportunities can be usefully treated as
a latent construct that is manifested in entrepreneurial action, namely the
exercise of judgment over the arrangement of heterogeneous capital assets.
The Austrian theory of capital, interpreted in the *attributes* framework
described above, provides a useful bridge between the Knightian theory of
entrepreneurship and the theory of economic organization. In short, this
chapter suggests a reorientation of the entrepreneurship literature toward
deeds, not words or dreams. In Rothbard's (1985, p. 283) words: "Entrepreneurial ideas without money are mere parlor games until the money
is obtained and committed to the projects." Of course, the subjectivist
concept of resources is inextricably tied to beliefs—vision, imagination,
new mental models, if you like—but these beliefs are relevant only to the
extent that they are manifest in action.

One objection to this approach is to invoke recent literature in behavioral economics and neuroeconomics. This literature takes preferences,
not choices, as its unit of analysis, seeking to understand the psychological
basis of preference, the consistency of preferences, and the like, rather than
taking preferences as an irreducible primary. Likewise, a theory of opportunity identification could mimic the methods of behavioral economics
and neuroeconomics. This is, indeed, a potentially fruitful avenue for
entrepreneurship research. However, like behavioral economics, such an
approach has more in common with applied psychology than economics.
It may contribute to a general, interdisciplinary approach to entrepreneurship, but is not an integral part of the economic theory of entrepreneurship
(see Gul and Pesendorfer, 2005, for a more general argument along these
lines).

CHAPTER 6

Risk, Uncertainty, and Economic Organization[†]

In a recent paper, "The Limits of Numerical Probability: Frank H. Knight and Ludwig von Mises and the Frequency Interpretation," Hans-Hermann Hoppe (2007) explores Mises's approach to probability and its implications for economic forecasting. Hoppe argues that Mises, like Frank Knight, subscribed to the "frequency interpretation" developed by Mises's brother, Richard von Mises (1939), along with others such as Ronald Fisher, Jerzy Neyman, and Egon Pearson. At first, this might seem surprising, as the frequency interpretation is usually contrasted with the "subjectivist" approach to probability advanced by Finetti (1937) and, among economists, usually associated with Keynes (1921). A thoroughgoing commitment to methodological subjectivism is, of course, a hallmark of the Austrian School. However, as Hoppe points out, Mises recognized two distinct kinds of probability, one applying to natural phenomena and another applying to human action. Just as Mises embraced "praxeology" in economics while endorsing the experimental method in the natural sciences, he thought a special kind of probability was relevant to economic decision making, while accepting his brother's frequency interpretation for other kinds.

[†]Published originally in Jörg Guido Hülsmann and Stephan Kinsella, eds., *Property, Freedom, and Society: Essays in Honor of Hans-Hermann Hoppe* (Auburn, Ala.: Ludwig von Mises Institute, 2009), pp. 325–37.

This chapter extends the discussion by drawing out implications for economic organization of Mises's approach to probability, particularly regarding the entrepreneur's role in guiding the economic process by establishing and dissolving firms, directing their operations, and organizing them to create and capture value. After a brief review of Hoppe's interpretation of Knight and Mises, I summarize recent literature on the Knight–Mises approach to entrepreneurship and the firm, closing with some suggestions for future research.

Knight, Mises, and Mises on Probability

Most economists are familiar with Knight's distinction between "risk" and "uncertainty." Risk refers to situations in which the outcome of an event is unknown, but the decision maker knows the range of possible outcomes and the probabilities of each, such that anyone with the same information and beliefs would make the same prediction. Uncertainty, by contrast, characterizes situations in which the range of possible outcomes, let alone the relevant probabilities, is unknown. In this case the decision maker cannot follow a formal decision rule but must rely on an intuitive understanding of the situation—what Knight calls "judgment"—to anticipate what may occur. Risk, in this sense, refers to "a quantity susceptible of measurement," and not a "true" uncertainty that cannot be quantified (Knight, 1921, p. 26). The essential function of the entrepreneur, in Knight's system, is to exercise judgment, particularly in the context of purchasing factors of production.

Mises, in similar fashion, distinguished between "class probability" and "case probability." The former describes situations in which an event may be classified as a unique element of a homogeneous class, the properties of which are known. No one can predict whether a particular house in a particular neighborhood will burn down this year, but insurance companies know how many similar houses in similar locations have burned in the past, and from this the likelihood of a particular house burning within a particular period can be estimated. Case probability applies to cases in which each event is unique, such that no general class probabilities can be defined.[1] Here Mises, as argued by Hoppe, builds on his brother's

---

[1] O'Driscoll and Rizzo (1985) adopt the terms "typical events" and "unique events" to get at this distinction.

defense of "frequentism," the idea that the probability of a particular event is the limit value of its relative frequency in a series of trials. In this understanding, probabilities can be defined only in cases in which repeated trials are feasible—i.e., in situations where each event can be meaningfully compared to other events in the same class. Moreover, and for this reason, probabilities can only be defined *ex post*, as learned through experience, and cannot exist *a priori*. Hence, Mises defines case probability, or uncertainty, as a case in which probabilities, in the frequentist sense, do not exist.[2]

Hoppe (2007) summarizes Knight's and Mises's views and argues persuasively that they are variants of Richard von Mises's position.[3] Hoppe also goes beyond Mises in explaining why human action, in Mises's sense of purposeful behavior, cannot be made part of a homogenous class. "Without a specified collective and an (assumedly) full count of its individual members and their various attributes no numerical probability statement is possible (or is, if made, arbitrary)" (Hoppe, 2007, p. 10). Of course, as Hoppe notes, we can define such classes in a technical sense—me writing this chapter is an element of the class "economists writing book chapters"—but defining the class is not sufficient for applying class probability to an event. There must also be randomness, or what Richard von Mises (1939, p. 24) calls "complete lawlessness," within the class. And yet, this is not possible with human action:

> It is in connection with this randomness requirement where Ludwig von Mises (and presumably Knight) see insuperable difficulties in applying probability theory to human actions. True, formal-logically for every single action a corresponding collective can be defined. However, ontologically, human actions (whether of individuals or groups) cannot be grouped in "true" collectives but must be conceived as unique events. Why? As Ludwig von Mises would presumably reply, the assumption that one knows nothing about any particular event except its membership in a known class is false

---

[2] Hence the use of the term "case probability" is misleading; what Mises really means is "case non-probability," or perhaps "case judgments without probabilities." Confusingly, Mises also argues elsewhere that "[o]nly preoccupation with the mathematical treatment could result in the prejudice that probability always means frequency" (Mises, 1949, p. 107). Van den Hauwe (2007) argues, in contrast to Hoppe, that Mises's position is in some ways closer to Keynes's.

[3] One might also include Shackle's notion of "self-destructive, non-seriable" decisions. See G.L.S. Schackle, *Decision, Order, and Time in Human Affairs* (Cambridge: Cambridge University Press, 1961).

in the case of human actions; or, as Richard von Mises would put it, in the case of human actions we know a "selection rule" the application of which leads to fundamental changes regarding the relative frequency (likelihood) of the attribute in question (thus ruling out the use of the probability calculus). (Hoppe, 2007, p. 11)

Hoppe touches briefly upon, without treating in detail, the subjective approach to probability, in which *a priori* probabilities are treated simply as beliefs, rather than the outcome of some objective process of repeated trial and observation. Hoppe quotes Richard von Mises's (1939, p. 75) remark that subjectivists such as Keynes fail to recognize "that if we know nothing about a thing, we cannot say anything about its probability." Adds Mises (1939, p. 76): "The peculiar approach of the subjectivists lies in the fact that they consider 'I presume that these cases are equally probable,' to be equivalent to 'These cases are equally probable,' since, for them, probability is only a subjective notion." Subjective probability has become central in contemporary microeconomic theory, however, particularly with the rise of Bayesian approaches to decision making. Agents acting under conditions of uncertainty are assumed to have prior beliefs—correct or incorrect—about the probabilities of various events. These prior beliefs are exogenous, they may be common to a group of agents or unique to a particular agent, and they may or may not correspond to objective probabilities (in the frequentist sense). The Bayesian approach focuses on the procedure by which agents update these prior beliefs based on new information, and this updating is assumed to take place according to a formal rule (i.e., according to Bayes's law). Hence, the *ex post* probability, in such a problem, contains an "objective" element, even if it is a revision of a purely subjective prior belief.[4]

Langlois (1982) argues for a tight connection between subjectivism in the Austrian sense of value theory and subjective probability theory, arguing that probabilities should be interpreted as beliefs about information structures, rather than objective events. "[I]t is not meaningful to talk about 'knowing' a probability or a probability distribution. A probability assessment reflects one's state of information about an event; it is not some-

---

[4]Bayesian updating can also be applied to objective prior probabilities, presumably to give guidance to the decision maker in cases where repeated trials to determine the new *ex post* probability are not possible. The "Monty Hall paradox" is a classic example.

thing ontologically separate whose value can be determined objectively" (Langlois, 1982, p. 8).

What distinguishes case from class probability, according to Langlois, is the character of the decision maker's information about the event. Objective probabilities (in the frequentist sense) are simply special cases of subjective probabilities in which the decision maker structures the problem in terms of classes of events. Entrepreneurship, in Langlois's interpretation, can be described as the act of formalizing the decision problem. To use the language of decision theory, a non-entrepreneur (call him, following Kirzner, 1973, a Robbinsian maximizer) is presented with a decision tree, a set of outcomes, and the probabilities for each outcome, and simply uses backwards induction to solve the problem. The entrepreneur, as it were, re-draws the tree, by noticing a possible option or outcome that other agents failed to see. The key distinction, according to Langlois, is not whether the decision tree is populated with objective or subjective probabilities, but whether the tree itself is exogenous (Knightian risk) or endogenous (Knightian uncertainty).

Hoppe follows Richard von Mises in rejecting the subjectivist position (and obviously sees no contradiction between the frequentist approach to probability and the subjective theory of value). It is not clear exactly what is gained by redefining probabilities as "subjective with one information set" or "subjective with another information set." As discussed in the next section, both Knight and Mises saw probability theory in economics as playing a particular role, namely allowing the theorist to distinguish situations in which prices are predictable, making profits and losses ephemeral, and situations in which prices can only be anticipated, using some form of judgment or *Verstehen*, by entrepreneurs. A subjectivist parameterization of *Verstehen* may be possible, without being useful.

Uncertainty and the Entrepreneur

Neither Knight nor Mises focused primarily on individual decision making *per se*, but on the role of decision making within the market system. "As economists," Hoppe (2007, p. 4) observes, Knight and Mises "come upon the subject of probability indirectly, in conjunction with the question concerning the source of entrepreneurial profits and losses."[5] Indeed, while

---

[5] See also Buchanan and Di Pierro (1980).

Knight devotes a chapter of *Risk, Uncertainty, and Profit* to a detailed discussion of knowledge, reasoning, and learning, his main purpose is not to analyze the ontology of judgment, but to explain the practical workings of the market. Specifically, his purpose in developing his account of probability was to decompose business income into two constituent elements, interest and profit. Interest is a reward for forgoing present consumption, is determined by the relative time preferences of borrowers and lenders, and would exist even in a world of certainty. Profit, by contrast, is a reward for anticipating the uncertain future more accurately than others (e.g., purchasing factors of production at market prices below the eventual selling price of the product), and exists only in a world of "true" uncertainty. In such a world, given that production takes time, entrepreneurs will earn either profits or losses based on the differences between factor prices paid and product prices received.

Ludwig von Mises, as discussed in chapter 5 above, gives uncertainty a central role in his theory of profit and loss, and his account of the impossibility of economic calculation under socialism. Because there are no factor markets under socialism, there are no factor prices, and hence no way for planners to choose efficiently among the virtually infinite range of possibilities for combining heterogeneous resources to make a particular set of consumer goods. Entrepreneurs under capitalism engage in this process of "appraisement" every day, weighing possible combinations of factors and trying to anticipate what consumers will buy and how much they'll pay once the final goods and services are ready. Profit and loss provides essential feedback for entrepreneurs as they "test" their conjectures on the market.

Why can't a central planning board mimic the operations of entrepreneurs? The key, for Mises, is that entrepreneurial appraisement is not a mechanical process of computing expected values using known probabilities, but a kind of *Verstehen* that cannot be formally modeled using decision theory. The entrepreneur, Mises (1949, p. 582) writes, "is a speculator, a man eager to utilize his opinion about the future structure of the market for business operations promising profits." The entrepreneur relies on his "specific anticipative understanding of the conditions of the uncertain future," an understanding that "defies any rules and systematization."

This concept of the entrepreneurial function is difficult to reconcile with the optimization framework of neoclassical economics. In this framework, either decision making is "rational," meaning that it can be represented by formal decision rules, or it is purely random. T. W. Schultz (1980, pp. 437–38) poses the problem this way:

> [I]t is not sufficient to treat entrepreneurs solely as economic agents who only collect windfalls and bear losses that are unanticipated. If this is all they do, the much vaunted free enterprise system merely distributes in some unspecified manner the windfalls and losses that come as surprises. If entrepreneurship has some economic value it must perform a useful function which is constrained by scarcity, which implies that there is a supply and a demand for their services.

The key to understanding this passage is to recognize Schultz's rejection, following Friedman and Savage (1948), of Knightian uncertainty. If all uncertainty can be parameterized in terms of (possibly subjective) probabilities, then decision making in the absence of such probabilities must be random. Any valuable kind of decision making must be modelable, must have a marginal revenue product, and must be determined by supply and demand. For Knight, however, decision making in the absence of a formal decision rule or model (i.e., judgment) is not random, it is simply not modelable. It does not have a supply curve, because it is a residual or controlling factor that is inextricably linked with resource ownership. As discussed above, it is a kind of understanding, or *Verstehen*, that defies formal explanation but is rare and valuable. In short, without the concept of Knightian uncertainty, Knight's idea of entrepreneurial judgment makes little sense.

Nor is judgment simply luck.[6] To be sure, one could imagine a model in which entrepreneurs are systematically biased, as in Busenitz and Barney (1997)—individuals become owner-entrepreneurs because they overestimate their own ability to anticipate future prices—and the supply of entrepreneurs is sufficiently large that at least a few guess correctly, and earn profits. In such an economy there would be entrepreneurs, firms, profits, and losses, and profit (under uncertainty) would be distinct from interest. However, as Mises (1951) emphasizes, some individuals are more adept than others, over time, at anticipating future market conditions, and these individuals tend to acquire more resources while those whose forecasting skills are poor tend to exit the market. Indeed, for Mises,

---

[6]Demsetz (1983) compares Kirznerian alertness to luck.

the entrepreneurial selection mechanism in which unsuccessful entrepreneurs—those who systematically overbid for factors, relative to eventual consumer demands—are eliminated from the market is the critical "market process" of capitalism.[7]

Conclusion

Uncertainty, in Knight's and Ludwig von Mises's sense, is thus fundamental to understanding not only the profit-and-loss system, and the market's process of allocating productive resources to their highest-valued users, but also the economic nature of the business firm itself. Unfortunately, contemporary neoclassical economics tends to reject both the distinction between case and class probability and the entrepreneur. If there is no "true" uncertainty, then profits are the result of monopoly power or random error. If any firm can do what any other firm does, if all firms are always on their production possibility frontiers, and if firms always make optimal choices of inputs, then there is little for the entrepreneur to do.

Fortunately, the modern entrepreneurship literature has begun to recognize the need for a more sophisticated treatment of uncertainty (along with other cognitive issues—see the discussion in Alvarez and Barney, 2007), and concepts of resource heterogeneity are common in the resource- and knowledge-based views of the firm, transaction-cost economics, and the real-options approach to the firm. Far from rehashing old controversies, with the reexamination of Ludwig von Mises's and Knight's views on uncertainty, Hoppe's paper provides fresh insight into the entrepreneur, the firm, and the market process.

---

[7] See chapter 7 below.

CHAPTER 7

Price Theory and Austrian Economics[†]

The Austrian approach underlies all the chapters in this volume. Austrian economics, I have argued, provides unique insight into the emergence, boundaries, and internal organization of the firm. Likewise, firms operate within a particular institutional context—they are the "islands of conscious power in [the] ocean of unconscious cooperation like lumps of butter coagulating in a pail of buttermilk" (D. H. Robertson, quoted in Coase 1937, p. 388). That "ocean of unconscious cooperation" is the market, and Austrians have developed a unique understanding of the market economy that sheds additional light into organizational and strategic issues.

Indeed, the Austrian school has experienced a remarkable renaissance over the last five decades (Vaughn, 1994; Rothbard, 1995; Oakley, 1999; Salerno, 1999b, 2002). Austrian economics flourished originally in Vienna during the last three decades of the nineteenth century, and in Europe and North America through the 1920s, and then entered a prolonged eclipse in the 1930s and 1940s. Kept alive by important contributions from Hayek (1948), Mises (1949), Lachmann (1956), Rothbard (1962), Kirzner (1973), and others, the Austrian tradition emerged once more as

---

[†]Published as "The Mundane Economics of the Austrian School" in *Quarterly Journal of Austrian Economics* 11, nos. 3–4 (2008): 165–87.

an organized movement in the 1970s, and remains today an important alternative to the "mainstream" tradition of neoclassical economics.

But what exactly is the distinct contribution of the Austrian school? How does it differ from other traditions, schools of thought, approaches, or movements within economics and its sister disciplines? As a social movement, the Austrian School possesses the formal markers usually taken to demarcate a school of thought, such as its own institutions—specialized journals, conferences, academic societies, and funding agencies—and the patterns of self-citation emphasized by Crane (1972). Here, though, I am concerned not with the sociology of the Austrian School, but with its core theoretical doctrines, propositions, and modes of analysis, particularly as they apply to everyday, pedestrian, ordinary economic problems. These are the basic problems of price theory, capital theory, monetary theory, business-cycle theory, and the theory of interventionism, problems that are central to any approach within economics.

Price theory—the theory of value, exchange, production, and market intervention—was what Mises (1933, p. 214) had in mind when he made the statement, often surprising to contemporary Austrians, that the Austrian, Walrasian, and Jevonian versions of marginalism "differ only in their mode of expressing the same fundamental idea and ... are divided more by their terminology and by peculiarities of presentation than by the substance of their teachings." These are not the words of a young, enthusiastic author yet to appreciate the important differences among rival schools of thought; the essay was written in 1932, when Mises was a mature scholar. Hayek, likewise, wrote in his 1968 entry for the *International Encyclopedia of the Social Sciences* that his (fourth) generation of the Austrian School

> can hardly any longer be seen as a separate school in the sense of representing particular doctrines. A school has its greatest success when it ceases as such to exist because its leading ideals have become a part of the general dominant teaching. The Vienna school has to a great extent come to enjoy such a success. Hayek (1968a, p. 52)

A few sentences later Hayek singles out "value and price theory" as the key Austrian contribution to modern economics (recognizing, of course, the influence of Marshall, and presumably Hicks, Allen, and Samuelson as well).

These statements hardly can mean that Mises and Hayek failed to recognize the important distinctions among the three marginalist traditions, given their substantial work on the methodology of the Austrian School (Mises, 1933, 1962; Hayek, 1952a). Instead, they indicate that both Mises and Hayek considered value and price theory to be central to the Austrian tradition, an emphasis broadly shared among all theoretical economists. Consider that Mises's 1932 essay focuses on the differences between theoretical economics and the historicism of the Younger German Historical School. Indeed, Mises's usual doctrinal targets were historicism, institutionalism, and other forms of what he considered to be "anti-economics," not alternative versions of theoretical economics (let alone different strands within the Austrian School). In the fight for theoretical economics, Mises considered the Lausanne and British neoclassical tradition as allies. All three marginalist traditions took value, price, exchange, and production theory to be their central core.[1]

Perhaps recognizing the close ties between Austrian value and price theory and that of mainstream economics, recent commentators have looked elsewhere for the distinguishing characteristics of the Austrian School. D. Klein (2008, p. 361), for example, identifies the Hayekian notion of "spontaneous order" as the main contribution of the Austrian tradition, urging that the label "Austrian," with its specific historical and geographical connotations, be replaced by "spontaneous order economics" or "Smith–Hayek economics." Austrian economics, he argues, is part of a broader tradition that includes key figures in the Scottish Enlightenment, French classical liberals of the eighteenth and nineteenth century, and twentieth-century thinkers such as Michael Polanyi.[2]

---

[1] Admittedly, Hayek's 1968 assessment of the Austrian School's influence is harder to reconcile with his own insistence (Hayek, 1937, 1945, 1946) that neoclassical economists had failed to appreciate the role of knowledge and expectations. Hayek remained ambivalent on this point; in an unfinished draft for the *New Palgrave Dictionary*, written around 1982 (and reprinted in Hayek, 1992, pp. 53–56), Hayek describes indifference-curve analysis as "the ultimate statement of more than half a century's discussion in the tradition of the Austrian School," adding that "by the third quarter of the twentieth century the Austrian School's approach had become the leading form of microeconomic theory." But he goes on to identify the school's "main achievement" as clarifying the differences between "disciplines that deal with relatively simple phenomena, like mechanics, ... and the sciences of highly complex phenomena."

[2] Koppl urges Austrian economists to join what he calls the "heterodox mainstream," a body of literature embracing bounded rationality, rule following, institutions, cognition, and evolution, or BRICE. Austrians have "an opportunity to contribute to the heterodox mainstream of today and join, thereby, the emerging new orthodoxy of tomorrow" (Koppl, 2006, pp. 237–38).

While I agree that the Austrian tradition is part of a larger, liberal movement, I see Austrian economics as nonetheless a distinct kind of economic analysis, and think that the essence of the Austrian approach is not subjectivism, the market process (disequilibrium), or spontaneous order, but what I call mundane economics—price theory, capital theory, monetary theory, business-cycle theory, and the theory of interventionism. Call this the "hard core" of Austrian economics. I maintain that this hard core is (1) distinct, and not merely a verbal rendition of mid-twentieth-century neoclassical economics; (2) the unique foundation for applied Austrian analysis (political economy, social theory, business administration, and the like); and (3) a living, evolving body of knowledge, rooted in classic contributions of the past but not bound by them.[3]

A different view is found in Vaughn's (1994) influential book on the modern Austrian movement. Vaughn's characterization of the post-1974 "Austrian revival" has proved controversial (Gordon, 1995; Rothbard, 1995; Ekelund, 1997; Thornton, 1999). Her interpretation of the first three generations of the Austrian School, by contrast, has received relatively little attention. Vaughn consistently characterizes the price theory of Menger, Böhm-Bawerk, Mises, and Rothbard as backward-looking, inconsistent, and often wrong. Their elaborations of mundane economics, she says, are mainly verbal "neoclassical" economics, because they rely heavily on equilibrium constructs; indeed, Menger's price theory is that of "half-formed neoclassical economist" (Vaughn, 1994, p. 19). Menger's distinctive Austrian contribution, Vaughn (1994, pp. 18–19) argues, is "his many references to problems of knowledge and ignorance, his discussions of the emergence and function of institutions, the importance of articulating processes of adjustment, and his many references to the progress of mankind." These issues, which attracted considerable attention during the "Austrian revival" of the 1970s, are discussed in Menger's 1883 book *Untersuchungen über die Methode der Socialwissenschaften und der politischen Oekonomie insbesondere* [Investigations into the method of the social sciences with special reference to economics]. They are largely absent from the *Principles*, however.

---

[3] My focus here is economic theory, not methodology, so my point is different from Rothbard's (1995) argument that Misesian praxeology, not the alternative Popperian, evolutionary epistemology of the later Hayek or the "radical subjectivism" of Lachmann, is the proper starting point for Austrian economics.

Specifically, Vaughn maintains that there is a fundamental contradiction in Menger and Mises's understanding of markets because they simultaneously employ equilibrium theorizing and talk about time, uncertainty, "process," and in Menger's case, institutions. Mises's *Human Action*, for example, combined "some fundamental Mengerian insights with the apparatus of neoclassical price theory to the detriment of both" (Vaughn, 1994, p. 70).

This chapter argues against this characterization of Menger, Mises, and their contemporaries. As explained below, Austrian economists from Menger to Rothbard were fully aware of time, uncertainty, knowledge, expectations, institutions, and market processes. Indeed, their understanding of these issues was sophisticated. They employed equilibrium theorizing, but in a precise and deliberate manner. They understood clearly the distinction between their own understandings of mundane economics and that of their Walrasian and Jevonian colleagues. They devoted their energies to developing and communicating the principles of mundane economics, not because they failed to grasp the importance of knowledge, process, and coordination, but because they regarded these latter issues as subordinate to the main task of economic science, namely the construction of a more satisfactory theory of value, production, exchange, price, money, capital, and intervention.

My contention is that mundane Austrian economics not only provides a solid foundation for addressing conventional economic questions about markets and industries, regulation, comparative economic systems, macroeconomic fluctuations, trade, and growth, but also helps place organizational and managerial issues in sharper relief. A mistaken focus on subjectivism, spontaneous order, radical uncertainty, and the like as the essence of the Austrian contribution has led management scholars to overlook the importance of the Austrian theories of price formation, capital, money, and economic fluctuations, theories that have important implications for firms and entrepreneurs.

Central Themes of Austrian Economics Before 1974

Before 1974, the bulk of Austrian economics dealt with mundane economic subjects. Menger's *Principles* (1871), for example, deals entirely with value, price, and exchange (plus a short section on money). Menger intended the *Principles* as an introduction to a longer, more comprehensive work. The planned sequel was never written, but from Menger's notes, Hayek (1934, p. 69) tells us, "we know that the second part was to treat 'interest, wages, rent, income, credit, and paper money,' a third 'applied' part the theory of production and commerce, while a fourth part was to discuss criticism of the present economic system and proposals for economic reform." The three volumes of Böhm-Bawerk's great treatise, *Capital and Interest* (1884–1912), deal primarily with capital and interest theory but also include the famous sections (in volume II, *Positive Theory of Capital*) on value and price, introducing the "marginal-pairs" approach to price formation. Wieser's *Social Economics* (1914) ranges more widely, as did Wieser throughout his career, but still focuses primarily on fundamental questions of value, exchange, production, factor pricing, and international trade. The Anglo-American economists influenced by the Austrians—Phillip Wicksteed, Frank Fetter, Henry Davenport, and J. B. Clark, for example—also viewed the core of Austrian economics as its theory of value and exchange, not knowledge, expectations, and disequilibrium.[4]

Possibly the most striking example of an Austrian commitment to mundane economics is Rothbard's *Man, Economy, and State* (1962). Of the 12 chapters in the original edition, all but two focus on the details of value, price, exchange, capital, money, competition, and the like. (Chapter 1 deals with methodological and ontological issues, chapter 12 with the theory of government intervention.) Production theory alone gets five chapters. Even if *Power and Market* is included, the book contains little about subjective expectations, learning, equilibration, emergent orders, and the like. Perhaps for this reason, Vaughn (1994, p. 96) states that

---

[4]Interestingly, the third- and fourth-generation Austrians were thoroughly steeped not only in the writings of their Viennese predecessors, but also those of the Anglo-American Mengerian price theorists. Hayek (1963a, p. 32) notes that "in the early post-war period the work of the American theorists John Bates Clark, Thomas Nixon Carver, Irving Fisher, Frank Fetter, and Herbert Joseph Davenport was more familiar to us in Vienna than that of any other foreign economists except perhaps the Swedes." Hayek quotes a letter from Clark to Robert Zuckerkandl in which Clark praises Zuckerkandl's *Theory of Price* (1899), saying "[n]othing gives me greater pleasure than to render full honor to the eminent thinkers, mainly Austrians, who were earlier in this field than myself, and who have carried their analysis to greater lengths" (Hayek, 1939a, p. 39) Hayek adds that "at least some of the members of the second or third generation of the Austrian School owed nearly as much to the teaching of J. B. Clark as to their immediate teachers." Salerno (2006) discusses Clark's influence on Mises.

Rothbard's treatise "must have seemed to a typical reader to be more or less familiar economics presented almost exclusively in words with a few controversial definitions, and some strange discontinuous graphs."

Man, Economy, and State was of course intended as a more elementary and systematic presentation of the contents of Mises's *Human Action* (1949), which covers a broader range of philosophical, historical, and sociological subjects (Stromberg, 2004). *Human Action* begins, for example, with a lengthy methodological and ontological sections and chapters on "Time" and "Uncertainty." Still, the bulk of the book—the 16 chapters comprising Parts 3, 4, and 5—deal with the core economic subjects of value, price, and exchange. The same is true, at least partly, of another important postwar contribution to Austrian economics, Lachmann's *Capital and Its Structure* (1956). Lachmann's book includes lengthy and insightful discussions of expectations (chapter 2) and "process analysis" (chapter 3), defined as "a causal-genetic method of studying economic change, tracing the effects of decisions made independently of each other by a number of individuals through time, and showing how the incompatibility of these decisions after a time necessitates their revision" (Lachmann, 1956, p. 39).[5] What Lachmann has in mind here is the continual readjustment of the economy's capital structure—he calls it "reshuffling" and "regrouping"—as firms experiment with various combinations of capital goods. Clearly, however, Lachmann has a specific purpose in mind, namely explaining the implications of capital heterogeneity for the theory of production, economic growth, and the business cycle. The book is not focused primarily on meta-theoretic concerns, but on the economic theory of capital itself.

The main exception to this pattern is Hayek, whose influential essays on knowledge (Hayek, 1937, 1945) and competition (Hayek, 1948) appeared in the middle of the century.[6] Of course, Hayek's reputation at this time was based on his technical contributions to monetary and business-cycle theory (see the essays collected in Hayek, 2008), and Hayek's main interests, from his first writings in the late 1920s until his move to Chicago

---

[5]Lachmann cites Hicks (1939), Lindahl (1939), and Lundberg (1937) as the main exponents of process analysis, though these theorists are not usually included in the contemporary "market process" tradition.

[6]Morgenstern (1935) also deals with expectations and their role in the formation of economic equilibria.

in 1950, remained economic theory, conventionally defined.[7] More generally, while many members and fellow travelers of the Austrian School wrote on broad social themes, all regarded technical economics as the heart of the Mengerian project.

By contrast, O'Driscoll and Rizzo's *Economics of Time and Ignorance* (1985) contains only a few references to Menger and none to Böhm-Bawerk (outside Roger Garrison's chapter on capital). After an introduction it contains chapters on "Static versus Dynamic Subjectivism," "Knowledge and Decisions," "The Dynamic Conception of Time," and "Uncertainty in Equilibrium." An application section follows, which features chapters on "Competition and Discovery," "The Political Economy of Competition and Monopoly," and chapters on capital and money. At least half of the book, then, deals with ontological or meta-theoretic issues while the core principles of valuation, price formation, and production theory occupy relatively little space. Or consider the edited volume *The Market Process: Essays in Contemporary Austrian Economics* (Boettke and Prychitko, 1994). Of the book's five main parts, only one, "Money and Banking," deals primarily with a conventional economic subject; a section on "Cost and Choice" includes a chapter on utility theory, but even this chapter is primarily ontological, while the remaining sections focus on meta-theoretic issues (with an applied section on political economy).

One might infer that these works take the basic body of causal-realist price theory as given, as so well established that further elaboration is unnecessary, thus preferring to concentrate on advanced applications, methodological foundations, critiques, and so on. However, as attested by the statements from Vaughn (1994) quoted above, Austrians after 1974 by

---

[7] By the 1950s, Hayek tells us,

> I had ... become somewhat stale as an economist and felt much out of sympathy with the direction in which economics was developing. Though I had still regarded the work I had done during the 1940s on scientific method, the history of ideas, and political theory as temporary excursions into another field, I found it difficult to return to systematic teaching of economic theory and felt it rather as a release that I was not forced to do so by my teaching duties. (1994, p. 126)

Throughout his career at the London School of Economics from 1932 to 1949, Hayek's main teaching obligation had been the required graduate course in economic theory. Of course, he did produce his first important work in classical liberal political economy, *The Road to Serfdom*, in 1944.

no means accepted the core principles of Austrian price theory as correct, or even as a distinct approach at all, as opposed to a verbal rendition of Walrasian and Marshallian economics. Instead, Austrians after 1974 have tended to regard issues like knowledge, uncertainty, and process as the distinct contribution of the Austrian School.

As noted above, for Vaughn (1994) the most "Austrian" of the classic Austrian texts is Menger's 1883 collection of methodological essays. These essays attempted to defend Menger's theoretical approach against the methods of the (Younger) German Historical School provoking the fierce reaction by Gustav Schmoller and his followers that became a full-blown *Methodenstreit*. Here Menger presents his theory of "organic" institutions, what Hayek (1973–79, p. 43) termed "spontaneous order."[8] How is it possible, Menger (1883, p. 146) asks, "that institutions which serve the common welfare and are extremely significant for its development come into being without a common will directed toward establishing them?" Menger's (1892) essay on money provides a detailed example of this process, in which a commonly accepted medium of exchange emerges as a by-product of individual traders' decisions to adopt particular commodities as money. A monetary standard, in this sense, is the "result of human action but not the result of human design" (Hayek, 1948, p. 7).[9] Do these ideas relate to the price theory outlined in Menger's *Principles*, from which they are largely absent?

First, note that the passage dealing with spontaneous order occupies just two short chapters (30 pages in the 1981 English edition) in a 16-chapter (237-page) book. These chapters are undeniably profound and have exerted an important influence on later Austrians' understanding of social phenomena (White, 1981). However, the bulk of the text deals with Menger's defense of economics as a "theoretical science," with "exact laws," rather than a historical science dealing with historically contingent, "national economies." Second, Menger's examples of organic phenomena are not limited to language, religion, law, competition, and money. Indeed, Menger introduces the concept of emergent social processes with a more mundane example: prices.

---

[8] See Klein (1997) and Klein and Orsborn (2009) on the differences between Menger's account of institutions and Hayek's understanding of spontaneous order. Klein (1997) argues that Menger's notion of coordination is closer to Schelling's (1978) than Hayek's.

[9] See also Klein and Selgin (2000).

[We] could point to a long series of phenomena of this kind. We intend, however, to set forth the above idea by an example that is so striking that it excludes any doubt of the meaning of what we plan to present here. We mean the example of the social prices [i.e., market prices] of goods. As is well known, there are in individual cases completely or at least in part the result of positive social factors, e.g., prices under the sway of tax and wage laws, etc. But as a rule these are formed and changed free of any state influence directed toward regulating them, free of any social agreement, as unintended results of social movement. The same thing holds true of interest on capital, ground rents, speculative profit, etc. (Menger, 1883, p. 146)

In other words, Menger's concept of spontaneous order is simply the process by which voluntary interaction establishes social regularities such as prices, wages, interest rates, and rents. Not only is the market system itself a product of spontaneous order, in this sense, but so are individual market prices.

Menger's presentation here challenges the usual distinction (Davis and North, 1971) between the institutional environment (or "rules of the game") and the institutional arrangements (the "play of the game") that emerge in that environment. The new institutional economics (Klein, 2000; Williamson, 2000) typically treats the former—the legal system, language, norms and customs—as the results of human action but not human design, while the latter—firms, contracts, the terms of specific transactions—are seen as the product of deliberate design by particular agents. Menger treats both kinds of institutions as "spontaneous," meaning (generally) undirected by state planners. In other words, for Menger, price theory is not a technical discipline independent of research on spontaneous orders; price theory is spontaneous-order research. Again, in Menger's (1883, pp. 158–59) words:

[M]arket prices, wages, interest rates, etc., have come into existence in exactly the same way as those social institutions which we mentioned in the previous section. For they, too, as a rule are not the result of socially teleological causes, but the unintended result of innumerable efforts of economic subjects pursuing individual interests.... The methods for the exact understanding of the origin of the "organically" created social structures and those for the solution of the main problems of exact economics are by nature identical.

Equilibrium in Austrian Price Theory

Menger's economics, as has been documented elsewhere (Caldwell, 1990; Salerno, 1999a; Klein, 2006), is causal-realist, marginalist, and subjectivist. Despite frequent assertions that Austrian economics is defined as "market process economics" or "disequilibrium economics," the concept of equilibrium features prominently in causal-realist economics (Hülsmann, 2000; MacKenzie, 2008) At least four distinct equilibrium constructs appear in Austrian analysis. Following Mises's terminology, as amended by Salerno (1994a), we can call them the *plain state of rest* (PSR), the *fully arbitraged state of rest* or *Wicksteedian state of rest* (WSR), the *final state of rest* (FSR), and the *evenly rotating economy* (ERE). Two of these, the PSR and WSR, describe real-world outcomes, while the FSR and ERE are what Mises called "imaginary constructions," hypothetical scenarios that do not obtain in reality, but are useful in economic reasoning, allowing the theorist to isolate the effects of particular actions or circumstances, holding all else constant.

The PSR obtains every day in the real world, each time a buyer and seller agree on a price and make an exchange, momentarily exhausting the gains from trade. (Menger called these "points of rest"; Böhm-Bawerk, "momentary equilibria.") A set of potential buyers and sellers interacting in a defined market space can also be described as being in a PSR once the trading period is completed. "When the stock market closes, the brokers have carried out all orders which could be executed at the market price. Only those potential sellers and buyers who consider the market prices too low or too high respectively have not sold or bought" (Mises, 1949, p. 245). At this point "[a] state of rest emerges." The PSR persists as long as market participants' relative valuations of the goods and services being exchanged (including speculative demands) remain constant.

PSR prices are not necessarily those that would emerge in the "final state of rest" (FSR), a hypothetical situation, never actually achieved, following a sequence of events in which the basic data of the market are frozen but market participants continue to trade, revising their beliefs about other participants' reservation prices and obtaining better information about technological possibilities and consumer demands, until all feasible gains from trade are exhausted. After analyzing the PSR, "[w]e go a step further. We pay attention to factors which are bound to bring about a tendency toward price changes. We try to find out to what goal this tendency must lead before all its driving force is exhausted and a new state of rest emerges" Mises (1949, p. 246). In the real economy, of course, these underlying factors are constantly changing, and hence the FSR is never achieved.[10]

The FSR is used to trace the effects of changes in tastes, technology, expectations, resource availability, and other exogenous variables on patterns of resource allocation by focusing on a sequence of PSR equilibria in which market participants adjust their behavior until all gains from trade have been exhausted. As Salerno (2006) explains,

> FSR analysis also begins from a fully adjusted economy in which profits are currently zero. However in this construction the past and future are relevant to economic planning. Alterations in the economic data are permitted to occur but only one at a time and with a lapse of time between changes sufficiently long to permit a complete adjustment of prices and production in the economy to each change, thus resulting in the emergence of a new zero-profit FSR before another change in the economic data can occur. During the transition to the new FSR, profits and losses appear across the economy spurring entrepreneurs to shuffle and reshuffle resources and capital combinations to take advantage of profit opportunities and avoid losses.

Salerno (2006) notes that Mises modeled his construct after Clark's notion of "dynamic" equilibrium, similar to what is called "comparative statics" in contemporary neoclassical economics. Mises "used Clark's construct in formulating a 'step-by step' or 'process' analysis logically demonstrating the sequence of changes which occur throughout the entire interdependent system of markets in the transition to the new FSR"—for example, in

---

[10]Machlup (1958, p. 57) seems to have the FSR in mind when he writes:

> To characterize a concrete situation "observed" in reality as one of "equilibrium" is to commit the fallacy of misplaced concreteness. At best, the observer may mean to assert that in his opinion the observed and duly identified situation corresponds to a model in his mind in which a set of selected variables determine a certain outcome, and that he finds no inherent cause of change—that is, that he believes only an outside disturbance, not in evidence at the moment, could produce a change in these variables. This, of course, is a personal judgment, meaningful only if the variables are fully enumerated and the assumptions about their interrelations are clearly stated.

tracing the effects of an increase in the money supply on prices and resource allocation. (Modern comparative statics, however, as formalized by Hicks, 1939, and Samuelson, 1947, abstracts from the element of time.)

It is important to emphasize that the movement from PSR to FSR takes place in analytical time, not calendar time; FSR analysis is a logical exercise, not meant to explain the sequence of events taking place in real markets, for the underlying "data" are in constant flux. This point is not well understood, even among Austrians. For example, Boettke and Prychitko (1994) caution against overreliance on equilibrium theorizing in Austrian economics, even characterizing some of the classic contributions to Austrian economics as "neoclassical Austrianism."[11] "When Austrians refer to proximity to an end state in their treatment of entrepreneurship they may be relying too much on the equilibrium construct" (Boettke and Prychitko, 1994, p. 65). However, the causal-realistic price theory of Menger and his followers does not make any assumptions about the "proximity" of PSR or WSR prices to their FSR values in calendar time. Instead, the theorist uses the imaginary construction of the FSR to explain what pattern of activities and ownership would obtain following an exogenous change in preferences, resource availability, or technological knowledge, holding all else constant. The causal-realist theorist does not assume that such adjustments take place in calendar time; indeed, this imaginary process would be impossible in a world in which preferences, stocks, technology, and the like are constantly changing.

Lying between the PSR and the FSR is the WSR, a realistic concept in which trading takes place while preferences remain constant, with market participants revising their beliefs about other participants' reservation prices until all feasible gains from trade are exhausted. Wicksteed's (1910, pp. 219–28) fruit market provides the canonical example.[12] By the end of each market day, a specified period in which preferences, stocks of goods, and the set of traders remains fixed, what Wicksteed calls "the equilibrating price" has been achieved. In this situation, "the marginal position of the commodity in question is identical upon the relative scales of all who have

---

[11]Though specific Austrian writings are not identified, a footnote refers to "relevant sections" of Mises (1949), Rothbard (1962), Kirzner (1973, 1979, 1985b) and High (1980, 1982, 1986) as "neoclassical Austrianism."

[12]See also Marget (1938–42, vol. 2), Kirzner (1963, pp. 105–35) and Salerno (1994a, pp. 97–106).

secured a supply, and higher on them all than it is on the scales of any of those who have secured no supply" (Wicksteed, 1910, p. 216). The market day is a hypothetical construct, in that it holds only as long as preferences, technical knowledge, stocks of goods available for exchange, and so on are held constant. And yet, the WSR is not a purely imaginary construction, as this process of equilibration takes place in real markets, at least over short periods of calendar time.

> Assuming the underlying data are unchanged, [this] approach yields a coherent explanation of how, as information becomes more complete and speculation more accurate, PSRs succeed one another until the intermediate equilibrium situation represented by a fully-arbitraged state of rest (or WSR) is brought into being. (Salerno, 1994a, p. 102)

The ERE, used by Mises (1949, pp. 247–51) and Rothbard (1962, pp. 320–28), serves a more limited function. The ERE is an imaginary construction in which preferences, technology, and resource availability are held constant and agents are assumed to repeat the same set of actions each market day. Economic activity takes place—there is production, consumption, saving, and investment—but entrepreneurs can predict the future with certainty. The main function of the ERE is to show that in the absence of uncertainty, factor prices would be bid up to their full discounted marginal revenue products, eliminating entrepreneurial profit and loss. Business owners would still earn interest income if they advance wages to workers and other factor owners before production is completed and sales receipts are realized, and they can earn implicit wages on the labor they supply to the firm, but there can be no profits and losses. Only by using such a construction, Mises argued, can the theorist decompose real-world business income into interest, the owner's implicit wage, and entrepreneurial profit.[13]

As noted above, the PSR and WSR are intended as realistic phenomena, not hypothetical constructs (like the FSR and ERE). Marshall's "market-day equilibrium" is also intended to explain real-world pricing in markets, something like Wicksteed's WSR, but includes arbitrary assump-

---

[13] For additional discussion see Cowen and Fink (1985), Gunning (1989), and MacKenzie (2008).

tions about the marginal utility of money (Walker, 1969).[14]   Likewise, Hicks's "temporary equilibrium"—a form of Walrasian general equilibrium that incorporates agents' expectations of prices that will obtain in future trading periods—shares elements of the Austrian WSR. However, it is, like Walrasian equilibrium, a deliberately artificial construct, not meant to explain actual market prices but as a modeling step in explaining a concept of intertemporal equilibrium (De Vroey, 2002).

Before 1974, then, Austrian economists used the realistic equilibrium constructs of the PSR and WSR, and the imaginary constructions of the FSR and ERE, to explain the basic phenomena of value, production, exchange, and price.   Their work was built on Menger's value theory and its underlying concepts of purpose, subjectivism, and uncertainty, and the extensions of the Mengerian approach to deal with price formation under direct exchange (Böhm-Bawerk's horse market, Wicksteed's fruit market), monetary calculation and indirect exchange, capital theory (the time structure of production and the heterogeneity of capital goods), FSR analysis, the effects of government intervention (business-cycle theory, regulation), and other mundane aspects of commercial life.

Knowledge, Expectations, and the Convergence to Equilibrium

Since the "Austrian revival" of the 1970s the mundane economic subjects described above have commanded relatively little attention. The most popular issues and topics among modern Austrians have included fractional-reserve "free banking," political economy, and the methodological foundations of the Austrian School.   During the 1980s, a lengthy debate took place over the existence of "equilibrating tendencies" in the market economy, with Kirzner and Lachmann representing opposite positions (Selgin, 1988). Kirzner argued that the existence of profit opportunities under disequilibrium, and that the tendency of alert entrepreneurs to discover and exploit these opportunities, was sufficient to establish a general, systematic tendency toward equilibrium. Lachmann, in contrast, maintained that in the face of "radical" uncertainty, including subjective expectations, equilibrating tendencies could not be assumed, absent some explanation for

---

[14]Just as Mises's (hypothetical) FSR results from a sequence of PSRs, Marshall's "normal equilibrium" is brought about by a series of market-day equilibria (De Vroey, 2002).

learning. Knowledge, expectations, and the convergence to equilibrium came to occupy center stage in the Austrian research program.

My purpose in this section is not to analyze this debate, but to ask why the problem of convergence to equilibrium received so little attention in early Austrian writings. Neither Menger, Böhm-Bawerk, Wieser, the Anglo-American Austrians, nor Mises devoted much effort to this issue. If the presence or absence of equilibrating tendencies in the entrepreneurial market process is the central problem of price theory, why did the early Austrians fail to recognize it?

First, the modern Austrian literature uses the term *equilibrium* quite broadly and often inconsistently. O'Driscoll and Rizzo (1985, p. 39), for example, refer to "correct" and "incorrect" prices, identifying the latter with "non-equilibrium" prices, although the equilibrium construct is not defined or discussed in detail until much later in the discussion. Vaughn (1994) refers to "equilibrium models" (p. 2), "equilibrium states" (p. 3), "equilibrium theorizing" (p. 8), "equilibrium constructs" (p. 11), and more—all within the first dozen pages!—but does not provide a formal definition of any equilibrium concept until the discussion of Mises in her fourth chapter (pp. 81–82). There she characterizes Mises's distinction among three equilibrium constructs (PSR, FSR, and ERE) as "surprisingly unsatisfying" (p. 81), seemingly treating the PSR and FSR as equivalent to Marshallian short-run and long-run partial equilibrium, respectively, and the ERE as Mises's own idiosyncratic, and unhelpful, construction.[15]

More generally, the modern Austrian literature on "disequilibrium" is not always careful to define the concept of equilibrium, and virtually never discusses distinctions among the PSR, WSR, FSR, or ERE. O'Driscoll and Rizzo (1985, pp. 80–85) argue that modern Austrians typically have some notion of "plan coordination" in mind. Indeed, all four equilibrium constructs described above involve a form of plan coordination, in the sense that individuals engaged in exchange hold shared beliefs about what is to be exchanged, what price will be paid, and so on. However, as O'Driscoll and Rizzo (1985, p. 80) observe, plan coordination—they call it "Hayekian equilibrium"—is a very general concept; it "can be partial or general, and

---

[15] Inexplicably, she accuses Rothbard (1962) of confusing the FSR and ERE, though without providing any specific page reference (Vaughn, 1994, p. 82, n 35). She also says Mises "seemed to confuse his two [*sic*] distinct notions of equilibrium."

can prevail over the various 'runs' of Marshallian time."[16] Plans can be said to be "coordinated" in the PSR, in the limited sense of coordination just mentioned, without being "coordinated" in any broader sense, as in a longer period of time, a larger set of potential traders or bundles of goods. As O'Driscoll and Rizzo (1985, pp. 80–81) put it: "Hayekian equilibrium therefore must entail homogenous expectations with respect to the time period within which equilibrium prevails. Outside of that period, however, expectations can, and sometimes must, be divergent." They go on to conclude that Hayekian equilibrium, in any form, cannot be obtained in real exchange. "Hayek and the other Austrians did not realize that equilibrium is not a directly operational construct and that the real world was never in equilibrium" (p. 81). This is clearly false, however, with respect to the PSR (and, to a weaker extent, the WSR), when expressed in "plan coordination" terms.

Rothbard (1962) is somewhat imprecise in distinguishing among equilibrium constructs. His discussion of price determination (pp. 79–186, and *passim*) focuses mainly on PSR prices, though he occasionally refers to prices that "tend toward" their (WSR) equilibrium values. As described above, every price paid in an actual transaction is a PSR price, so the concept of a market price tending toward its PSR value makes little sense. PSR prices can, of course, be what the Walrasian literature calls "false prices," meaning that they differ from their WSR or FSR values.

In his treatment of expectations Rothbard (1962, pp. 130–37) notes that the formation of PSR prices does not assume perfect knowledge. Indeed, the supply and demand curves underlying PSR analysis incorporate market participants' expectations of future price changes, expectations that may or may not be consistent with those of other market participants. If expectations are incorrect, then shortages and surpluses emerge as market participants trade at PSR prices—Rothbard (1962, p. 134) calls them "provisional resting point[s]"—that differ from their values once these price differences have been arbitraged away (a state of affairs presumably like the WSR, though Rothbard is not explicit on this point). As these shortages and surpluses are revealed, market participants will adjust their

---

[16]Kirzner (2000) argues for a more nuanced appreciation of Hayek's commitment to "plan coordination," arguing (against O'Driscoll, 1977) that Hayek was ambivalent on the proper notion of coordination in economics. For more on concepts of coordination see Klein (1997) and Klein and Orsborn (2009).

expectations until the fully arbitraged price, what Rothbard here calls the "genuine equilibrium price," emerges. Rothbard does, then, assume a simple learning process, though he does not spell out the details of this process. However, his assumptions about knowledge and the ability of market participants to learn from their mistakes ("speculative errors") are minimal. Market participants are assumed to adjust their expectations about the PSR prices that emerge moment-to-moment, in the markets in which these traders are active. In other words, these are very short-run expectations, not long-run expectations (in the Marshallian sense of the long run).

Likewise, the Austrian price theory of Böhm-Bawerk, Wicksteed, Fetter, Mises, and Rothbard treats the movement of prices from PSR to WSR values as a straightforward process. It does not require "perfect knowledge," only that agents are aware of surpluses and shortages (from trading at false prices) and that they adjust their bids accordingly. As noted above, agents' expectations about other agents' preferences are already incorporated into the reservation bids and asks. While these writers were not as explicit about their assumptions concerning knowledge and expectations as Mayer (1932), Hayek (1937, 1945) and the later Austrians, they were hardly unaware of processes underlying market clearing. Wicksteed, for example, is explicit that forecast errors explain the deviation of PSR prices (the "actual price") from their WSR equivalents (the "ideal price"):

> A market is the machinery by which those on whose scales of preference any commodity is relatively high are brought into communication with those on whose scales it is relatively low, in order that exchanges may take place to mutual satisfaction until equilibrium is established. But this process will always and necessarily occupy time. The persons potentially constituting the market will not all be present at the same time, and therefore the composition of the collective scale (on which, together with the total amount of the commodity in existence, the ideal point of equilibrium depends) must be a matter of estimate and conjecture. The transactions actually conducted at any moment will be determined in relation to the anticipated possibilities of transactions at other moments. Speculation as to these fixture possibilities will be more or less elaborate and conscious according to the nature of the market and the length of time over which the adjustment will be likely to extend. But speculation is always present when any possessor of the commodity refuses to sell at the moment at a price which he knows he will be

> prepared to accept ultimately (whether an hour or eleven months
> hence), if satisfied that he can do no better; or if any purchaser
> refuses at the moment to give a price to which he knows he will
> ultimately be willing to rise should the alternative be to go with-
> out the commodity; or if any one buys at a price below which he
> would ultimately sell sooner than keep the stock for his own use.
> (Wicksteed, 1910, p. 236)

These forecast errors are revealed, Wicksteed (1910, p. 236) continues, as
traders exchange at non-WSR prices in real time:

> If no one at first has a correct conception of the facts, a series of
> tentative estimates, and the observation of the transactions that
> take place under their influence, may gradually reveal them; and if
> we could eliminate all error from speculative estimates and could
> reduce derivative preferences to exact correspondence with the
> primary preferences which they represent, and on which they are
> based, the actual price would always correspond with the ideal
> price.

Salerno (1994a, p. 105) notes that Mises, in *The Theory of Money and
Credit*, invokes arbitrage in his account of purchasing power parity (Mises,
1912, pp. 195–203). "The money price of any commodity in any place,
under the assumption of completely unrestricted exchange and disregard-
ing the differences arising from the time taken in transit, must be the same
as the price at any other place, augmented or diminished by the money
cost of transport" (Mises, 1912, pp. 196–97). Hence, Mises argues,

> the purchasing power of money shows a tendency to come to the
> same level throughout the world, and that *the alleged differences
> in it are almost entirely explicable by differences in the quality of the
> commodities offered and demanded*, so that there is only a small and
> almost negligible remainder left over, that is due to differences in
> the quality of the offered and demanded money.
> The existence of the tendency itself is hardly questioned.
> (p. 198; emphasis in original)

Mises continues:

> Nobody would wish to dispute the fact that costs of production
> differ greatly from one another in different localities. But it must be
> denied that this exercises an influence on the price of commodities
> and on the purchasing power of money. The contrary follows too

clearly from the principles of the theory of prices, and is too clearly
demonstrated day by day in the market, to need any special proof
in addition. The consumer who seeks the cheapest supply and the
producer who seeks the most paying sale concur in the endeavor
to liberate prices from the limitations of the local market. (Mises,
1912, pp. 199–200)

Note that Mises treats the "tendency" of the purchasing power of money
to equalize across and within markets, less transportation costs, as "clearly
demonstrated day by day in the market," i.e., as an empirical fact not
requiring special explanation.

Here it is worth emphasizing a methodological point. For modern, neoclassical economists, the instrumentalist approach (Friedman,
1953) renders moot many such questions about the mechanics underlying
market-clearing processes. The goal of economic theory, in this approach,
is not to explain actual prices, but to explain hypothetical prices (for example, full-information prices, Nash equilibrium prices, perfectly competitive
prices, and the like). It is unlikely that Menger and his followers, steeped
in the causal-realist tradition, would simply assume that "equilibrium"
obtains—after all, they were seeking to explain real prices, not hypothetical
ones. They saw the processes of buyers and sellers making bids and asks,
of revising their offers in light of new information, and so on as real-world
phenomena, not instrumental constructs like the Walrasian *tâtonnement*.[17]

Lachmann (1977, p. 189), while expressing reservations about the log-

---

[17] De Vroey (2002, pp. 406–07) argues that Marshall, too, regarded his market-day
equilibrium construct as both realistic and practical, i.e., not requiring an underlying
adjustment process:

> Two adjustment processes are present in Marshall: the adjustment toward
> market-day equilibrium and the adjustment toward normal equilibrium.
> In my view ... the former should be interpreted as proceeding instanta-
> neously, whereas the latter (to be called intertemporal adjustment) arises
> across several trading rounds....
>
> The stationary equilibrium concept of equilibrium is in accord with
> the common-sense understanding of equilibrium—i.e., it is a point of
> rest. It is implied that this point does not need to be effectively reached;
> it suffices that reacting forces are triggered whenever it is not reached.
> Equilibrium is thus viewed as an attractor.... Note also that in this line of
> thought, assessing the existence of equilibrium or disequilibrium amounts
> to making a statement about reality.

ical consistency of market-level equilibrium constructs such as the WSR, nonetheless recognized that Menger's points of rest, Böhm-Bawerk's momentary equilibrium, and Mises's plain state of rest represent real phenomena:

> The Austrians were concerned, in the first place, with the individual in household and business. There is no doubt that here equilibrium has a clear meaning and real significance. Men really aim at bringing their various actions into consistency. Here a tendency towards equilibrium is not only a necessary concept of praxeology, but also a fact of experience. It is part of the logic inherent in human action. Interindividual equilibrium, such as that on a simple market, like Böhm-Bawerk's horse market, already raises problems but still makes sense. "Equilibrium of an industry" à la Marshall is already more precarious. "Equilibrium of the economic system as a whole," as Walras and Pareto conceived of it, is certainly open to Mises's [anti-equilibrium] strictures.

In other words, the deliberately unrealistic character of the equilibrium constructs that dominate neoclassical economics—and, by implication, Austrian concepts like the FSR and ERE—does not render the equilibrium concept itself unrealistic.

Clearly, the Mengerian price theorists did not assume that real prices were FSR or ERE prices. They allowed for subjective, heterogeneous beliefs about changes in demand, resource availability, and knowledge. And Mises (1949, p. 247) is clear that the movement from the PSR to the FSR takes place in analytical time, not calendar time. "Between the appearance of a new datum and the perfect adjustment of the market to it some time must pass. (And, of course, while this period of time elapses, other new data appear.)" In other words, the real economy does not converge on a FSR because as the market is adjusting to one change in the data, another takes place, the combined effects of which cannot be known *ex ante*. Hence the accuracy of real-world expectations is not central to this approach. These theorists make no assumptions about the tendency or PSR and WSR prices to converge toward some "final" values.

What about "radical uncertainty"? One can perhaps imagine a market in which PSR prices do not "converge" toward WSR prices because of endogenous, subjective expectations. However, as discussed above, it is not clear that such a case has much practical significance, because the movement from the PSR to the WSR requires only modest assumptions about knowledge (namely, the ability of market participants to learn from their mistakes). Even in the simplest, pure-exchange economy, Mengerian price theory allows traders to have subjective expectations relevant to that particular market (i.e., beliefs about other traders' preferences), expectations that are incorporated into the PSR supply and demand curves.

Vaughn (1994, p. 91) argues that much stronger assumptions about knowledge and expectations are necessary for economic analysis, even (presumably) for Mengerian price theory:

> If all action is speculation, if people are constantly reevaluating their preferences, if entrepreneurs make losses as well as profits, can we be so certain that markets are fundamentally orderly? Perhaps our world is one in which individual rationality leads to overall waste and error.... Even more to the point, in a world of constant change, how can people's plans come to be realized? Why are speculators likely to be more right about entrepreneurial prospects than the entrepreneurs themselves? And how is successful rational action distinguishable from pure luck? What are the regularities in economic life that can be counted on to lend stability and predictability to an otherwise bewildering world?

Most likely Menger, Böhm-Bawerk, Wieser, Mises, and their Viennese contemporaries would have been baffled by the last statement in the quotation above. The science of economics, in Menger's formulation, is about the explanation of regularities—the "exact laws" of reality described in the Investigations. As Menger wrote to Walras in 1884:

> It is rather necessary that we go back to the most simple elements of the mostly very complex phenomena that are here in question—that we thus determine in an analytical manner the ultimate factors that constitute the phenomena, the prices, and that we then accord to these elements the importance that corresponds to their nature, and that, in keeping with this importance, we try to establish the laws according to which the complex phenomena of human interaction result from simple phenomena. (Quoted in Hülsmann, 2007, p. 106)

As Bastiat (1850) observed, Paris gets fed. The task of economics is to explain why.

The early Austrians' emphasis on order helps us understand Mises's and Hayek's statements, quoted at the beginning of the chapter, about the close relationship between Austrian and neoclassical economics. Menger, Walras, and Jevons all sought to explain the regularities of economic life. The historicists, by contrast, saw the economy as a chaotic flood that defied rational explanation. Indeed, some contemporary interpretations of Austrian economics seem to place it closer to the German Historical School than the Austrian School. Vaughn (1994, p. 90) for example, writes of Mises:

> [W]hat about sources of discoordination and disorder in [free, un-hampered] markets? Mises really had very little to say about such problems, and in fact one concludes that he thought disorder was a relatively minor problem.... [T]he only obvious sources of in-stability or disorder in his system were the consequences of bad banking institutions and destabilizing intervention on the part of government. Trade cycles were brought about by misguided credit policies. Unemployment was a consequence of minimum wage rates. Inflation was an increase in the quantity of money brought about by government policy. Externalities were the consequence of imperfectly specified property rights. He never considered possible sources of disorder internal to the market; disorder was an exoge-nous phenomenon brought about by government regulation....
>
> In this attitude ... Mises is really not very different from many neoclassical economic theorists (although perhaps more consistent and more outspoken than others who shared his basic evaluation of the market).

I think Vaughn is correct that Mises thought "disorder," in the sense she describes above, was a "relatively minor problem." For Mises, economic theory is the analysis of coordination—not the idea of "plan coordination" often associated with Hayek, or what O'Driscoll and Rizzo (1985) call "pattern coordination," but what Mises, following W. H. Hutt, described as "price coordination" (Salerno, 1991). This coordination, as noted below does not require any assumptions about the tendency of PSR or WSR prices to converge to FSR values. Full coordination of plans occurs only in the ERE, a hypothetical state of affairs that does not (indeed, could not) occur in the real economy. For Mises, following Clark (1899), the FSR is an analytical device used to isolate the effects of specific changes in preferences, beliefs, resource availability, productive technology, and the like on the allocation of resources.[18]

What does Mises mean by coordination, outside an imaginary world of perfect knowledge, consistent expectations, "rational" behavior, and the other assumptions of the First and Second Welfare Theorems of neoclassical economics? How, in other words, can Mises justify the efficiency of resource allocation under capitalism without making strong assumptions about the closeness of real-world prices to some idealized, or "correct," prices?

Central to the neoclassical notion of efficiency is the idea that only FSR prices count for assessing the welfare properties of the market.[19] A primary objective of Kirzner's account of the entrepreneurial market process is to show that the movement from PSR prices to their Marshallian/Walrasian FSR equivalents is not automatic and instantaneous, but the result of entrepreneurial behavior. In Kirzner's framework, the market does possess equilibrating tendencies, but these tendencies are not exogenous, but result from the actions of entrepreneurs alert to the profit opportunities created by temporary trading at false, i.e., non-FSR, prices. For Kirzner, PSR prices themselves are not particularly important; what matters is whether they tend to converge toward their FSR values. Kirzner's concept of alertness can thus be seen as an addendum to the neoclassical understanding of market equilibrium. Kirzner's approach, as Boettke and Prychitko (1994, p. 3) describe it, "provided the disequilibrium foundations of equilibrium economics that were required to complete the neoclassical project of explicating the operating principles of the price system." Kirzner's objective, in this sense, is to justify the use of FSR, or near-FSR, prices in welfare analysis. If the market possesses equilibrating tendencies, then the welfare theorems of neoclassical economics are reasonable criteria for assessing market performance, and the main talk of welfare economics should be the analysis of these tendencies and of market interventions that inhibit the process of equilibration (Kirzner, 1988b).[20]

---

[18]Note that Clark (1907, p. 96) describes simple FSR analysis or comparative statics—e.g., if the supply increases, the price will fall, *ceteris paribus*—as obvious, as what he calls a "commercial fact."

[19]And these FSR prices are only "efficient" in perfectly competitive markets; any degree of asymmetric information renders economic outcomes inefficient (Grossman, 1980).

[20]Adds Boettke (2005):

Why is all this important? Well as Franklin Fischer pointed out in his very

Salerno (1991, 1999b) offers a different interpretation of Mises, arguing that Mengerian price theory is primarily a theory of PSR prices, not FSR prices. In this view, the existence or nonexistence of equilibrating tendencies in the unhampered market—the issue that divided "Kirznerians" and "Lachmannians," and dominated much of the Austrian discussion in the 1980s—is relatively unimportant. For Mises, the critical "market process" is not the convergence to equilibrium, but the selection mechanism in which unsuccessful entrepreneurs—those who systematically overbid for factors, relative to eventual consumer demands—are eliminated from the market (Mises, 1951). In this context, the recent debate over "de-homogenizing" Mises and Hayek (Rothbard, 1991; Salerno, 1993, 1994b, 1996b; Yeager, 1994, 1995, 1997; Herbener, 1996; Hoppe, 1996; Stalebrink, 2004) deals not simply with the socialist calculation debate or second-order distinctions between "calculation" and "knowledge," but with a fundamentally new interpretation of Austrian price theory, a causal-realist approach to the market that differs in important ways from the Marshallian/Walrasian analysis that fills the contemporary textbooks. Austrian economics, in this view, is not simply neoclassical microeconomics—what Caldwell (2004, pp. 328–88) calls "basic economic reasoning"—plus the Mises–Hayek theory of the business cycle plus knowledge, process, plan coordination, and spontaneous order, but a fundamentally different kind of microeconomics.[21]

---

important book *The Disequilibrium Foundations of Equilibrium Economics* (1983) that unless we have good reasons to believe in the systemic tendency toward equilibrium we have no justification at all in upholding the welfare properties of equilibrium economics. In other words, without the sort of explanation that Kirzner provides the entire enterprise of neoclassical equilibrium is little more than a leap of faith.

If one rejects the neoclassical equilibrium concept as a welfare benchmark, though, this justification is unnecessary.

[21] Caldwell (2004, p. 333) argues that Austrians accept "the simple (although unrealistic) models used for basic economic reasoning," such as supply-and-demand analysis, at least for market-level predictions. But Menger's analysis, while "abstract," is not "unrealistic" in the sense of Walras's or Marshall's models of market exchange. In Long's (2006) terminology, Austrians reject "precisive abstraction," in which false assumptions are deliberately included to simplify the analysis, while embracing "non-precisive abstraction," in which certain characteristics of the situation are simply not specified. In other words, the "basic economic reasoning" of the Austrians is different from the basic economic reasoning of neoclassical economics.

In a recent response to Salerno, Kirzner (1999) takes a characteristically subtle position on the relationship between PSR and FSR prices. He argues the PSR is an "equilibrium" only in a trivial sense and that PSR prices are not meaningful for assessing the welfare properties of markets. He also recognizes that PSR analysis was important to Mises. To solve this seeming contradiction, he says that Mises used the PSR only to defend the concept of consumer sovereignty, not for analysis of the market process. However, if PSR prices are sufficient to assure that production is satisfying consumer wants, it is unclear why FSR prices are important, and why one would care about the alleged tendency of PSR prices to reach them.

A New Way Forward for Austrian Economics: Developing Austrian Price Theory

The main argument of this chapter is that Austrian economics is primarily mundane economics—the theory and applications of value, production, exchange, price, capital, money, the firm, regulation, comparative institutions, and other "mainstream" topics. What makes Austrian economics unique is its causal-realist approach to these issues, not its attention to adjustment processes, the formation of knowledge and expectations, spontaneous order, plan or pattern coordination, radical subjectivism, and other manifestations of "disequilibrium" economics. Such issues are interesting and potentially important, but are ultimately subordinate to the main task of economic analysis, the development, extension, application, and refinement of the mundane Austrian tradition established by Menger. Naturally, this means that students of Austrian economics must invest significant time in mastering the existing literature before engaging in their own creative restatement and revision.

As noted in chapters 4 and 5, Austrian economics is attracting increasing attention among applied researchers in strategic management, organizational economics, and the theory of the firm. Often the value-added of Austrian economics in these fields is seen as its emphasis on disequilibrium, which seems to fit the profit-seeking approach of strategic management better than do neoclassical partial- and general-equilibrium models. Here a more sophisticated and nuanced understanding of equilibrium would be helpful, however. Organizational structures that are implemented, contracts that are signed and executed, and other business arrangements that take place in real markets are equilibrium phenomena, in the PSR sense of equilibrium. They should be explainable using the same causal-realistic mechanism used by the Austrians to explain real prices and quantities. FSR analysis, as practiced by Mises, should also apply here: how, for instance, does the profit-and-loss mechanism provide incentives for agents to restructure PSR arrangements so that they move toward their FSR equivalents? How do changes in regulation or other aspects of public policy, or exogenous changes in the competitive or technological environments, replace one PSR with another?

Unfortunately, despite the pleas of modern Austrians for more analysis of "process," very little progress has been made in this area within the Austrian literature. Indeed, the bulk of the work during the last few decades in evolutionary economics, dynamic programming, evolutionary game theory, Bayesian learning models, agent-based simulations, complexity theory, and so on, is fundamentally acausal and nonrealistic, an extension of the mathematical economics of the late nineteenth and early twentieth centuries. O'Driscoll and Rizzo (1985, pp. 65–66) cite some examples of these literatures, implying that they are "Hayekian" in spirit; however, despite sharing certain keywords with Austrian economics, it is unclear that these research programs have been influenced in any way by the core contributions or approach of the Austrian School.

Of course, the argument here is not that knowledge, expectations, and process are unimportant, or that they should be ignored by Austrians (or by any social scientists), but that they are secondary, and valuable only to the extent they help construct a more satisfactory theory of markets and prices. Austrian economics emerged as a causal, realistic alternative to the historicism of its day, and remains today an alternative both to mechanistic neoclassical economics and to the non-economics of old-style institutionalism. Without a commitment to preserving and extending the hard core of Austrian price theory, the distinct place of the Austrian School will be lost.

CHAPTER 8

Commentary

A   Government Did Invent the Internet, But the Market Made it Glorious[†]

Libertarians often cite the Internet as a case in point that liberty is the mother of innovation. Opponents quickly counter that the Internet was a government program, proving once again that markets must be guided by the steady hand of the state. In one sense, the critics are correct, though not in ways they understand.

The Internet indeed began as a typical government program, the ARPANET, designed to share mainframe computing power and to establish a secure military communications network. Of course, the designers could not have foreseen what the (commercial) Internet has become. Still, this reality has important implications for how the Internet works—and explains why there are so many roadblocks in the continued development of online technologies. It is only thanks to market participants that the Internet became something other than a typical government program, characterized by inefficiency, overcapitalization, and irrelevance.

In fact, the role of the government in the creation of the Internet is

---

[†]Published originally on Mises.org, June 12, 2006.

often understated. The Internet owes its very existence to the state and to state funding. The story begins with ARPA, created in 1957 in response to the Soviets' launch of Sputnik, and established to research the efficient use of computers for civilian and military applications.

During the 1960s, the RAND Corporation had begun to think about how to design a military communications network that would be invulnerable to a nuclear attack. Paul Baran, a RAND researcher whose work was financed by the Air Force, produced a classified report in 1964 proposing a radical solution to this communication problem. Baran envisioned a decentralized network of different types of "host" computers, without any central switchboard, designed to operate even if parts of it were destroyed. The network would consist of several "nodes," each equal in authority, each capable of sending and receiving pieces of data.

Each data fragment could thus travel one of several routes to its destination, such that no one part of the network would be completely dependent on the existence of another part. An experimental network of this type, funded by ARPA and thus known as ARPANET, was established at four universities in 1969. Researchers at any one of the four nodes could share information, and could operate any one of the other machines remotely, over the new network. (Actually, former ARPA head Charles Herzfeld says that distributing computing power over a network, rather than creating a secure military command-and-control system, was the ARPANET's original goal, though this is a minority view.)

By 1972, the number of host computers connected to the ARPANET had increased to 37. Because it was so easy to send and retrieve data, within a few years the ARPANET became less a network for shared computing than what has been called "a high-speed, federally subsidized, electronic post office." The main traffic on the ARPANET did not consist of long-distance computing, but news and personal messages.

As parts of the ARPANET were declassified, commercial networks began to be connected to it. Any type of computer using a particular communications standard, or "protocol," was capable of sending and receiving information across the network. The design of these protocols was contracted out to private universities such as Stanford and the University of London, and was financed by a variety of federal agencies. The major thoroughfares or "trunk lines" continued to be financed by the Department of Defense. By the early 1980s, private use of the ARPA communications protocol—what is now called "TCP/IP"—far exceeded military use. In 1984 the National Science Foundation assumed the responsibility of building and maintaining the trunk lines or "backbones." (ARPANET formally expired in 1989; by that time hardly anybody noticed). The NSF's Office of Advanced Computing financed the Internet's infrastructure from 1984 until 1994, when the backbones were privatized.

In short, both the design and implementation of the Internet have relied almost exclusively on government dollars. The fact that its designers envisioned a packet-switching network has serious implications for how the Internet actually works. For example, packet switching is a great technology for file transfers, email, and web browsing but not necessarily the best for real-time applications like video and audio feeds, and, to a lesser extent, server-based applications.

Furthermore, without any mechanism for pricing individual packets, the network is overused, like any public good. Every packet is assigned an equal priority. A packet containing a surgeon's diagnosis of an emergency medical procedure has exactly the same chance of getting through as a packet containing part of a pop star's latest single or an online gamer's instruction to smite his foe. Because the sender's marginal cost of each transmission is effectively zero, the network is overused, and often congested. Like any essentially unowned resource, an open-ended packet-switching network suffers from what Garrett Hardin famously called the "Tragedy of the Commons."

In no sense can we say that packet-switching is the "right" technology. One of my favorite quotes on this subject comes from Michael Hauben and Ronda Hauben's *Netizens: On the History and Impact of Usenet and the Internet* (1995):

> The current global computer network has been developed by scientists and researchers and users who were free of market forces. Because of the government oversight and subsidy of network development, these network pioneers were not under the time pressures or bottom-line restraints that dominate commercial ventures. Therefore, they could contribute the time and labor needed to make sure the problems were solved. And most were doing so to contribute to the networking community.

In other words, the designers of the Internet were "free" from the constraint that whatever they produced had to satisfy consumer wants.

We must be very careful not to describe the Internet as a "private" technology, a spontaneous order, or a shining example of capitalistic ingenuity. It is none of these. Of course, almost all of the Internet's current applications—unforeseen by its original designers—have been developed in the private sector. (Unfortunately, the original web and the web browser are not among them, having been designed by the state-funded European Laboratory for Particle Physics (CERN) and the University of Illinois's NCSA.) And today's Internet would be impossible without the heroic efforts at Xerox PARC and Apple to develop a useable graphical user interface (GUI), a lightweight and durable mouse, and the Ethernet protocol. Still, none of these would have been viable without the huge investment of public dollars that brought the network into existence in the first place.

Now, it is easy to admire the technology of the Internet. I marvel at it every day. But technological value is not the same as economic value. That can only be determined by the free choice of consumers to buy or not to buy. The ARPANET may well have been technologically superior to any commercial networks that existed at the time, just as Betamax may have been technologically superior to VHS, the MacOS to MS-DOS, and Dvorak to QWERTY. (Actually Dvorak wasn't.) But the products and features valued by engineers are not always the same as those valued by consumers. Markets select for economic superiority, not technological superiority (even in the presence of nefarious "network effects," as shown convincingly by Liebowitz and Margolis, 1990, 1995, 1999).

Libertarian Internet enthusiasts tend to forget the fallacy of the broken window. We see the Internet. We see its uses. We see the benefits it brings. We surf the web and check our email and download our music. But we will never see the technologies that weren't developed because the resources that would have been used to develop them were confiscated by the Defense Department and given to Stanford engineers. Likewise, I may admire the majesty and grandeur of an Egyptian pyramid, a TVA dam, or a Saturn V rocket, but it doesn't follow that I think they should have been created, let alone at taxpayer expense.

What kind of global computer network would the market have selected? We can only guess. Maybe it would be more like the commercial online networks such as Comcast or MSN, or the private bulletin boards of the 1980s. Most likely, it would use some kind of pricing schedule, where different charges would be assessed for different types of transmissions. Unfortunately, the whole idea of pricing the Internet as a scarce resource—though we usually don't notice this, bandwidth is scarce given current technology—is ignored in most proposals to legislate network neutrality, a form of "network socialism" that can only stymie the Internet's continued growth and development. The net neutrality debate takes place in the shadow of government intervention. So too the debate over the division of the spectrum for wireless transmission. Any resource the government controls will be allocated based on political priorities.

Let us conclude: yes, the government was the founder of the Internet. As a result, we are left with a panoply of lingering inefficiencies, misallocations, abuses, and political favoritism. In other words, government involvement accounts for the Internet's continuing problems, while the market should get the credit for its glories.

B   Networks, Social Production, and Private Property[†]

Yochai Benkler's *The Wealth of Networks* is a comprehensive, informative, and challenging meditation on the rise of the "networked information economy" and its implications for society, politics, and culture. Benkler is a leading authority on the law, economics, and politics of networks, innovation, intellectual property, and the Internet, and he puts his wide knowledge and deep understanding to good use. He argues that the digital revolution is more revolutionary than has been recognized, even by its most passionate defenders. The new information and communications technologies do not simply make the old ways of doing things more efficient, but also support fundamentally new ways of doing things. In particular, the past few years have seen the rise of social production, a radically decentralized, distributed mode of interaction that Benkler calls "commons-based peer production."

Peer production involves the creation and dissemination of "user-generated content," including Wikipedia and open-source software, such as

---

[†]Published originally as a review of Yochai Benkler, *The Wealth of Networks: How Social Production Transforms Markets and Freedom*, reviewed in *The Independent Review* 13, no. 3 (Winter 2009).

Linux, that allow users to generate their own entries and modify those created by others. Commons-based peer production is characterized by weak property rights, an emphasis on intrinsic rather than extrinsic (monetary) rewards, and the exploitation of dispersed, tacit knowledge. (Some readers will immediately think of Hayek's concept of the market as generator and transmitter of knowledge, though Hayek does not figure prominently in the book.)

The Wealth of Networks is divided into three main parts. The first deals with the economics of the networked information economy. This is well-trod ground, having been explored in detail in Shapiro and Varian (1998), Liebowitz and Margolis (1999), and other works, but Benkler's treatment is nevertheless insightful, intelligent, and engaging. The characteristics of information as an economic good—high fixed costs and low marginal costs; the ability to be consumed without exhaustion; the difficulty of excluding "free-riders"—support the widespread use of commons-based peer production.

Benkler proposes social production as an alternative to the traditional organizational modes of *market* and *hierarchy*, in Oliver Williamson's terminology. Indeed, open-source production differs in important ways from spot-market interaction and production within the private firm. But here, as elsewhere, Benkler tends to overstate the novelty of social production. Firms, for example, have long employed internal markets; delegated decision rights throughout the organization; formed themselves into networks, clusters, and alliances; and otherwise taken advantage of openness and collaboration. Many different organizational forms proliferate within the matrix of private-property rights. Peer production is not new; rather, the relevant question concerns the magnitude of the changes.

Here, the book suffers from a problem common to others in this genre. Benkler provides a wealth of anecdotes to illustrate the new economy's revolutionary nature, but little information on magnitudes. How new? How large? How much? Cooperative, social production itself is hardly novel, as any reader of "I, Pencil" (Read, 1958) can attest. Before the web page, there was the pamphlet; before the Internet, the telegraph; before the Yahoo directory, the phone book; before the personal computer, electric service, the refrigerator, the washing machine, the telephone, and the VCR. In short, such breathlessly touted phenomena as network effects, the rapid diffusion of technological innovation, and highly valued intangible assets are not novel. (Tom Standage's [1998] history of the telegraph and its revolutionary impact, *The Victorian Internet*, is well worth reading in this regard.)

Part two, "The Political Economy of Property and Commons," is the book's most original, provocative, and—for me—frustrating section. Benkler sees social production as a powerful force for individual liberty. People used to be passive recipients of news, information, norms, and culture; now they are active creators. Each participant in an open-source project, each creator of user-generated content on Wikipedia or YouTube, "has decided to take advantage of some combination of technical, organizational, and social conditions within which we have come to live, and to become an active creator in his or her world, rather than merely to accept what was already there. The belief that it is possible to make something valuable happen in the world, and the practice of actually acting on that belief, represent a qualitative improvement in the condition of individual freedom" (Benkler, 2006, p. 137).

What Benkler means by "freedom" and "liberty," however, is not the classical liberal notion of the absence of state coercion, but the modern liberal view of "autonomy," individuals' ability to achieve their goals without restraints, voluntary or otherwise. This understanding of liberty, which originates with Kant and Rousseau, is central to Benkler's political economy. *Autonomy* means that "individuals are less susceptible to manipulation by a legally defined class of others—the owners of communications infrastructure and media" (Benkler, 2006, p. 9)—hence Benkler's sympathy for the commons, an institutional framework in which property rights are held not by individuals, but by a collective. It does not matter for Benkler whether the collective is a private club, such as the participants of an open-source project or the subscribers to a particular information service or the state. What matters is how the commons facilitates "freedom of action" in comparison to how a system of private-property rights affords freedom.

Benkler strongly opposes privatizing the information commons by allowing owners to exercise property rights. He chides Cisco Systems, for example, for designing and deploying "smart routers" that allow broadband service providers to control the flows of packets through their systems (for example, giving priority to some forms of content over others). This action is akin to erecting toll gates on the Information Superhighway. To ensure open access to the networked economy, Benkler (2006,

p. 21) favors a public ownership network infrastructure, loose enforcement of intellectual property rights, subsidized R&D, and "strategic regulatory interventions to negate monopoly control over essential resources in the digital environment."

This approach has some problems. First, although information itself cannot be "owned," the tangible media in which information is embedded and transmitted are scarce economic goods. Information may yearn to be "free," but cables, switches, routers, disk drives, microprocessors, and the like yearn to be owned. Such innovations do not spring from nowhere; they are the creations of profit-seeking entrepreneurs that consumers or other entrepreneurs purchase to use as they see fit. Of course, private property can be nationalized. Federal, state, and local governments can own broadband lines as they own streets and highways, or they can treat network infrastructure as a regulated public utility. If these resources are to be treated as public goods, then what about computers, iPods, and cell phones? Are these gateways to the Information Superhighway also part of the digital commons? If individuals can own cell phones, can they sign contracts with service providers to deliver whatever content is mutually agreed upon? Content providers and consumers are free to terminate their agreements if they are unhappy. In this sense, a private property regime allows as much "autonomy," in the libertarian sense, as a commons-based system. Moreover, if one takes into account the problems of collective ownership, about which Benkler is largely silent, the case for the commons becomes even more problematic.

Second, Benkler appears to adopt the Frankfurt school view of consumers as passive recipients of culture, easily manipulated by powerful corporate interests. "From the perspective of liberal political theory, the kind of open-participatory, transparent folk culture that is emerging in the networked environment is normatively more attractive than was the industrial cultural production system typified by Hollywood and the recording industry" (Benkler, 2006, p. 277). However, as Cowen (1998), Cantor (2001), and others have argued convincingly, commercial culture—which properly includes Elizabethan theater, classical music, and the Victorian novel, as well as television, movies, and popular music—has always been participatory in the broad sense Benkler describes. Far from being passive consumers of culture, individuals have played an active role in shaping the plays, books, songs, and shows made available to them simply by deciding to buy or not to buy, to patronize or not to patronize, to support or reject particular producers and particular products. The main difference today is that technological change—the advent of digital technology, cheap infrastructure, and the like—has lowered the costs of entry (production costs, distribution costs, and so forth), giving consumers additional options besides voice and exit. Is this difference one of degree or kind?

Moreover, in any model of social and cultural production, opinion makers play an important role. Even today, on political blogs and other forms of user-generated content, the range of acceptable opinion among the dominant sites, the ones at the left-hand side of Anderson's (2006) "long tail," is hardly broader than what one finds in the *New York Times* or the *Wall Street Journal*. Yes, a great deal of user-generated content exists, but most of it is ignored and is unlikely to have any lasting influence. An elite group of gatekeepers, Hayek's "second-hand dealers in ideas," continues to exercise an important influence on social, political, and cultural trends. In this sense, Benkler seems influenced, ironically, by the perfectly competitive general equilibrium model of neoclassical economics, with its assumption that all agents possess complete, perfect information. He worries: private ownership of digital resources "gives some people the power to control the options perceived by, or the preferences of, others, [which] is ... a law that harms autonomy" (Benkler, 2006, p. 149). In a world of subjective knowledge and beliefs and of dispersed, tacit knowledge, how can everyone have the same perceived options? Elsewhere he dismisses the effectiveness of competition as a means of enabling "autonomy" under private ownership because of transaction costs. In other words, competition must be "perfect" to be effective. But he undertakes little comparative institutional analysis. What are the transaction costs associated with commons-based peer production?

The book concludes with a section on public policy, summarizing Benkler's (2006, p. 25) concerns about privatizing the digital commons—what he calls a "second enclosure movement"—and outlining a positive role for the state, whose most important job, he argues, is to maintain openness, or "neutrality," within the economy's digital infrastructure. Here, as elsewhere, I find the treatment of government failure much too glib. Information itself is not scarce, but, as noted earlier, is embodied in tangible resources that are subject to the usual economic laws of supply and demand. Public ownership implies that a host of agency, information, and calculation problems need to be treated in an appropriately comparative manner, and Benkler does not do so. Despite these difficulties, *The Wealth of Networks* is a useful guide to the networked information economy and an eloquent statement of the left-liberal conception of the Internet's "institutional ecology." Benkler clearly believes that social production is more than a fad and has potentially revolutionary implications. I remain unconvinced, but I feel better informed about the relevant issues after reading Benkler's book.

C   Why Intellectuals Still Support Socialism[†]

Intellectuals, particularly academic intellectuals, tend to favor socialism and interventionism. How was the American university transformed from a center of higher learning to an outpost for socialist-inspired culture and politics? As recently as the early 1950s, the typical American university professor held social and political views quite similar to those of the general population. Today—well, you've all heard the jokes that circulated after the collapse of central planning in Eastern Europe and the former USSR, how the only place in the world where Marxists were still thriving was the Harvard political science department.

More generally, US higher education is now dominated by the students who were radicalized in the 1960s and who have now risen to positions of influence within colleges and universities. One needs only to observe the aggressive pursuit of "diversity" in admissions and hiring, the abandonment of the traditional curriculum in favor of highly politicized "studies" based on group identity, the mandatory workshops on sensitivity training, and so on. A 1989 study for the Carnegie Foundation for the Advancement of Teaching used the categories "liberal" and "conservative." It found that 70 percent of the professors in the major liberal arts colleges and research universities considered themselves liberal or moderately liberal, with less than 20 percent identifying themselves as conservative or moderately conservative (cited in Lee, 1994). (Of course, the term "liberal" here means left-liberal or socialist, not classical liberal.)

[†] Published originally on Mises.org, November 16, 2006.

Cardiff and Klein (2005) examined academics' political affiliations using voter-registration records for tenure-track faculty at 11 California universities. They find an average Democrat:Republican ratio of 5:1, ranging from 9:1 at Berkeley to 1:1 at Pepperdine. The humanities average 10:1, while business schools are at only 1.3:1. (Needless to say, even at the heartless, dog-eat-dog, sycophant-of-the-bourgeoisie business schools the ratio doesn't dip below 1:1.) While today's Republicans are hardly anti-socialist—particularly on foreign policy—these figures are consistent with a widespread perception that university faculties are increasingly un-representative of the communities they supposedly serve.

Now here's a surprise: even in economics, 63 percent of the faculty in the Carnegie study identified themselves as liberal, compared with 72 percent in anthropology, political science, and sociology, 76 percent in ethnic studies, history, and philosophy, and 88 percent in public affairs. The Cardiff and Klein study finds an average D:R ratio in economics departments of 2.8:1—lower than the sociologists' 44:1, to be sure, but higher than that of biological and chemical engineering, electrical engineering, computer science, management, marketing, accounting, and finance. A survey of American Economic Association members, examined by Klein and Stern (2006), finds that most economists support safety regulations, gun control, redistribution, public schooling, and anti-discrimination laws. Another survey, reported in the *Southern Economic Journal*, reveals that "71 percent of American economists believe the distribution of income in the US should be more equal, and 81 percent feel that the redistribution of income is a legitimate role for government. Support for these positions is even stronger among economists with aca-demic affiliations, and stronger still among economists with elite academic affiliations" (Lee, 1994, p. 21).

Why do so many university professors—and intellectuals more gener-ally—favor socialism and interventionism? F. A. Hayek offered a partial explanation in his 1949 essay "The Intellectuals and Socialism." Hayek asked why "the more active, intelligent and original men among [Ameri-can] intellectuals ... most frequently incline toward socialism." His answer is based on the opportunities available to people of varying talents.

Academics tend to be highly intelligent people. Given their leftward leanings, one might be tempted to infer from this that more intelligent people tend to favor socialism. However, this conclusion suffers from what empirical researchers call "sample selection bias." Intelligent people hold a variety of views. Some are lovers of liberty, defenders of property, and supporters of the "natural order"—i.e., defenders of the market. Others are reformers, wanting to remake the world according to their own visions of the ideal society. Hayek argues that exceptionally intelligent people who favor the market tend to find opportunities for professional and financial success outside the Academy (i.e., in the business or professional world). Those who are highly intelligent but ill-disposed toward the market are more likely to choose an academic career. For this reason, the universities come to be filled with those intellectuals who were favorably disposed toward socialism from the beginning.

This also leads to the phenomenon that academics don't know much about how markets work, since they have so little experience with them, living as they do in their subsidized ivory towers and protected by academic tenure. As Joseph Schumpeter explained in *Capitalism, Socialism, and Democracy* (1942, p. 17), it is "the absence of direct responsibility for practical affairs" that distinguishes the academic intellectual from others "who wield the power of the spoken and the written word." This absence of direct responsibility leads to a corresponding absence of first-hand knowledge of practical affairs. The critical attitude of the intellectual arises, says Schumpeter, "no less from the intellectual's situation as an onlooker—in most cases also as an outsider—than from the fact that his main chance of asserting himself lies in his actual or potential nuisance value."

Hayek's account is incomplete, however, because it doesn't explain why academics have become more and more interventionist throughout the twentieth century. As mentioned above, during the first half of the twentieth century university faculty members tended to hold political views similar to those held by the general population. What caused the change?

To answer, we must realize first that academics receive many direct benefits from the welfare state, and that these benefits have increased over time. Excluding student financial aid, public universities receive about 50 percent of their funding from federal and state governments, dwarfing the 18 percent they receive from tuition and fees. Even "private" universities like Stanford or Harvard receive around 20 percent of their budgets from federal grants and contracts (US Department of Education, 1996). Including student financial aid, the figure is almost 50 percent. According to the US Department of Education, about a third of all students at public, 4-

year colleges and universities, and half the students at private colleges and universities, receive financial aid from the federal government.

In this sense, the most dramatic example of "corporate welfare" in the US is the GI Bill, which subsidized the academic sector, bloating it far beyond the level the market would have provided. The GI Bill, signed by President Roosevelt in 1944 to send returning soldiers to colleges and universities, cost taxpayers $14.5 billion between 1944 and 1956 (Skocpol, 1996). The latest (2008) version of the GI Bill is expected to cost $52 billion over the next ten years.

To see why this government aid is so important to the higher education establishment, we need only stop to consider for a moment what academics would do in a purely free society. The fact is that most academics simply aren't that important. In a free society, there would be far fewer of them than there are today. Their public visibility would no doubt be quite low. Most would be poorly paid. Though some would be engaged in scholarly research, the vast majority would be teachers. Their job would be to pass the collective wisdom of the ages along to the next generation. In all likelihood, there would also be far fewer students. Some students would attend traditional colleges and universities, but many more students would attend technical and vocational schools, where their instructors would be men and women with practical knowledge.

Today, many professors at major research universities do little teaching. Their primary activity is research, though much of that is questionable as real scholarship. One needs only to browse through the latest specialty journals to see what passes for scholarly research in most disciplines. In the humanities and social sciences, it is likely to be postmodern gobbledygook; in the professional schools, vocationally oriented technical reports. Much of this research is funded in the United States by government agencies, such as the National Science Foundation, National Institutes of Health, the National Endowment for the Humanities, the USDA, and others. The large universities have tens of thousands of students, themselves supported by government-subsidized loans and grants.

Beyond university life, academics also compete for prestigious posts within government agencies. Consider economics. The US federal government employs at least 3,000 economists—about 15% of all members of the American Economic Association. The Federal Reserve System itself employs several hundred. There are also advisory posts, affiliations with important government agencies, memberships of federally appointed commissions, and other career-enhancing activities. These benefits are not simply financial. They are also psychological. As Lee (1994, p. 22) puts it:

> Like every other group, academics like to exert influence and feel important. Few scholars in the social sciences and humanities are content just to observe, describe, and explain society; most want to improve society and are naive enough to believe that they could do so if only they had sufficient influence. The existence of a huge government offers academics the real possibility of living out their reformist fantasies.[1]

It's clear, then, that for academics, there are many benefits to living in a highly interventionist society. It should be no wonder, then, that academics tend to support those interventions. Economists, in particular, play active roles as government advisers, creating and sustaining the welfare state that now surrounds us. Naturally, when government funds their research, economists in applied fields such as agricultural economics and monetary economics are unlikely to call for serious regulatory reform in their specialty areas.

Murray Rothbard devotes an interesting chapter of *Man, Economy, and State*, to the traditional role of the economist in public life. Rothbard notes that the functions of the economist on the free market differ strongly from those of the economist on the hampered market. "What can the economist do on the purely free market?" Rothbard asks. "He can explain the workings of the market economy (a vital task, especially since the untutored person tends to regard the market economy as sheer chaos), but he can do little else."

Furthermore, economists are not traditionally popular as policy advisors. Economics teaches that resources are limited, that choices made imply opportunities forgone, that our actions can have unintended consequences. This is typically not what government officials want to hear. When they propose an import tariff to help domestic manufacturers, we economists explain that this protection will come only at the expense of domestic consumers. When they suggest a minimum-wage law to raise the incomes of low-wage workers, we show that such a law hurts the very people it purports to help by forcing them out of work. Over the last several

---

[1] See also Pasour (2004) and White (2005) on the influence of government spending on research in agricultural economics and monetary economics, respectively.

decades, however, the role of the economist has expanded dramatically. Partly for the reasons we discussed earlier, the welfare state has partly co-opted the profession of economics. Just as a higher murder rate increases the demand for criminologists, so the growth of the welfare/regulatory state increases the demand for policy analysts, antitrust consultants, tax and regulatory experts, and various forecasters.

To some degree, the increasing professionalization of the economics business must share the blame for this change. The economists' premier professional society, the American Economic Association, was itself created as an explicitly "progressive" organization. Its founder, the religious and social reformer Richard T. Ely, planned an association, he reported to a colleague, of "economists who repudiate laissez-faire as a scientific doctrine" (Coats, 1960, p. 556). The other founding members, all of whom had been trained in Germany under Gustav Schmoller and other members of the younger German Historical School—the so-called Socialists of the Chair—were similarly possessed with reformist zeal. The constitution of the AEA still contains references to the "positive role of the church, the state and science in the solution of social problems by the development of legislative policy" (Coats, 1960, p. 558). Fortunately, the AEA subsequently distanced itself from the aims of its founders, although its annual distinguished lecture is still called the "Richard T. Ely lecture."[2]

If asked to select a single event that most encouraged the transformation of the average economist from a critic of intervention to a defender of the welfare state, I would name the Second World War. To be sure, it was the Progressive Era that saw the permanent introduction of the income tax and the establishment of the Federal Reserve System. And it was during the Great Depression that Washington, D.C., first began to employ a substantial number of economists to join such central planning organizations as the National Resources Planning Board. Still, even in those years, the average economist favored free trade, low taxes, and sound money.

World War II, however, was a watershed event for the profession. For the first time, professional economists joined the ranks of government planning bureaus en masse. One job was to control prices, as with the Office of Price Administration, led by Leon Henderson and later John

---

[2]For more on the professionalization of economics see Bernstein (2001).

Kenneth Galbraith. This group included prominent free-market econo-mists such as Herbert Stein and George Stigler. Another role was to study military procurement (what later became known as "operations research") with Columbia University's Statistical Research Group (including Stigler, Milton Friedman, Harold Hotelling, Abraham Wald, Leonard Savage), or with the Army's Statistical Control Group, which was led by Tex Thornton, later president of Litton Industries, and his "Whiz Kids." The most famous Whiz Kid was Robert McNamara, Thornton's leading protégé, who later applied the same techniques to the management of the Vietnam War.[3]

Moreover, before World War II the primary language of economics, in the English-speaking world, was English. Since then, however, economic theory has come to be expressed in obscure mathematical jargon, while economic history has become a branch of applied statistics. It is common to attribute this change to the publication of Paul Samuelson's mathemat-ical treatise (Samuelson, 1947), and to the development of computers. These are no doubt important. However, it is likely the taste for central planning that economists—even nominally free-market economists—got during World War II that forever changed the direction of the discipline.

What about other public figures, what Hayek called "second-hand dealers in ideas"—the journalists, book editors, high-school teachers, and other members of the "opinion-molding" class? First, intelligent and ar-ticulate liberals (in the classical sense) tend to go into business and the professions (Hayek's selection-bias argument). Second, many journalists trade integrity for access; few are brave enough to challenge the state, because they crave information, interviews, and time with state officials.

What does the future hold? It is impossible to say for sure, but there are encouraging signs. The main reason is technology. The web has challenged the state university and state media cartels as never before. You don't need a PhD to write for Wikipedia. What does the rise of the new media, new means of sharing information, new ways of establishing authority and cred-ibility, imply for universities as credential factories? Moreover, as universi-ties become more vocationally oriented, they will find it hard to compete with specialized, technology-intensive institutions such as DeVry Univer-sity and the University of Phoenix, the fastest-growing US universities.

---

[3]On Litton see also Sobel (1984, pp. 68–72). On the relationship between Thornton and McNamara see Shapley (1993) and Byrne (1993).

The current crises in higher education and the media are probably good things, in the long run, if they force a rethinking of educational and intellectual goals and objectives, and take power away from the establishment institutions. Then, and only then, we may see a rebirth of genuine scholarship, communication, and education.

——————— ⌘ ———————

D   Management Theory and the Business Cycle[†]
(with Nicolai J. Foss)

Is management theory to blame for the current crisis in the world economy? Some commentators think that business schools' focus on shareholder wealth maximization, performance-based pay, and the virtue of self-interest have led banks, corporations, and governments astray. Hefty bonuses promoted excessive risk-taking, and the free-market philosophy taught in business schools removed the final ethical checks and balances on such behavior. "It is the type of thinking," worry Raymond Fisman and Rakesh Khurana (2008), "that is now bringing capitalism to its knees."

The populist crackdown on executive pay is linked to such thinking. The late Sumantra Ghoshal of the London Business School, widely hailed as one of the world's foremost management gurus, was a forceful critic of performance pay and its allegedly destructive consequences. More generally, Ghoshal thought that management theory was "bad for practice" financially, ethically, and politically Ghoshal and Moran (1996); Ghoshal (2005).

We think, however, that management theory has much to offer policymakers, practitioners, and analysts seeking to understand the current crisis. Take, for example, the notion of heterogeneity. The idea that resources, firms, and industries are different from each other—that capital and labor are specialized for particular projects and activities, that people are distinct—is ubiquitous in the theory and practice of management. What strategists call competitive advantage arises from heterogeneity, from doing something differently from the competition. Human-resource managers

---

[†]Published originally as "Management Theory is Not to Blame," Mises.org, March 19, 2009. See also Agarwal, Barney, Foss, and Klein (2009) for further details.

deal with an increasingly diverse workforce and people with highly specialized talents. Firms that expand internationally learn the lessons of market,
cultural, and institutional heterogeneity. As a consequence, management
scholars think of firms as bundles of heterogeneous resources or assets.
Assets can be specific to certain firms. Assets may be "co-specialized" with
other assets, such that they generate value only in certain combinations.
And as any accountant knows, assets have different (economic) life ex-
pectancies. Such unique and specialized assets can also be intangible, such
as worker-specific knowledge or firm-specific capabilities.

To the uninitiated this may sound trite. But look at economics. Here
homogeneity, not heterogeneity, rules the roost. Economic models of industries and economies typically start with "representative firms," implying
that all firms in an industry are alike. This may be a handy starting point if
one is interested in the industry *per se* rather than in individual firms, but
can be seriously misleading if one is interested in the relative performance
of firms or industries.

And, here, macroeconomists are the worst transgressors. Their models
of an entire economy treat factors of production as homogeneous within
categories. Thus, "labor" means homogeneous labor inputs. "Capital" has
the same interpretation. Nobel Laureate Robert Solow adopted the notion
of "shmoo" from the comic Lil' Abner—shmoos are identical creatures
shaped like bowling pins with legs—to capture this kind of homogeneity.
This style of reasoning originated with Ricardo, who found it a useful
simplification. And it can be. But sometimes economists' assumption of
homogeneity leads them into trouble, as is the case with the current crisis.

The macroeconomic problem, we are told, is that "banks" made unwise
investments, and now aren't "lending" enough. "Businesses" and "consumers" can't get "loans." "Firms" have too many "bad assets" on their
books. The key question, though, is which ones? Which banks aren't lending to which customers? Which firms have made poor investments? A loan
isn't a loan isn't a loan. The relevant question, in analyzing the credit mess,
is which loans aren't being made, to whom, and why? The critical issues are
the composition of lending, not the amount. Total lending, total liquidity,
average equity prices, and the like obscure the key questions about how
resources are being allocated across sectors, firms, and individuals, whether
bad investments are being liquidated, and so on. Such aggregate notions
homogenize—and in doing so, suppress critical information about relative

prices. The main function of capital markets, after all, is not to moderate the total amount of financial capital, but to allocate capital across activities.

The US stimulus package and similar proposals around the world are likewise stymied by their crude, Keynesian-style reliance on macroeconomic aggregates. According to the common wisdom, the bank crisis led to a collapse of effective aggregate demand, and only massive increases in government expenditure (and government debt) can kick-start the economy. Expenditures—on what? It doesn't matter: just spend. The only criterion is whether the projects are "shovel-ready."

But a shovel isn't a shovel isn't a shovel. As Hayek—Keynes's most important intellectual opponent—argued in the 1930s and 1940s, the economy's capital structure is a complex and delicate structure, one that cannot be mashed and pushed like putty. Resources cannot be shifted costlessly from one activity to another, particularly in a modern economy in which much of those resources are embodied in industry-specific, firm-specific, and worker-specific capabilities. Even idle resources can be misallocated—what Hayek and Mises called "malinvestment"—if invested in activities that don't produce the goods and services the economy needs.

Every manager knows that directing specialized resources to the wrong projects is a bad bet, even if it leads to a slight boost in short-term earnings. In the same way, the path to economic recovery is to allow markets to channel specialized resources to their highest-valued uses, not to dump taxpayer funds on whatever firms and industries happen to be ready for them—or politically connected. In an important sense, banks' failure to distinguish among heterogeneous borrowers got us into this mess. A mistaken focus on homogeneity, in pursuit of a quick fix, will only bring more of the same.

E   Menger the Revolutionary[†]

"There never lived at the same time," wrote Ludwig von Mises (1949, p. 869), "more than a score of men whose work contributed anything essential to economics." One of those men was Carl Menger (1840–1921),

[†]Published originally as the Foreword to Carl Menger, *Principles of Economics* (reprint edition, Auburn, Ala.: Ludwig von Mises Institute, 2006).

Professor of Political Economy at the University of Vienna and founder of the Austrian school of economics. Menger's path-breaking *Grundsätze der Volkswirtschaftslehre* [Principles of Economics], published in 1871, not only introduced the concept of marginal analysis, it presented a radically new approach to economic analysis, one that still forms the core of the Austrian theory of value and price.

Unlike his contemporaries William Stanley Jevons and Léon Walras, who independently developed concepts of marginal utility during the 1870s, Menger favored an approach that was deductive, teleological, and, in a fundamental sense, humanistic. While Menger shared his contemporaries' preference for abstract reasoning, he was primarily interested in explaining the real-world actions of real people, not in creating artificial, stylized representations of reality. Economics, for Menger, is the study of purposeful human choice, the relationship between means and ends. "All things are subject to the law of cause and effect," he begins his treatise. "This great principle knows no exception" (Menger, 1871, p. 51). Jevons and Walras rejected cause and effect in favor of simultaneous determination, the idea that complex systems can be modeled as systems of simultaneous equations in which no variable can be said to "cause" another. This has become the standard approach in contemporary economics, accepted by nearly all economists but the followers of Menger.

Menger sought to explain prices as the outcome of the purposeful, voluntary interactions of buyers and sellers, each guided by their own, subjective evaluations of the usefulness of various goods and services in satisfying their objectives (what we now call marginal utility, a term later coined by Friedrich von Wieser). Trade is thus the result of people's deliberate attempts to improve their well-being, not an innate "propensity to truck, barter, and exchange," as suggested by Adam Smith (1776, I, p. 24). The exact quantities of goods exchanged—their prices, in other words—are determined by the values individuals attach to marginal units of these goods. With a single buyer and seller, goods are exchanged as long as participants can agree on an exchange ratio that leaves each better off than he was before.

In a market with many buyers and sellers, the price reflects the valuations of the buyer least willing to buy and the seller least willing to sell, what Böhm-Bawerk would call the "marginal pairs." With each voluntary exchange, then, the gains from trade are momentarily exhausted, regardless of the exact structure of the market. Menger's highly general explanation of price formation continues to form the core of Austrian microeconomics.

Menger's analysis has been labeled "causal-realistic," partly to emphasize the distinction between Menger's approach and that of the neoclassical economists (see chapter 7 for a detailed discussion of Menger's economic theory). Besides its focus on causal relations, Menger's analysis is realistic in the sense that he sought not to develop formal models of hypothetical economic relationships, but to explain the actual prices paid every day in real markets. The classical economists had explained that prices are the result of supply and demand, but they lacked a satisfactory theory of valuation to explain buyers' willingness to pay for goods and services. Rejecting value subjectivism, the classical economists tended to treat demand as relatively unimportant and concentrated on hypothetical "long-run" conditions, in which "objective" characteristics of goods—most importantly, their costs of production—would determine their prices. The classical economists also tended to group factors of production into broad categories—land, labor, and capital—leaving them unable to explain the prices of discrete, heterogeneous units of these factors. Menger realized that the actual prices paid for goods and services reflect not some objective, "intrinsic" characteristics, but rather the uses to which discrete units of goods and services can be put as perceived, subjectively, by individual buyers and sellers.

The *Principles* was written as an introductory volume in a proposed multi-volume work. As noted in chapter 7 above, however, no later volumes were written. Menger did not in the *Principles* develop explicitly the concept of opportunity cost, he did not extend his analysis to explain the prices of the factors of production, and he did not develop a theory of monetary calculation. Those advances would come later from his students and disciples Böhm-Bawerk, Wieser, J. B. Clark, Wicksteed, Fetter, Davenport, Mises, and Hayek. Many of the most important ideas are implicit in Menger's analysis, however. For example, his distinction among goods of lower and higher "orders," referring to their place in the temporal sequence of production, forms the heart of Austrian capital theory, one of its most distinctive and important elements. Indeed, Menger emphasizes the passage of time throughout his analysis, an emphasis that has not yet made its way into mainstream economic theorizing.

While most contemporary economics treatises are turgid and dull, Menger's book is remarkably easy to read, even today. His prose is lucid, his analysis is logical and systematic, his examples clear and informative. The *Principles* remains an excellent introduction to economic reasoning and, for the specialist, the classic statement of the core principles of the Austrian school.

As Hayek (1976, p. 12) writes, the significance of the Austrian school is "entirely due to the foundations laid by this one man." However, while Menger is universally recognized as the Austrian school's founder, his causal-realistic approach to price formation is not always appreciated, even within contemporary Austrian economics. As we saw in chapter 7, Vaughn (1994) finds Menger's price theory unoriginal, identifying as the distinctive "Austrian" contribution in Menger his brief references to institutions, evolution, and the like. My view is different: Menger's main contribution to the Austrian tradition is his price theory, his "mundane" economics, which is distinct from that of the neoclassical tradition and which is the fundamental building block of Austrian economic analysis.

Another remarkable feature of Menger's contribution is that it appeared in German, while the then-dominant approach in the German-speaking world was that of the "younger" German historical school, which eschewed theoretical analysis altogether in favor of inductive, ideologically driven, historical case studies. The most accomplished theoretical economists, the British classicals such as J. S. Mill, were largely unknown to German-speaking writers. As Hayek (1976, p. 13) notes, "[i]n England the progress of economic theory only stagnated. In Germany a second generation of historical economists grew up who had not only never become really acquainted with the one well-developed system of theory that existed, but had also learnt to regard theoretical speculations of any sort as useless if not positively harmful." Menger's approach—haughtily dismissed by the leader of the German historical school, Gustav Schmoller, as merely "Austrian," the origin of that label—led to a renaissance of theoretical economics in Europe and, later, in the US.

In short, the core concepts of contemporary Austrian economics—human action, means and ends, subjective value, marginal analysis, methodological individualism, the time structure of production, and so on—along with the Austrian theory of value and price, which forms the heart of Austrian analysis, all flow from Menger's pathbreaking work. As Salerno (1999a, p. 71) has written, "Austrian economics always was and will forever remain Mengerian economics."

F   Hayek the Innovator[†]

F. A. Hayek is undoubtedly the most eminent of the modern Austrian economists. Student of Friedrich von Wieser, protégé and colleague of Mises, and foremost representative of an outstanding generation of Austrian school theorists, Hayek was more successful than anyone else in spreading Austrian ideas throughout the English-speaking world. "When the definitive history of economic analysis during the 1930s comes to be written," said John Hicks in 1967, "a leading character in the drama (it was quite a drama) will be Professor Hayek.... [I]t is hardly remembered that there was a time when the new theories of Hayek were the principal rival of the new theories of Keynes" (Hicks, 1967, p. 203). Unfortunately, Hayek's theory of the business cycle was eventually swept aside by the Keynesian revolution. Ultimately, however, this work was again recognized when Hayek received, along with the Swede Gunnar Myrdal, the 1974 Nobel Memorial Prize in Economic Science. Hayek was a prolific writer over nearly seven decades; his Collected Works, currently being published by the University of Chicago Press and Routledge, are projected at nineteen volumes.

Life and work

Hayek's life spanned the twentieth century, and he made his home in some of the great intellectual communities of the period.[4] Born Friedrich August von Hayek in 1899 to a distinguished family of Viennese intellectuals,[5] Hayek attended the University of Vienna, earning doctorates in 1921 and 1923. Hayek came to the University at age 19 just after World War I, when it was one of the three best places in the world to study economics (the others being Stockholm and Cambridge, England). Though he was enrolled as a law student, his primary interests were economics and psychology, the latter due to the influence of Mach's theory of perception on Wieser

---

[†]Published originally as "F. A. Hayek: Austrian Economist and Social Theorist," in Randall G. Holcombe, ed., *Fifteen Great Austrian Economists*. Auburn, Ala.: Mises Institute, 1999, pp. 181–94.

[4]Hayek (1994), and the introduction by Stephen Kresge.

[5]Hayek's father was a physician and botanist. One grandfather, a statistician, was a friend of Eugen von Böhm-Bawerk; the philosopher Ludwig Wittgenstein was a second cousin.

and Wieser's colleague Othmar Spann, and the former stemming from the reformist ideal of Fabian socialism so typical of Hayek's generation.

Like many students of economics then and since, Hayek chose the subject not for its own sake, but because he wanted to improve social conditions—the poverty of postwar Vienna serving as a daily reminder of such a need. Socialism seemed to provide a solution. Then in 1922 Mises published his *Die Gemeinwirtschaft*, later translated as *Socialism.* "To none of us young men who read the book when it appeared," Hayek recalled, "the world was ever the same again" (Hayek, 1956, p. 133). *Socialism*, an elaboration of Mises's pioneering article from two years before, argued that economic calculation requires a market for the means of production; without such a market there is no way to establish the values of those means and, consequently, no way to find their proper uses in production. Mises's devastating attack on central planning converted Hayek to laissez-faire, along with contemporaries like Wilhelm Röpke, Lionel Robbins, and Bertil Ohlin. It was around this time that Hayek began attending Mises's famed *Privatseminar*. Regular participants, who received no academic credit or other official recognition for their time, included Hayek, Gottfried Haberler, Fritz Machlup, Oskar Morgenstern, Paul Rosenstein-Rodan, Richard von Strigl, Karl Schlesinger, Felix Kaufmann, Alfred Schütz, Eric Voegelin, Karl Menger, Jr., and others not so famous. For several years the *Privatseminar* was the center of the economics community in Vienna, attracting such visitors as Robbins from London and Howard S. Ellis from Berkeley. Later, Hayek became the first of this group to leave Vienna; most of the others, along with Mises himself, were also gone by the start of World War II.

Mises had done earlier work on monetary and banking theory, successfully applying the Austrian marginal utility principle to the value of money and then sketching a theory of industrial fluctuations based on the doctrines of the British Currency School and the ideas of the Swedish economist Knut Wicksell. Hayek used this last as a starting point for his own research on fluctuations, explaining the origin of the business cycle in terms of bank credit expansion and its transmission in terms of capital malinvestments. His work in this area eventually earned him an invitation to lecture at the London School of Economics and Political Science and then to occupy its Tooke Chair in Economics and Statistics, which he accepted in 1931. There he found himself among a vibrant and exciting group: Robbins, J. R. Hicks, Arnold Plant, Dennis Robertson, T. E. Gregory, Abba Lerner, Kenneth Boulding, and George Shackle, to name only the most prominent. Hayek brought his (to them) unfamiliar views,[6] and gradually, the "Austrian" theory of the business cycle became known and accepted. At the LSE Hayek lectured on Mises's business-cycle theory, which he was refining and which, until Keynes's *General Theory* came out in 1936, was rapidly gaining adherents in Britain and the US and was becoming the preferred explanation of the Depression. Hayek and Keynes had sparred in the early 1930s in the pages of the *Economic Journal* over Keynes's *Treatise on Money*. As one of Keynes's leading professional adversaries, Hayek was well situated to provide a full refutation of the *General Theory*. But he never did. Part of the explanation for this no doubt lies with Keynes's personal charm and legendary rhetorical skill, along with Hayek's general reluctance to engage in direct confrontation with his colleagues.[7] Hayek also considered Keynes an ally in the fight against wartime inflation and did not want to detract from that issue (Hayek, 1994, p. 91). Furthermore, as Hayek later explained, Keynes was constantly changing his theoretical framework, and Hayek saw no point in working out a detailed critique of the *General Theory*, if Keynes might change his mind again (Hayek, 1963b, p. 60; Hayek, 1966, pp. 240–41). Hayek thought a better course would be to produce a fuller elaboration of Böhm-Bawerk's capital theory, and he began to devote his energies to this project. Unfortunately, *The Pure Theory of Capital* was not completed until 1941, and by then the Keynesian macro model had become firmly established.[8]

Within a very few years, however, the fortunes of the Austrian school

---

[6]Hicks (1967, p. 204) noted, in reference to Hayek's first (1931) English book, that "*Prices and Production* was in English, but it was not English economics."

[7]In addition, Hayek (1963b, p. 60) cited his own "tiredness from controversy"; he had already engaged the market socialists on economic calculation, Knight on capital theory, and Keynes on money.

[8]For more on Hayek's failure to respond to the *General Theory* see Caldwell (1995), especially pp. 40–6. Hayek (1963b, pp. 60–61; 1966, pp. 240–41) also believed that an effective refutation of Keynes would have to begin with a thorough critique of aggregate, or "macro" economics more generally. Caldwell (1988) suggests another reason: it was during this time that Hayek was losing faith in equilibrium theory and moving toward a "market process" view of economic activity, making it difficult for him to engage Keynes on the same terms in which they had debated earlier. McCormick (1992, pp. 99–134) and Blaug (1993, pp. 53–55) propose an entirely different reason: Hayek couldn't respond because the Austrian capital theory, on which the cycle theory was built, was simply wrong.

suffered a dramatic reversal. First, the Austrian theory of capital, an integral part of the business-cycle theory, came under attack from the Italian-born Cambridge economist Piero Sraffa and the American Frank Knight, while the cycle theory itself was forgotten amid the enthusiasm for the *General Theory*. Second, beginning with Hayek's move to London and continuing until the early 1940s, the Austrian economists left Vienna for personal and then for political reasons, so that a school ceased to exist there as such.[9] Mises left Vienna in 1934 for Geneva and then New York, where he continued to work in isolation; Hayek remained at the LSE until 1950, when he joined the Committee on Social Thought at the University of Chicago. Other Austrians of Hayek's generation became prominent in the US—Gottfried Haberler at Harvard, Fritz Machlup and Oskar Morgenstern at Princeton, Paul Rosenstein-Rodan at MIT—but their work no longer seemed to show distinct traces of the tradition founded by Menger.

At Chicago, Hayek again found himself among a dazzling group: the economics department, led by Knight, Milton Friedman, and later George Stigler, was one of the best anywhere, and Aaron Director at the law school soon set up the first law and economics program.[10] But economic theory, in particular its style of reasoning, was rapidly changing; Paul Samuelson's *Foundations* had appeared in 1947, establishing physics as the science for economics to imitate, and Friedman's 1953 essay on "positive economics" set a new standard for economic method. In addition, Hayek had ceased to work on economic theory, concentrating instead on psychology, philosophy, and politics, and Austrian economics entered a prolonged eclipse.[11] Important work in the Austrian tradition was done during this period by Rothbard (1956, 1962, 1963a,b), Kirzner (1963, 1966, 1973), and Lachmann (1956), but at least publicly, the Austrian tradition lay mostly dormant.

---

[9] On the emigration of the Austrian economists see Craver (1986).

[10] However, at Chicago Hayek was considered something of an outsider; his post was with the Committee on Social Thought, not the economics department, and his salary was paid by a private foundation, the William Volker Fund (the same organization that paid Mises's salary as a visiting professor at New York University).

[11] By this time, Hayek (1994, p. 126) said, "I had ... become somewhat stale as an economist and felt much out of sympathy with the direction in which economics was developing. Though I had still regarded the work I had done during the 1940s on scientific method, the history of ideas, and political theory as temporary excursions into another field, I found it difficult to return to systematic teaching of economic theory and felt it rather as a release that I was not forced to do so by my teaching duties."

When the 1974 Nobel Prize in economics went to Hayek, interest in the Austrian school was suddenly and unexpectedly revived. While this was not the first event of the so-called "Austrian revival," the memorable South Royalton conference having taken place earlier the same year, the rediscovery of Hayek by the economics profession was nonetheless a decisive event in the renaissance of Austrian economics.[12] Hayek's writings were taught to new generations, and Hayek himself appeared at the early Institute for Humane Studies conferences in the mid-1970s. He continued to write, producing *The Fatal Conceit* in 1988, at the age of 89. Hayek died in 1992 in Freiburg, Germany, where he had lived since leaving Chicago in 1961.

Contributions to economics

Hayek's legacy in economics is complex. Among mainstream economists, he is mainly known for his popular *The Road to Serfdom* (1944) and for his work on knowledge in the 1930s and 1940s (Hayek, 1937, 1945). Specialists in business-cycle theory recognize his early work on industrial fluctuations, and modern information theorists often acknowledge Hayek's work on prices as signals, although his conclusions are typically disputed.[13] Hayek's work is also known in political philosophy (Hayek, 1960), legal theory (Hayek, 1973–79), and psychology (Hayek, 1952b). Within the Austrian school of economics, Hayek's influence, while undeniably

---

[12] The proceedings of the South Royalton conference were published as *The Foundations of Modern Austrian Economics* (Dolan, 1976). A follow-up volume appeared two years later: *New Directions in Austrian Economics* (Spadaro, 1978). For perspectives on the Austrian revival see Rothbard (1995), and Vaughn (1994). Salerno (1996b) argues that the Austrian revival should be dated not from 1974, but from 1962–63, when Rothbard published *Man, Economy, and State* (1962), *America's Great Depression* (1963a), and *What Has Government Done to Our Money?* (1963b), the works that sparked the younger South Royalton participants' interest in Austrian economics.

[13] Lucas (1977) cites Hayek as a leading exponent of pre-Keynesian business-cycle theory. Grossman and Stiglitz (1976) and Grossman (1980; 1989) argue that contrary to Hayek, market prices are not "sufficient statistics" for changes in tastes and technology. This literature tries to test the "informative content" of price signals, and contends that in general only perfectly competitive prices convey useful information. Farrell and Bolton (1990) claim that Hayek overstates the coordinating properties of decentralized market exchange. Hayek's 1945 paper is also frequently cited in the new institutional literature emphasizing process and adaptation, although coordination through markets is seen as only one type of desirable coordination. See, for example, Williamson (1991c).

immense, has very recently become the subject of some controversy. His emphasis on spontaneous order and his work on complex systems have been widely influential among many Austrians. Others have preferred to stress Hayek's work in technical economics, particularly on capital and the business cycle, citing a tension between some of Hayek's and Mises's views on the social order. (While Mises was a rationalist and a utilitarian, Hayek focused on the limits to reason, basing his defense of capitalism on its ability to use limited knowledge and learning by trial and error.)

BUSINESS-CYCLE THEORY. Hayek's writings on capital, money, and the business cycle are widely regarded as his most important contributions to economics (Hicks, 1967; Machlup, 1976b). Building on Mises's *Theory of Money and Credit* (1912), Hayek showed how fluctuations in economy-wide output and employment are related to the economy's capital structure. In *Prices and Production* (1931) he introduced the famous "Hayekian triangles" to illustrate the relationship between the value of capital goods and their place in the temporal sequence of production. Because production takes time, factors of production must be committed in the present for making final goods that will have value only in the future after they are sold. However, capital is heterogeneous. As capital goods are used in production, they are transformed from general-purpose materials and components to intermediate products specific to particular final goods. Consequently, these assets cannot be easily redeployed to alternative uses if demands for final goods change. The central macroeconomic problem in a modern capital-using economy is thus one of *intertemporal coordination*: how can the allocation of resources between capital and consumer goods be aligned with consumers' preferences between present and future consumption? In *The Pure Theory of Capital* (1941), perhaps his most ambitious work, Hayek describes how the economy's structure of production depends on the characteristics of capital goods—durability, complementarity, substitutability, specificity, and so on. This structure can be described by the various "investment periods" of inputs, an extension of Böhm-Bawerk's notion of "roundaboutness," the degree to which production takes up resources over time.[14]

---

[14] Hayek ultimately rejected Böhm-Bawerk's "average period of production" as a useful concept, though he had used it earlier in *Prices and Production* (1931). See Hayek (1994), p. 141, and White (1996)

In *Prices and Production* (1931) and *Monetary Theory and the Trade Cycle* (1933b) Hayek showed how monetary injections, by lowering the rate of interest below what Mises (following Wicksell) called its "natural rate," distort the economy's intertemporal structure of production.[15] Most theories of the effects of money on prices and output (then and since) consider only the effects of the total money supply on the price level and aggregate output or investment. The Austrian theory, as developed by Mises and Hayek, focuses on the way money enters the economy ("injection effects") and how this affects relative prices and investment in particular sectors. In Hayek's framework, investments in some stages of production are "malinvestments" if they do not help to align the structure of production to consumers' intertemporal preferences. The reduction in interest rates caused by credit expansion directs resources toward capital-intensive processes and early stages of production (whose investment demands are more interest-rate elastic), thus "lengthening" the period of production. If interest rates had fallen because consumers had changed their preferences to favor future over present consumption, then the longer time structure of production would have been an appropriate, coordinating response. A fall in interest rates caused by credit expansion, however, would have been a "false signal," causing changes in the structure of production that do not accord with consumers' intertemporal preferences.[16] The boom generated by the increase in investment is artificial. Eventually, market participants come to realize that there are not enough savings to complete all the new projects; the boom becomes a bust as these malinvestments are discovered and liquidated.[17] Every artificial boom induced by credit

---

[15] Hayek thought the more important case was when the market interest rate was kept constant despite a rise in the natural interest rate. In his writings, however, he focused on the expositionally easier case when credit expansion lowers the market interest rate below an unchanged natural rate.

[16] For most of his career Hayek viewed a system of fractional-reserve banking as inherently unstable, endorsing a role (in principle) for government stabilization of the money supply. In later writings, beginning with *The Constitution of Liberty* (1960) and culminating in *Denationalisation of Money* (1976), he argued in favor of competition among private issuers of fiat money. See White (1999).

[17] Anticipating modern cycle theories, Hayek (1939b) recognized that the behavior of the cycle depends on expectations about future price and interest rate movements. As Garrison and Kirzner put it (1987, p. 612), for Hayek "prices are signals, not marching orders." But Hayek did not believe agents could know the real structure of the economy, to correctly distinguish movements in interest rates generated by changes in consumers'

expansion, then, is self-reversing. Recovery consists of liquidating the malinvestments induced by the lowering of interest rates below their natural levels, thus restoring the time structure of production so that it accords with consumers' intertemporal preferences.[18]

KNOWLEDGE, PRICES, AND COMPETITION AS A DISCOVERY PROCEDURE. Hayek's writings on dispersed knowledge and spontaneous order are also widely known, but more controversial. In "Economics and Knowledge" (1937) and "The Use of Knowledge in Society" (1945) Hayek argued that the central economic problem facing society is not, as is commonly expressed in textbooks, the allocation of given resources among competing ends. "It is rather a problem of how to secure the best use of resources known to any of the members of society, for ends whose relative importance only those individuals know. Or, to put it briefly, it is a problem of the utilization of knowledge not given to anyone in its totality" (Hayek, 1945, p. 78).

Much of the knowledge necessary for running the economic system, Hayek contended, is in the form not of "scientific" or technical knowledge—the conscious awareness of the rules governing natural and social phenomena—but of "tacit" knowledge, the idiosyncratic, dispersed bits of understanding of "circumstances of time and place." This tacit knowledge is often not consciously known even to those who possess it and can never be communicated to a central authority. The market tends to use this tacit knowledge through a type of "discovery procedure" (Hayek, 1968b), by which this information is unknowingly transmitted throughout the economy as an unintended consequence of individuals' pursuing their own ends.[19] Indeed, Hayek's (1948) distinction between the neoclassical no-

---

intertemporal preferences from those generated by changes in the money supply.

[18] For general overviews of Hayek's macroeconomic views see O'Driscoll (1977), and Garrison and Kirzner (1987). For expositions and interpretations of the Austrian trade-cycle theory, particularly as it relates to modern cycle theories, see Garrison (1978, 2000); Beilante and Garrison (1988); van Zijp (1993); and Foss (1994b), pp. 39–55.

[19] Hayek's use of an argument from ignorance as a defense of the market is unusual. Modern economists typically require assumptions of hyperrationality—complete and perfect information, rational expectations, perfect markets, and so on—to justify market allocations as "efficient." In the new microeconomics literature on information and incentives, theorists like Joseph Stiglitz have used deviations from these assumptions of perfection to

tion of "competition," identified as a set of equilibrium conditions (number of market participants, characteristics of the product, and so on), and the older notion of competition as a rivalrous process, has been widely influential in Austrian economics (Kirzner, 1973; Machovec, 1995).

For Hayek, market competition generates a particular kind of order—an order that is the product "of human action but not human design" (a phrase Hayek borrowed from Adam Smith's mentor Adam Ferguson). This "spontaneous order" is a system that comes about through the independent actions of many individuals, and produces overall benefits unintended and mostly unforeseen by those whose actions bring it about. To distinguish between this kind of order and that of a deliberate, planned system, Hayek (1968c) used the Greek terms *cosmos* for a spontaneous order and *taxis* for a consciously planned one.[20] Examples of a *cosmos* include the market system as a whole, money, the common law, and even language. A *taxis*, by contrast, is a designed or constructed organization, like a firm or bureau; these are the "islands of conscious power in [the] ocean of unconscious cooperation like lumps of butter coagulating in a pail of buttermilk" (D. H. Robertson, quoted in Coase, 1937, p. 35).[21]

Most commentators view Hayek's work on knowledge, discovery, and competition as an outgrowth of his participation in the socialist calculation debate of the 1920s and 1930s. The socialists erred, in Hayek's view, in failing to see that the economy as a whole is necessarily a spontaneous order and can never be deliberately made over in the way that the operators of a planned order can exercise control over their organization. This is because planned orders can handle only problems of strictly limited complexity. Spontaneous orders, by contrast, tend to evolve through a process of natural selection, and therefore do not need to be designed or even understood by a single mind.[22]

---

reach a verdict of *market failure* and to provide a rationale for government intervention (see note 13 above). For Hayek, by contrast, the fact that agents are not hyperrational is an argument not against individual freedom, but against state planning and social control.

[20]Earlier Hayek (1933b, p. 27) had used "organism" and "organization," borrowed from Mises, to distinguish the two; this is the distinction cited by Coase in his famous 1937 article, "The Nature of the Firm."

[21]On the relationship between the socialist calculation debate and the theory of the firm see chapter 1 above.

[22]For more on spontaneous order see Fehl (1986). Vanberg (1994) argues that Hayek's

Hayek and Austrian economics

Clearly, the Austrian revival owes as much to Hayek as to anyone. But are Hayek's writings really "Austrian economics"—part of a separate, recognizable tradition—or should we regard them, instead, as an original, deeply personal, contribution?[23] Some observers charge that Hayek's later work, particularly after he began to turn away from technical economics, shows more influence of his friend Sir Karl Popper than of Carl Menger or Mises: one critic speaks of "Hayek I" and "Hayek II"; another writes on "Hayek's Transformation."[24]

It is true that Popper had a significant impact on Hayek's mature thought. Of greater interest is the precise nature of Hayek's relationship with Mises. Undoubtedly, no economist has had a greater impact on Hayek's thinking than Mises—not even Wieser, from whom Hayek learned his craft but who died in 1927 when Hayek was still a young man. In addition, Mises clearly considered Hayek the brightest of his generation.[25] Yet, as Hayek (1978) noted, he was from the beginning always something less than a pure follower: "Although I do owe [Mises] a decisive stimulus at a crucial point of my intellectual development, and continuous inspiration through a decade, I have perhaps most profited from his teaching because I was not initially his student at the university, an innocent young man who took his word for gospel, but came to him as a trained economist, versed in a parallel branch of Austrian economics

---

notion of spontaneous order via group selection is incompatible with methodological individualism.

[23]Wieser's have generally been considered a personal contribution, by Hayek himself and others. For a contrary view, see Ekelund (1986).

[24]For Hayeks I and II see Hutchison (1981), pp. 210–19; for the "transformation" see Caldwell (1988). The secondary literature contains some debate about whether Hayek's 1937 article "Economics and Knowledge" represents a decisive break with Mises in favor of a Popperian "falsificationist" approach, one holding that empirical evidence can be used to falsify a theory (though not to "verify" it by induction). For the case that 1937 is a crucial turning point see Hutchison (1981, p. 215) and Caldwell (1988, p. 528); for the reverse see Gray (1984, pp. 16–21) and Garrison and Kirzner (1987, p. 610). Hayek (1992, pp. 55–56; 1994, pp. 72–74) himself supported the former interpretation, maintaining that it was indeed Mises he had hoped to persuade in the 1937 article. If true, Hayek's attempt was remarkably subtle, for Mises apparently welcomed Hayek's argument, unaware that it was directed at him.

[25]Margit von Mises (1984, p. 133) recalls of her husband's seminar in New York that he "met every new student hopeful that one of them might develop into a second Hayek."

[the Wieser branch] from which he gradually, but never completely, won me over."

Much has been written on Hayek's and Mises's views on the socialist calculation debate. The issue is whether a socialist economy is "impossible," as Mises charged in 1920, or simply less efficient or more difficult to implement. Hayek (1992, p. 127) maintained later that Mises's "central thesis was not, as it is sometimes misleadingly put, that socialism is impossible, but that it cannot achieve an efficient utilization of resources." That interpretation is itself subject to dispute. Hayek is arguing here against the standard view on economic calculation, found for instance in Schumpeter (1942, pp. 172–186) or Bergson (1948). This view holds that Mises's original statement of the impossibility of economic calculation under socialism was refuted by Oskar Lange, Fred Taylor, and Abba Lerner, and that later modifications by Hayek and Robbins amounted to an admission that a socialist economy is possible in theory but difficult in practice because knowledge is decentralized and incentives are weak. Hayek's response in the cited text, that Mises's actual position has been exaggerated, receives support from the primary revisionist historian of the calculation debate, Don Lavoie, who states that the "central arguments advanced by Hayek and Robbins did not constitute a 'retreat' from Mises, but rather a clarification directing the challenge to the later versions of central planning.... Although comments by both Hayek and Robbins about computational difficulties of the [later approaches] were responsible for misleading interpretations of their arguments, in fact their main contributions were fully consistent with Mises's challenge" (Lavoie, 1985, p. 20). Kirzner (1988a) similarly contends that Mises's and Hayek's positions should be viewed together as an early attempt to elaborate the Austrian "entrepreneurial-discovery" view of the market process. Salerno (1990a) argues, by contrast, in favor of the traditional view—that Mises's original calculation problem is different from the discovery-process problem emphasized by Lavoie and Kirzner.[26]

Furthermore, Hayek's later emphasis on group selection and spontaneous order is not shared by Mises, although there are elements of this line of thought in Menger. A clue to this difference is in Hayek's (1978)

---

[26] Hayek's writings on socialist economic calculation are collected in Hayek (1997). See Caldwell (1997) for an overview.

statement that "Mises himself was still much more a child of the rationalist tradition of the Enlightenment and of continental, rather than of English, liberalism ... than I am myself." This is a reference to the "two types of liberalism" to which Hayek frequently refers: the continental rationalist or utilitarian tradition, which emphasizes reason and man's ability to shape his surroundings, and the English common-law tradition, which stresses the limits to reason and the "spontaneous" forces of evolution.[27]

Recently, the relationship between Mises and Hayek has become a full-fledged "de-homogenization" debate. Salerno (1990a,b, 1993, 1994a) and Rothbard (1991, 1995) see Hayek's emphasis on knowledge and discovery as substantially different from Mises's emphasis on purposeful human action. Salerno (1993), for example, argues that there are two strands of modern Austrian economics, both descended from Menger. One, the Wieser–Hayek strand, focuses on dispersed knowledge and the price system as a device for communicating knowledge. Another, the Böhm-Bawerk–Mises strand, focuses on monetary calculation (or "appraisal," meaning anticipation of future prices) based on existing money prices. Kirzner (1994, 1995, 1996, 1997) and Yeager (1994, 1995) argue, by contrast, that the differences between Hayek and Mises are more matters of emphasis and language than substance.[28]

---

[27] For more on the complex and subtle Mises–Hayek relationship see Klein (1992, pp. 7–13) and the references cited therein.

[28] Kirzner (1995, p. 1244), for example, writes that Mises's and Hayek's critiques of socialism "are simply different ways of expounding the same basic, Austrian, insight.... To fail to see the common economic understanding shared by Mises and Hayek, is to have been needlessly misled by superficial differences in exposition and emphasis. To compound this failure by perceiving a clash, among modern Austrians, of 'Hayekians' versus 'Misesians,' is to convert an interpretive failure into a *dogmengeschichtliche* nightmare." For more on the de-homogenization debate see Herbener (1991, 1996), Salerno (1994a, 1996b), Hoppe (1996), Boettke (1998), and Yeager (1995). Rothbard (1994, p. 559) identifies three "distinctive and often clashing paradigms within Austrian economics: Misesian praxeology; the Hayek–Kirzner emphasis on the market as transmission of knowledge and coordination of plans—rather than the Misesian emphasis on continuing coordination *of prices*; and the ultra-subjectivism of [Ludwig] Lachmann."

Interestingly, Hayek himself sought to de-homogenize his work from that of free-market thinkers with whom he disagreed methodologically. In an interview in the 1980s he described Milton Friedman as a "logical positivist," who "believe[s] economic phenomena can be explained as macrophenomena, that you can ascertain cause and effects from aggregates and averages [Friedman] is on most things, general market problems, sound. I want him on my side. You know, one of the things I often have publicly said is that one

Regardless, there is widespread agreement that Hayek ranks among the greatest members of the Austrian school, and among the leading economists of the twentieth century. His work continues to be influential in business-cycle theory, comparative economic systems, political and social philosophy, legal theory, and even cognitive psychology. Hayek's writings are not always easy to follow—he describes himself as "puzzler" or "muddler" rather than a "master of his subject"—and this may have contributed to the variety of interpretations his work has aroused.[29] Partly for this reason, Hayek remains one of the most intriguing intellectual figures of our time.

---------------------- ☙ ----------------------

G Williamson and the Austrians[†]

Oliver Williamson's 2009 Nobel Prize, shared with Elinor Ostrom, is great news for Austrians. Williamson's pathbreaking analysis of how alternative organizational forms—markets, hierarchies, and hybrids, as he calls them—emerge, perform, and adapt, has defined the modern field of organizational economics. Williamson is no Austrian, but he is sympathetic to Austrian themes (particularly the Hayekian understanding of tacit knowledge and market competition), his concept of "asset specificity" enhances and extends the Austrian theory of capital, and his theory of firm boundaries has almost single-handedly displaced the benchmark model of perfect competition from important parts of industrial organization and antitrust economics. He is also a pragmatic, careful, and practical economist who is concerned, first and foremost, with real-world economic phenomena,

---

of the things I most regret is not having returned to a criticism of Keynes's treatise, but it is as much true of not having criticized Milton's *[Essays in] Positive Economics*, which in a way is quite as dangerous a book." Quoted in Hayek (1994), pp. 144–45.

[29] On puzzlers and masters of their subjects see Hayek (1975). Along with himself, Hayek named Wieser and Frank Knight as representative puzzlers, and Böhm-Bawerk, Joseph Schumpeter, and Jacob Viner as representative masters of their subjects. As Hayek (1975, p. 51) recalled, "I owed whatever worthwhile new ideas I ever had to not being able to remember what every competent specialist is supposed to have at his fingertips. Whenever I saw a new light on something it was as the result of a painful effort to reconstruct an argument which most competent economists would effortlessly and instantly reproduce."

[†] Published originally on Mises.org, October 14, 2009.

choosing clarity and relevance over formal mathematical elegance. For these and many other reasons, his work deserves careful study by Austrians.

Opening the black box

In economics textbooks, the "firm" is a production function or production possibilities set, a "black box" that transforms inputs into outputs. Given the existing state of technology, the prices of inputs, and a demand schedule, the firm maximizes money profits subject to the constraint that its production plans must be technologically feasible. The firm is modeled as a single actor, facing a series of uncomplicated decisions: what level of output to produce, how much of each factor to hire, and the like. These "decisions," of course, are not really decisions at all; they are trivial mathematical calculations, implicit in the underlying data. In short: the firm is a set of cost curves, and the "theory of the firm" is a calculus problem.

Williamson attacks this conception of the firm, what he calls the "firm-as-production-function" view. Building on Coase's (1937) transaction-cost or "contractual" approach, Williamson argues that the firm is best regarded as a "governance structure," a means of organizing a set of contractual relations among individual agents. The firm, then, consists of an entrepreneur-owner, the tangible assets he owns, and a set of employment relationships—a realistic and thoroughly Austrian view. Williamson emphasizes "asset specificity"—the degree to which resources are specialized to particular trading partners—as the key determinant of the firm's boundaries, defined as the set of transactions that are internal to the firm (or, put differently, the set of assets owned by the entrepreneur). More generally, he holds that entrepreneurs will tend to choose the form of organization—a loose network of small firms, trading in the open market; a franchise network, alliance, or joint-venture; or a large, vertically integrated firm—that best fits the circumstances.

Some Austrians have argued, following Alchian and Demsetz (1972), that Coase and Williamson wrongly claim that firms are not part of the market, that entrepreneurs substitute coercion for voluntary consent, and that corporate hierarchies are somehow inconsistent with the free market (e.g., Ellig and Gable, 1993; Minkler, 1993a; Langlois, 1994a; Mathews, 1998). I think this is a misreading of Coase and of Williamson. It is true that Coase speaks of firms "superseding" the market and entrepreneurs "suppressing" the price mechanism, while Williamson says firms emerge to overcome "market failure." But they do not mean that the firm is out-side the market in some general sense, that the market system as a whole is inefficient relative to government planning, or anything of the sort. Moreover, Williamson does not use the term "market failure" in the usual left-interventionist sense, but means simply that real-world markets are not "perfect" as in the perfectly competitive general-equilibrium model, which explains why firms exist. Indeed, Williamson's work on vertical integration can be read as a celebration of the market. Not only are firms part of the market, broadly conceived, but the variety of organizational forms we observe in markets—including large, vertically integrated enterprises—is a testament to the creativity of entrepreneurs in figuring out the best way to organize production.

What about Williamson's claim that markets, hierarchies, and hybrids are alternative forms of governance? Does he mean that firms and hybrid organizations are not part of the market? No. Coase and Williamson are talking about a completely different issue, namely the distinction between types of contracts or business relationships within the larger market con-text. The issue is simply whether the employment relationship is different from, say, a spot-market trade or a procurement arrangement with an inde-pendent supplier. Alchian and Demsetz (1972) famously argued that there is no essential difference between the two—both are voluntary contrac-tual relationships, there is no "coercion" involved, no power, etc. Coase (1937), Williamson, Herbert Simon (1951), Grossman and Hart (1986), my own work, and most of the modern literature on the firm argues that there are important, qualitative differences. Coase and Simon emphasize "fiat," by which they mean simply that employment contracts are, within limits, open-ended. The employer does not negotiate with the employee about performing task A, B, or C on a given day; he simply instructs him to do it. Of course, the employment contract itself is negotiated on the labor market, just as any contract is negotiated. But, once signed, it is qualita-tively different from a contract that says "independent contractor X will perform task A on day 1." An employment relationship is characterized by what Simon (1951) called the "zone of authority." Williamson emphasizes the legal distinction, namely that disputes between employers and employ-ees are settled differently from disputes between firms, between firms and customers, between firms and independent suppliers or distributors, etc. Grossman and Hart, and my own work with Nicolai Foss, emphasize the distinction between asset owners and non-owners. If I hire you to work with my machine, I hold residual control and income rights to the use of the machine that you do not have, and thus your ability to use the machine as you see fit is limited. If you own your own machine, and I hire you to produce services with that machine, then you (in this case, an independent contractor) hold these residual income and control rights, and this affects many aspects of our relationship.

While Coase, Simon, Hart, and other organizational economists do not draw explicitly on the Austrians, this distinction can also be interpreted in terms of Menger's distinction between *orders* and *organizations*, or Hayek's *cosmos* and *taxis*. Coase and Williamson are simply saying that the firm is a *taxis*, the market a *cosmos*. This does not deny that there are "unplanned" or "spontaneous" aspects of the internal organization of firms, or that there is purpose, reason, the use of monetary calculation, etc., in the market.

Asset specificity and Austrian capital theory

As we have seen in prior chapters, the black-box approach to the firm that dominated neoclassical economics omits the critical organizational details of production. Production is treated as a one-stage process, in which factors are instantly converted into final goods, rather than a complex, multi-stage process unfolding through time and employing rounds of intermediate goods. Capital is treated as a homogeneous factor of production. Williamson, by contrast, emphasizes that resources are heterogeneous, often specialized, and frequently costly to redeploy. What he calls asset specificity refers to "durable investments that are undertaken in support of particular transactions, the opportunity cost of which investments are much lower in best alternative uses or by alternative users should the original transaction be prematurely terminated" (Williamson, 1985, p. 55). This could describe a variety of relationship-specific investments, including both specialized physical and human capital, along with intangibles such as R&D and firm-specific knowledge or capabilities. Like Klein, et al. (1978), Williamson emphasizes the "holdup" problem that can follow such investments, and the role of contractual safeguards in securing the returns (what Klein, et al. call "quasi-rents") to those assets.

Austrian capital theory focuses on a different type of specificity, namely the extent to which resources are specialized to particular places in the time-structure of production. Menger famously characterized goods in terms of "orders": goods of lowest order are those consumed directly. Tools and machines used to produce those consumption goods are of a higher order, and the capital goods used to produce the tools and machines are of an even higher order. Building on his theory that the value of all goods is determined by their ability to satisfy consumer wants (i.e. their marginal utility), Menger showed that the value of the higher-order goods is given or 'imputed' by the value of the lower-order goods they produce. Moreover, because certain capital goods are themselves produced by other, higher-order capital goods, it follows that capital goods are not identical, at least by the time they are employed in the production process. The claim is not that there is no substitution among capital goods, but that the degree of substitution is limited; as Lachmann (1956) put it, capital goods are characterized by "multiple specificity." Some substitution is possible, but only at a cost.

Mises and Hayek used this concept of specificity to develop their theory of the business cycle. Williamson's asset specificity focuses on specialization not to a particular production process, but to a particular set of trading partners. His aim is to explain the business relationship between these partners (arms-length transaction, formal contract, vertical integration, etc.). The Austrians, in other words, focus on assets that are specific to particular uses, while Williamson focuses on assets that are specific to particular users. But there are obvious parallels, and opportunities for gains from trade. Austrian business-cycle theory can be enhanced by considering how vertical integration and long-term supply relations can mitigate, or exacerbate, the effects of credit expansion on the economy's structure of production. Likewise, transaction cost economics can benefit from considering not only the time-structure of production, but also Kirzner's (1966) refinement that defines capital assets in terms of subjective, individual production plans, plans that are formulated and continually revised by profit-seeking entrepreneurs (and Edith Penrose's, 1959, concept of the firm's "subjective opportunity set").

Vertical integration, strategizing, and economizing

The general thrust of Williamson's teaching on vertical integration is not that markets somehow "fail," but that they succeed, in rich, complex, and often unpredictable ways. A basic conclusion of transaction cost economics is that vertical mergers, even when there are no obvious technological synergies, may enhance efficiency by reducing governance costs. Hence Williamson (1985, p. 19) takes issue with what he calls the "inhospitality tradition" in antitrust—namely, that firms engaged in non standard business practices like vertical integration, customer and territorial restrictions, tie ins, franchising, and so on, must be seeking monopoly gains. Indeed, antitrust authorities have become more lenient in evaluating such practices, evaluating them on a case-by-case basis rather than imposing *per se* restrictions on particular forms of conduct. While this change may reflect sensitivity to Chicago School claims that vertical integration and restraints need not reduce competition, rather than to claims that such arrangements provide contractual safeguards (Joskow, 1991, pp. 79–80), the Chicago position on vertical restraints relies largely (though not explicitly) on transaction-cost reasoning (Meese, 1997). In this sense, Williamson's work can be construed as a frontal attack on the perfectly competitive model, particularly when used as a benchmark case for antitrust and regulatory policy.

Likewise, Williamson argues that for managers, "economizing" is the best form of "strategizing." The literature on business strategy, following Porter (1980), has tended to emphasize "market-power" as the source of firm-level competitive advantage. Building directly on the old structure–conduct–performance model of industrial organization, Porter and his followers argued that firms should seek to limit rivalry by enacting entry barriers, forming coalitions, limiting the bargaining power of buyers and suppliers, etc. Williamson challenges this strategic positioning approach in an influential 1991 article, "Strategizing, Economizing, and Economic Organization," Williamson (1991d) where he claims that managers should focus on increasing economic efficiency, by choosing appropriate governance structures, rather than increasing their market power. Here again, moves by firms to integrate, cooperate with upstream and downstream partners, form alliances, and such are not only profitable for the firms, but for consumers as well. Deviations from perfect competition are, in this sense, part of the market process of allocating resources to their highest-valued uses, all to the benefit (as Mises emphasized) of the consumer.

Coda

On a personal level, Williamson is friendly and sympathetic to Austrians and to Austrian concerns. He encourages students to read the Austrians (particularly Hayek, whom he cites often). Williamson chaired my PhD dissertation committee, and one of my first published papers, "Economic Calculation and the Limits of Organization," was originally presented in Williamson's Institutional Analysis Workshop at Berkeley. Williamson did not buy my argument about the distinction between calculation and incentive problems—he maintained (and continues to maintain) that agency costs, not Mises's calculation argument, explain the failure of central planning—but his reactions helped me shape my argument and refined my understanding of the core Misesian and Hayekian literatures. (Also, the great Sovietologist Alec Nove, visiting Berkeley that semester, happened to be in the audience that day, and gave me a number of references and counter-arguments.) Williamson, knowing my interest in the Austrians, once suggested that I write a dissertation on the Ordo School, the influence of Hayek on Eucken and Röpke, and the role of ideas in shaping economic policy. He cautioned me that writing on such a topic would not be an advantage on the job market, but urged me to follow my passions, not to follow the crowd. I ended up writing on more prosaic topics but never forgot that advice, and have passed it along to my own students.

References

Abell, P., Teppo Felin, and Nicolai J. Foss. 2008. "Building microfoundations for the routines, capabilities, and performance links." *Managerial and Decision Economics* 29: 489–502.

Acs, Zoltan J., and D. B. Audretsch. 1990. *Innovation and Small Firms.* Cambridge, MA: MIT Press.

Acs, Zoltan J., and Daniel A. Gerlowski. 1996. *Managerial Economics and Organization.* Englewood Cliffs, N.J.: Prentice-Hall.

Agarwal, Rajshree, Jay B. Barney, Nicolai Foss, and Peter G. Klein. 2009. "Heterogeneous resources and the financial crisis: Implications of strategic management theory." *Strategic Organization* 7: 467–84.

Alchian, Armen A. 1965. "Some economics of property rights." *Il Politico* 30. Reprinted in Alchian, *Economic Forces at Work*. Indianapolis, IN: Liberty Press, 1977.

———. 1969. "Corporate management and property rights." In Henry G. Manne, ed. *Economic Policy and the Regulation of Corporate Securities.* Washington, D.C.: American Enterprise Institute, 1969.

Alchian, Armen A., and Harold Demsetz. 1972. "Production, information costs, and economic organization." *American Economic Review* 62: 777–95.

Aldrich, H. E. 1990. "Using an ecological perspective to study organizational founding rates." *Entrepreneurship Theory and Practice* 14: 7–24.

Aldrich, Howard E., and Gabriele Wiedenmayer. 1993. "From traits to rates: An ecological perspective on organizational foundings." In Jerome A. Katz and Robert H. Brockhaus, eds. *Advances in Entrepreneurship, Firm Emergence, and Growth.* Greenwich, CT: JAI Press, 1993.

Alvarez, Sharon, and Lowell W. Busenitz. 2001. "The entrepreneurship of resource-based theory." *Journal of Management* 27: 755-75.

Alvarez, Sharon A., and Jay B. Barney. 2004. "Organizing rent generation and appropriation: Toward a theory of the entrepreneurial firm." *Journal of Business Venturing* 19: 621–35.

———. 2007. "Discovery and creation: Alternative theories of entrepreneurial action." *Strategic Entrepreneurship Journal* 1: 33–48.

Anderson, Chris. 2006. *The Long Tail: Why the Future of Business Is Selling Less of More.* New York: Hyperion.

Andrade, Gregor, Mark Mitchell, and Erik Stafford. 2001. "New evidence and perspectives on mergers." *Journal of Economic Perspectives* 15: 103–20.

Andrade, Gregor, and Erik Stafford. 2004. "Investigating the economic role of mergers." *Journal of Corporate Finance* 10: 1–36.

Arrow, Kenneth J. 1974. *The Limits of Organization.* New York: W. W. Norton.

Audretsch, D. B., M. Keilbach, and E. Lehmann. 2005. *Entrepreneurship and Economic Growth.* Oxford, UK: Oxford University Press.

Barber, Brad M., Donald Palmer, and James Wallace. 1995. "Determinants of conglomerate and predatory acquisitions: Evidence from the 1960s." *Journal of Corporate Finance* 1: 283–318.

Barney, Jay B. 1986. "Strategic factor markets: Expectations, luck and business strategy." *Management Science* 42: 1231–1241.

———. 1991. "Firm resources and sustained competitive advantage." *Journal of Management* 17: 99–120.

Barone, Enrico. 1908. "The ministry of production in the collectivist state." In F. A. Hayek, ed., *Collectivist Economic Planning.* Clifton, N.J.: Augustus M. Kelley. 1975.

Barzel, Yoram. 1968. "Optimal timing of innovation." *Review of Economic and Statistics* 50: 348–355.

―――. 1987. "The entrepreneur's reward for self-policing." *Economic Inquiry* 25: 103–16.

―――. 1997. *Economic Analysis of Property Rights.* Cambridge: Cambridge University Press.

Bastiat, Frédéric. 1850. *Economic Harmonies.* Irvington-on-Hudson, N.Y.: Foundation for Economic Education. Trans. W. Hayden Boyers. 1996.

Batemarco, Robert. 1985. "Positive economics and praxeology: The clash of prediction and explanation." *Atlantic Economic Journal* 13: 31–37.

Baumol, William J. 1990. "Entrepreneurship: Productive, unproductive, and destructive." *Journal of Political Economy* 98: 893–921.

Begley, T., and D. Boyd. 1987. "Psychological characteristics associated with performance in entrepreneurial firms and smaller businesses." *Journal of Business Venturing* 2: 79–93.

Beilante, Don, and Roger W. Garrison. 1988. "Phillips curves and Hayekian triangles: Two perspectives on monetary dynamics." *History of Political Economy* 20: 207–34.

Benkler, Yochai. 2006. *The Wealth of Networks: How Social Production Transforms Markets and Freedom.* New Haven: Yale University Press.

Berger, Allen N., Rebecca S. Demsetz, and Philip E. Strahan. 1999. "The consolidation of the financial services industry: Causes, consequences, and implications for the future." *Journal of Banking and Finance* 23: 135–94.

Berger, Philip G., and Eli Ofek. 1995. "Diversification's effect on firm value." *Journal of Financial Economics* 37: 39–65.

Bergson, Abram. 1948. "Socialist economics." In Howard S. Ellis, ed., *A Survey of Contemporary Economics.* Vol. 1. Homewood, Ill.: Richard D. Irwin, 1948.

Berle, Adolph A., and Gardiner C. Means. 1932. *The Modern Corporation and Private Property.* New York: Macmillan.

Bernstein, Michael A. 2001. *A Perilous Progress: Economists and Public Purpose in Twentieth-Century America.* Princeton, N.J.: Princeton University Press.

Bernstein, Peter L. 1992. *Capital Ideas: The Improbable Origins of Modern Wall Street.* New York: Free Press.

Besanko, David, David Dranove, and Mark Shanley. 1998. *Economics of Strategy*. New York: Wiley.

Bhagat, Sanjai, Andrei Shleifer, and Robert W. Vishny. 1990. "Hostile takeovers in the 1980s: The return to corporate specialization." *Brookings Papers on Economic Activity: Microeconomics* 1–72.

Bhidé, Amar. 1990. "Reversing corporate diversification." *Journal of Applied Corporate Finance* 3: 70–81.

Bittlingmayer, George. 1996. "Merger as a form of investment." *Kyklos* 49: 127–53.

Black, J. A., and K. E. Boal. 1994. "Strategic resources: Traits, configurations and paths to sustainable competitive advantage." *Strategic Management Journal* 15: 131–48.

Blaug, Mark. 1993. "Hayek revisited." *Critical Review* 7: 51–60.

Boettke, Peter J., ed. 1994. *The Elgar Companion to Austrian Economics*. Aldershot, UK: Edward Elgar.

———. 1998. "Economic calculation: The Austrian contribution to political economy." *Advances in Austrian Economics* 5: 131–58.

———. 2005. "Kirzner?" The Austrian Economists, Sept. 10 2005. URL: http://austrianeconomists.typepad.com/weblog/2005/09/kirzner.html (accessed September 16, 2008)

Boettke, Peter J., and David L. Prychitko, eds. 1994. *The Market Process: Essays in Contemporary Austrian Economics*. Aldershot: Edward Elgar.

Böhm-Bawerk, Eugen von. 1884–1912. *Capital and Interest*. South Holland, Ill: Libertarian Press. 1959.

———. 1889. *Positive Theory of Capital*. Vol. 2 of Böhm-Bawerk, *Capital and Interest*. South Holland, Ill: Libertarian Press. 1959.

Boland, Lawrence A. 1979. "A critique of Friedman's critics." *Journal of Economic Literature* 17: 503–22.

Boot, Arnoud W. A. 1992. "Why hang on to losers? Divestitures and takeovers." *Journal of Finance* 48: 1401–23.

Boot, Arnoud W. A., Todd T. Milbourn, and Anjan V. Thakor. 1999. "Mega-mergers and expanded scope: Theories of bank size and activity diversity." *Journal of Banking and Finance* 23: 195–214.

Boudreaux, Donald J., and Randall G. Holcombe. 1989. "The Coasian and Knightian theories of the firm." *Managerial and Decision Economics* 10: 147–54.

Boulding, Kenneth. 1956. *The Image: Knowledge in Life and Society.* Ann Arbor, MI: University of Michigan Press.

Brickley, James, Clifford W. Smith, and Jerold Zimmerman. 1997. *Managerial Economics and Organizational Architecture.* Chicago: Irwin-McGraw-Hill.

Brousseau, Eric, and Jean-Michel Glachant, eds. 2008. *New Institutional Economics: A Guidebook.* Cambridge: Cambridge University Press.

Buchanan, James, and Alberto Di Pierro. 1980. "Cognition, choice, and entrepreneurship." *Southern Economic Journal* 46: 693–701.

Busenitz, Lowell W. 1996. "Research on Entrepreneurial Alertness." *Journal of Small Business Management* 34: 35–44.

Busenitz, Lowell W., and Jay B. Barney. 1997. "Differences between entrepreneurs and managers in large organizations: Biases and heuristics in strategic decision making." *Journal of Business Venturing* 12: 9–30.

Byrne, John A. 1993. *The "Whiz Kids": Ten Founding Fathers of American Business, and the Legacy They Left Us.* New York, NY: Doubleday.

Caldwell, Bruce J. 1980. "A critique of Friedman's methodological instrumentalism." *Southern Economic Journal* 47: 366–74.

———. 1984. *Appraisal and Criticism in Economics: A Book of Readings.* Boston: Allen and Unwin.

———. 1988. "Hayek's transformation." *History of Political Economy* 20: 513–41.

———, ed. 1990. *Carl Menger and His Legacy in Economics: Annual Supplement to Volume 22: History of Political Economy.* Durham, NC: Duke University Press.

———. 1995. "Introduction." In F. A. Hayek, *Contra Keynes and Cambridge: Essays, Correspondence.* Vol. 9 of *The Collected Works of F. A. Hayek.* Chicago: University of Chicago Press. Bruce Caldwell (ed.)

————. 1997. "Hayek and socialism." *Journal of Economic Literature* 35: 1856–90.

————, ed. 2004. *Hayek's Challenge: An Intellectual Biography of F. A. Hayek.* Chicago: University of Chicago Press.

Cantillon, Richard. 1755. *Essai sur la Nature du Commerce en Général.* London: Macmillan. Henry Higgs (ed.) 1931.

Cantor, Paul. 2001. *Gilligan Unbound: Pop Culture in the Age of Globalization.* Lanham, MD: Rowman and Littlefield.

Cardiff, Christopher and Daniel B. Klein. 2005. "Faculty partisan affiliations in all disciplines: A voter-registration study." *Critical Review* 17: 237–255.

Casson, M. C. 1982. *The Entrepreneur: An Economic Theory.* Oxford: Martin Robertson.

————. 1993. "Entrepreneurship." In David H. Henderson, ed., *The Fortune Encyclopedia of Economics.* New York: Warner Books.

————. 1997. *Information and Organization.* Oxford: Oxford University Press.

————. 2000. "An entrepreneurial theory of the firm." In Nicolai J. Foss and Volke Mahnke, eds., *Competence, Governance and Entrepreneurship: Advances in Economic Strategy Research.* New York: Oxford University Press.

Casson, Mark C., and Nigel Wadeson. 2007. "The discovery of opportunities: Extending the economic theory of the entrepreneur." *Small Business Economics* 28: 285–300.

Chambers, Molly L. 2007. "Organizational spawning: Investment in farmer-controlled businesses." Ph.D. diss., University of Missouri, Columbia, MO.

Chandler, Alfred D., Jr. 1977. *The Visible Hand: The Managerial Revolution in American Business.* Cambridge, Mass.: Harvard University Press.

Chandler, Gaylen N., and Erik Jansen. 1992. "The founder's self-assessed competence and venture performance." *Journal of Business Venturing* 7: 223–36.

Chiles, Todd H. 2003. "Process theorizing: Too important to ignore in a kaleidic world." *Academy of Management Learning & Education* 2: 288–91.

Chiles, Todd H., Allen C. Bluedorn, and Vishal K. Gupta. 2007. "Beyond creative destruction and entrepreneurial discovery: a radical Austrian approach to entrepreneurship." *Organization Studies* 28: 467–93.

Chiles, Todd H., and Thomas Y. Choi. 2000. "Theorizing TQM: an Austrian and evolutionary economics interpretation." *Journal of Management Studies* 37: 185–212.

Chiles, Todd H., Allen D. Meyer, and Todd J. Hench. 2004. "Organizational emergence: the origin and transformation of Branson, Missouri's musical theaters." *Organization Science* 15: 499–519.

Chiles, Todd H., and T. G. Zarankin. 2005. "A 'kaleidic' view of entrepreneurship: Developing and grounding radical Austrian economics' master metaphor." Working Paper. Department of Management, University of Missouri.

Clark, John Bates. 1899. *The Distribution of Wealth: A Theory of Wages Interest and Profits*. New York: Macmillan.

———. 1907. *Essentials of Economic Theory*. New York: Macmillan.

Coase, Ronald H. 1937. "The nature of the firm." *Economica* NS 4: 386–405.

———. 1960. "The problem of social cost." *Journal of Law and Economics* 3: 1–44.

———. 1972. "Industrial organization: A proposal for research." In Coase, *The Firm, The Market, and the Law*. Chicago: University of Chicago Press. 1988.

———. 1988. *The Firm, The Market, and the Law*. Chicago: University of Chicago Press.

———. 1991. "The institutional structure of production." *American Economic Review* 82: 713–19.

Coats, A. W. 1960. "The first two decades of the American Economic Association." *American Economic Review* 50: 555–74.

Comment, Robert, and Gregg A. Jarrell. 1995. "Corporate focus and stock returns." *Journal of Financial Economics* 37: 67–87.

Companys, Yosem, and Jeffrey S. McMullen. 2007. "Strategic entrepreneurs at work: the nature, discovery, and exploitation of entrepreneurial opportunities." *Small Business Economics* 28: 301–322.

Cook, Michael L. 1995. "The future of U.S. Agricultural cooperatives: a neo-institutional approach." *American Journal of Agricultural Economics* 77: 1153–59.

Cook, Michael L., Molly J. Burress, and Peter G. Klein. 2008. "The clustering of organizational innovation: Developing governance models for vertical integration." *International Food and Agribusiness Management Review* 11: 49–75.

Cook, Michael L., and Fabio R. Chaddad. 2004. "Redesigning cooperative boundaries: the emergence of new models." *American Journal of Agricultural Economics* 86: 1249–53.

Cook, Michael L., and C. Iliopoulos. 2000. "Ill-defined property rights in collective action: the case of U.S. Agricultural cooperatives." In Claude Ménard, ed., *Institutions, Contracts and Organizations*. Cheltenham, UK: Edward Elgar.

Cook, Michael L., and Bradley Plunkett. 2006. "Collective entrepreneurship: an emerging phenomenon in producer-owned organizations." *Journal of Agricultural and Applied Economics* 38: 421–28.

Cooper, Arnold C., Timothy B. Folta, and Yoon S. Baik, "Entrepreneurial Information Search." *Journal of Business Venturing* 10: 107–20.

Cowen, Tyler. 1998. *In Praise of Commercial Culture*. Cambridge, Mass: Harvard University Press.

Cowen, Tyler and Richard Fink. 1985. "Inconsistent equilibrium constructs: The evenly rotating economy of Mises and Rothbard." *American Economic Review* 75: 866–69.

Crane, Diana. 1972. *Invisible Colleges: Diffusion of Knowledge in Scientific Communities*. Chicago: University of Chicago Press.

Craver, Earlene. 1986. "The emigration of the Austrian economists." *History of Political Economy* 18: 1–32.

Crocker, Keith J., and Scott E. Masten. 1991. "Pretia ex machina? Prices and process in long-term contracts." *Journal of Law and Economics* 34: 69–99.

Crocker, Keith J., and K. J. Reynolds. 1993. "The efficiency of incomplete contracts: an empirical analysis of Air Force engine procurement." *Rand Journal of Economics* 36: 126–46.

Dane, Erik, and Michael G. Pratt. 2007. "Exploring intuition and its role in managerial decision making." *Academy of Management Review* 32: 33–54.

Dasgupta, Partha and Joseph E. Stiglitz. 1980. "Industrial structure and the nature of innovative activity." *Economic Journal* 90: 266–93.

Davis, Lance E., and Douglass C. North. 1971. *Institutional Change and American Economic Growth*. Cambridge: Cambridge University Press.

De Marchi, Neil, ed. 1988. *The Popperian Legacy in Economics*. Cambridge: Cambridge University Press.

De Vroey, Michel. 2002. "Equilibrium and disequilibrium in Walrasian and neo-Walrasian economics." *Journal of the History of Economic Thought* 24: 405–22.

Demsetz, Harold. 1964. "The exchange and enforcement of property rights." *Journal of Law and Economics* 7: 11–26.

―――. 1967. "Toward a theory of property rights." *American Economic Review* 57: 347–59.

―――. 1983. "The neglect of the entrepreneur." In Joshua Ronen, ed., *Entrepreneurship*. Lexington, MA: Lexington Press.

―――. 1988a. "Profit as a functional return: Reconsidering Knight's views." In Demsetz, *Ownership, Control and the Firm: The Organization of Economic Activity*. Oxford and New York: Basil Blackwell.

―――. 1988b. "The nature of the firm revisited." *Journal of Law, Economics, and Organization* 4: 141–62.

―――. 1991. "The theory of the firm revisited." In Oliver E. Williamson and Sidney G. Winter, eds., *The Nature of the Firm*. Oxford: Blackwell, 1993.

Dickinson, Henry Douglas. 1933. "Price formation in a socialist community." *Economic Journal* 43: 237–50.

Dierickx, Ingemar, and Karel Cool. 1989. "Asset stock accumulation and sustainability of competitive advantage." *Management Science* 35: 1505–11.

Dolan, Edwin G., ed. 1976. *The Foundations of Modern Austrian Economics*. Kansas City: Sheed and Ward.

Earl, Peter E. 2003. "The entrepreneur as a constructor of connections." *Advances in Austrian Economics* 6: 113–30.

Eatwell, John, Murray Milgate, and Peter Newman, eds. 1998. *The New Palgrave Dictionary of Law and Economics*. London: Macmillan.

Eccles, Robert, and Harrison White. 1988. "Price and authority in inter-profit center transactions." *American Journal of Sociology* 94: S17–48.

Ekelund, Robert B. 1986. "Wieser's social economics: A link to modern Austrian theory." *Austrian Economics Newsletter* 6: 4, 9–11.

––––––. 1997. "Review of Vaughn, Austrian Economics in America." *Review of Austrian Economics* 10: 133–38.

Ekelund, R. B., Jr and D. S. Saurman. 1988. *Advertising and the Market Process: A Modern Economic View*. San Francisco: Pacific Research Institute for Public Policy Research.

Ellig, Jerry. 1993. "Internal pricing for corporate services." Working Paper. Center for the Study of Market Processes, George Mason University.

Ellig, Jerry and Wayne Gable. 1993. *Introduction to Market-Based Management*. Fairfax, Va.: Center for Market Processes.

Ericson, Richard E. 1991. "The classical soviet-type economy: Nature of the system and implications for reform." *Journal of Economic Perspectives* 5: 11–27.

Fama, Eugene F. 1980. "Agency problems and the theory of the firm." *Journal of Political Economy* 88: 288–307.

Fama, Eugene F., and Michael C. Jensen. 1983. "Separation of ownership and control." *Journal of Law and Economics* 26: 301–26.

Farrell, Joseph and Patrick Bolton. 1990. "Decentralization, duplication, and delay." *Journal of Political Economy* 98: 803–26.

Fehl, Ulrich. 1986. "Spontaneous order and the subjectivity of expectations: A contribution to the Lachmann–O'Driscoll problem." In Israel M. Kirzner, ed., *Subjectivism, Intelligibility, and Economic Understanding*. New York: New York University Press.

Finetti, Bruno de. 1937. "Foresight: Its logical laws, its subjective sources." In Henry E. Kyburg and Howard E. Smokier, eds., *Studies in Subjective Probability*. New York: Wiley, 1964.

Fisher, Franklin M. 1983. *Disequilibrium Foundations of Equilibrium Economics*. Cambridge: Cambridge University Press.

Fisman, Raymond, and Rakesh Khurana. 2008. "The Marie Antoinettes of corporate America." *Forbes* 12 (December).

Foss, Kirsten, and Nicolai J. Foss. 2001. "Assets, attributes and ownership." *International Journal of the Economics of Business* 8: 19–37.

————. 2002. "Economic organization and the tradeoffs between productive and destructive entrepreneurship." In Nicolai J. Foss and Peter G. Klein, eds., *Entrepreneurship and the Firm: Austrian Perspectives on Economic Organization.* Aldershot: Edward Elgar.

————. 2005. "Transaction costs and value: How property rights economics furthers the resource-based view." *Strategic Management Journal* 26: 541–53.

Foss, Kirsten, Nicolai J. Foss, and Peter G. Klein. 2007a. "Original and derived judgment: an entrepreneurial theory of economic organization." *Organization Studies* 28: 1893–1912.

Foss, Kirsten, Nicolai J. Foss, Peter G. Klein, and Sandra K. Klein. 2007b. "The entrepreneurial organization of heterogeneous capital." *Journal of Management Studies* 44: 1165–86.

Foss, Nicolai J. 1993a. "More on Knight and the theory of the firm." *Managerial and Decision Economics* 14: 269–76.

————. 1993b. "Theories of the firm: Contractual and competence perspectives." *Journal of Evolutionary Economics* 3: 127–44.

————. 1993c. "The two Coasian traditions." *Review of Political Economy* 4: 508–32.

————. 1994a. "The theory of the firm: The Austrians as precursors and critics of contemporary theory." *Review of Austrian Economics* 7: 31–65.

————. 1994b. *The Austrian School and Modern Economics: A Reassessment.* Copenhagen: Handelshøjskolens Forlag.

Foss, Nicolai J., and Peter G. Klein. 2005. "Entrepreneurship and the economic theory of the firm: Any gains from trade?" In Rajshree Agarwal, Sharon A. Alvarez, and Olav Sorenson, eds., *Handbook of Entrepreneurship: Disciplinary Perspectives.* Norwell, Mass: Kluwer.

————. 2010. "Austrian economics and the theory of the firm." In Peter G. Klein and Michael E. Sykuta, eds., *The Elgar Companion to Transaction Cost Economics.* Aldershot, UK: Edward Elgar.

Foss, Nicolai J., and Peter G. Klein, eds. 2002. *Entrepreneurship and the Firm: Austrian Perspectives on Economic Organization.* Aldershot, UK: Edward Elgar.

Foss, Nicolai J., Peter G. Klein, Yasemin Y. Kor, and Joseph T. Mahoney. 2008. "Entrepreneurship, subjectivism, and the resource-based view: Towards a new synthesis." *Strategic Entrepreneurship Journal* 2: 13–94.

Foss, Nicolai J., and Volker Mahnke. 2000. "Strategy and the market process perspective." In Jackie Krafft, ed., *The Process of Competition*. Aldershot: Edward Elgar.

Friedman, Milton, and Leonard Savage. 1948. "Utility analysis of choices involving risk." *Journal of Political Economy* 56: 279–304.

Friedman, Milton M. 1953. "The methodology of positive economics." In Friedman, *Essays in Positive Economics*. Chicago: University of Chicago Press.

Furubotn, Eirik, and Rudolf Richter. 1997. *Institutions and Economic Theory: The Contribution of the New Institutional Economics*. Ann Arbor: University of Michigan Press.

Gabor, André. 1984. "On the theory and practice of transfer pricing." In A. Ingham and Alistair M. Ulph, eds., *Demand, Equilibrium, and Trade: Essays in Honor of Ivor F. Pearce*. New York: St. Martin's Press.

Gabor, André, and Ivor F. Pearce. 1952. "A new approach to the theory of the firm." *Oxford Economic Papers* 4: 252–65.

———. 1958. "The place of money capital in the theory of production." *Quarterly Journal of Economics* 72: 537–57.

Gaglio, M., and J. A. Katz. 2001. "The psychological basis of opportunity identification: Entrepreneurial alertness." *Small Business Economics* 16: 95–111.

Galloway, L. 1996. *Operations Management: The Basics*. London: International Thomson Business Press.

Garrison, Roger W. 1978. "Austrian macroeconomics: A diagrammatical exposition." In Louis M. Spadaro, ed., *New Directions in Austrian Economics*. Kansas City, Mo.: Sheed Andrews and McMeel.

———. 2000. *Time and Money: The Macroeconomics of Capital Structure*. London: Routledge.

Garrison, Roger W., and Israel M. Kirzner. 1987. "Hayek, Friedrich August von." In John Eatwell, Murray Milgate, and Peter Newman, eds., *The New Palgrave Dictionary of Law and Economics*. London: Macmillan. 1998.

Gaver, Jennifer J., and Kenneth M. Gaver. 1993. "Additional evidence on the association between the investment opportunity set and corporate financing, dividend, and compensation policies." *Journal of Accounting and Economics* 16: 125–60.

Gertner, Robert H., David S. Scharfstein, and Jeremy C. Stein. 1994. "Internal versus external capital markets." *Quarterly Journal of Economics* 109: 1211–30.

Ghoshal, Sumantra. 2005. "Bad management theories are destroying good management practices." *Academy of Management Learning and Education* 4: 75–91.

Ghoshal, Sumantra, and Peter Moran. 1996. "Bad for practice: A critique of the transaction cost theory." *Academy of Management Review* 21: 13–47.

Gilson, Ronald J. 1996. "Corporate governance and economic efficiency: When do institutions matter?" *Washington University Law Quarterly* 74: 327–45.

Gilson, Ronald J., and Bernard S. Black. 1998. "Venture capital and the structure of capital markets: Banks versus stock markets." *Journal of Financial Economics* 47: 243–77

Goldberg, Victor. 1980. "Relational exchange: Economics and complex contracts." *American Behavioral Scientist* 23: 337–52.

Gompers, Paul A. 1995. "Optimal investment, monitoring, and the staging of venture capital." *Journal of Finance* 50: 1461–89.

Gordon, David. 1995. "Review of Vaughn, Austrian Economics in America." *Mises Review* 1: 19–25.

Grant, Robert M. 1996. "Prospering in dynamically-competitive environments: Organizational capability as knowledge integration." *Organization Science* 7: 375–87.

Gray, Alexander. 1946. *The Socialist Tradition: Moses to Lenin.* London: Longmans, Green.

Gray, John. 1984. *Hayek on Liberty.* Second edition, Oxford: Basil Blackwell, 1986.

Greve, Arent, and Janet W. Salaff. 2003. "Social networks and entrepreneurship." *Entrepreneurship Theory and Practice* 28: 1–22.

Grossman, Sanford J. 1980. "On the impossibility of informational efficient markets." *American Economic Review* 70: 393–408.

———. 1989. *The Informational Role of Prices.* Cambridge, Mass., and London: MIT Press.

Grossman, Sanford J., and Oliver D. Hart. 1986. "The costs and benefits of ownership: A theory of vertical and lateral integration." *Journal of Political Economy* 94: 691–719.

Grossman, Sanford J., and Joseph E. Stiglitz. 1976. "Information and competitive price systems." *American Economic Review* 66: 246–53.

Gul, Faruk and Wolfgang Pesendorfer. 2005. "The case for mindless economics." Working paper. Department of Economics, Princeton University.

Gunning, J. Patrick. 1989. "Mises on the evenly rotating economy." *Review of Austrian Economics* 3: 123–35.

Hamilton, Barton H. 2000. "Does entrepreneurship pay? An empirical analysis of the returns to self-employment." *Journal of Political Economy* 108: 604–31.

Hansmann, H. 1996. *The Ownership of Enterprise.* Cambridge, Mass.: Harvard University Press.

Harper, David. 1995. *Entrepreneurship and the Market Process: An Inquiry into the Growth of Knowledge.* London: Routledge.

Hart, Oliver. 1995. *Firms, Contracts and Financial Structure.* Oxford: Clarendon Press.

Hart, Oliver D., and John Moore. 1990. "Property rights and the nature of the firm." *Journal of Political Economy* 98: 1119–58.

Hauben, Michael, and Ronda Hauben. 1995. *Netizens: On the History and Impact of Usenet and the Internet.* At `http://www.columbia.edu/~rh120/` (accessed March 25, 2010).

Hauwe, Ludwig van den. 2007. "John Maynard Keynes and Ludwig von Mises on probability." *MPRA* Paper No. 6965.

Hayek, F. A. 1931. *Prices and Production.* Second revised edition, London: Routledge and Kegan Paul, 1935.

————. 1933a. "Socialist calculation." In Hayek, ed., *Collectivist Economic Planning.* Clifton, N.J.: Augustus M. Kelley. 1975.

————. 1933b. *Monetary Theory and the Trade Cycle.* London: Jonathan Cape.

————. 1933c. "The trend of economic thinking." In Hayek, *The Trend of Economic Thinking: Essays on Political Economists and Economic History.* Vol. 3 of *The Collected Works of F. A. Hayek.* Chicago: University of Chicago Press, 1991. W. W. Bartley III and Stephen Kresge (eds.)

———. 1934. "Carl Menger (1840–1921)." In Hayek, *The Fortunes of Liberalism: Essays on Austrian Economics and the Ideal of Freedom*. Vol. 4 of *The Collected Works of F. A. Hayek*. Chicago: University of Chicago Press. Peter G. Klein (ed.)

———, ed. 1935. *Collectivist Economic Planning*. Clifton, N.J.: Augustus M. Kelley. 1975.

———. 1937. "Economics and knowledge." *Economica* NS 4: 33–54.

———. 1939a. "Review of John Bates Clark: A memorial." In Hayek, *The Fortunes of Liberalism: Essays on Austrian Economics and the Ideal of Freedom*. Vol. 4 of *The Collected Works of F. A. Hayek*. Chicago: University of Chicago Press. Peter G. Klein (ed.)

———. 1939b. "Price expectations, monetary disturbances, and malinvestments." In Hayek, *Profits, Interest, and Investment*. London: Routledge and Kegan Paul.

———. 1940. "The competitive solution." In Hayek, *Individualism and Economic Order*. Chicago: University of Chicago Press. 1948.

———. 1941. *The Pure Theory of Capital*. Chicago: University of Chicago Press.

———. 1944. *The Road to Serfdom*. Chicago: University of Chicago Press.

———. 1945. "The use of knowledge in society." *American Economic Review* 35: 519–30.

———. 1946. "The meaning of competition." In Hayek, *Individualism and Economic Order*. Chicago: University of Chicago Press. 1948.

———. 1948. *Individualism and Economic Order*. Chicago: University of Chicago Press.

———. 1952a. *The Counter-Revolution of Science: Studies on the Abuse of Reason*. Glencoe, Ill.: The Free Press.

———. 1952b. *The Sensory Order*. Chicago: University of Chicago Press.

———. 1956. "In honour of Professor Mises." In Hayek, *The Fortunes of Liberalism: Essays on Austrian Economics and the Ideal of Freedom*. Vol. 4 of *The Collected Works of F. A. Hayek*. Chicago: University of Chicago Press. Peter G. Klein (ed.)

———. 1960. *The Constitution of Liberty*. Chicago: University of Chicago Press.

————. 1963a. "The economics of the 1920s as seen from Vienna." In Hayek, *The Fortunes of Liberalism: Essays on Austrian Economics and the Ideal of Freedom.* Vol. 4 of *The Collected Works of F. A. Hayek.* Chicago: University of Chicago Press. Peter G. Klein (ed.)

————. 1963b. "The economics of the 1930s as seen from London." In F. A. Hayek, *Contra Keynes and Cambridge: Essays, Correspondence.* Vol. 9 of *The Collected Works of F. A. Hayek.* Chicago: University of Chicago Press. Bruce Caldwell (ed.)

————. 1966. "Personal recollections of Keynes and the 'Keynesian revolution.'" In F. A. Hayek, *Contra Keynes and Cambridge: Essays, Correspondence.* Vol. 9 of *The Collected Works of F. A. Hayek.* Chicago: University of Chicago Press. Bruce Caldwell (ed.)

————. 1968a. "The Austrian school of economics." In Hayek, *The Fortunes of Liberalism: Essays on Austrian Economics and the Ideal of Freedom.* Vol. 4 of *The Collected Works of F. A. Hayek.* Chicago: University of Chicago Press. Peter G. Klein (ed.)

————. 1968b. "Competition as a discovery procedure." *Quarterly Journal of Austrian Economics* 5: 9–23. Translated by Marcellus S. Snow.

————. 1968c. "The confusion of language in political thought." In Hayek, *New Studies in Philosophy, Politics and Economics.* Chicago: University of Chicago Press, 1978.

————. 1973–79. *Law, Legislation, and Liberty.* Chicago: University of Chicago Press. Three volumes.

————. 1975. "Two types of mind." In Hayek, *The Trend of Economic Thinking: Essays on Political Economists and Economic History.* Vol. 3 of *The Collected Works of F. A. Hayek.* Chicago: University of Chicago Press, 1991. W. W. Bartley III and Stephen Kresge (eds.)

————. 1976. *Denationalisation of Money : An Analysis of the Theory and Practice of Concurrent Currencies.* London: Institute of Economic Affairs.

————. 1978. "Coping with ignorance." *Imprimis* 7: 1–6.

————. 1989. *The Fatal Conceit: The Errors of Socialism.* Vol. 1 of *The Collected Works of F. A. Hayek.* Chicago: University of Chicago Press. W. W. Bartley III (ed.)

———. 1992. *The Fortunes of Liberalism: Essays on Austrian Economics and the Ideal of Freedom.* Vol. 4 of *The Collected Works of F. A. Hayek.* Chicago: University of Chicago Press. Peter G. Klein (ed.)

———. 1994. *Hayek on Hayek: An Autobiographical Dialogue.* Chicago: University of Chicago Press. Stephen Kresge and Leif Wenar (eds.)

———. 1997. *Socialism and War: Essays, Documents, Reviews.* Vol. 10 of *The Collected Works of F. A. Hayek.* Chicago: University of Chicago Press. Bruce Caldwell (ed.)

———. 2008. *Prices and Production and Other Works on Money, the Business Cycle, and the Gold Standard.* Auburn, Ala.: Ludwig von Mises Institute. Joseph T. Salerno (ed.)

Heide, Jan B., and George John. 1988. "The role of dependence balancing in safeguarding transaction-specific assets." *Journal of Marketing* 52: 20–35.

Heilbroner, Robert L. 1970. *Between Capitalism and Socialism: Essays in Political Economics.* New York: Random House.

———. 1990. "Reflections after communism." *The New Yorker*: 91–100.

Herbener, Jeffrey M. 1991. "Ludwig von Mises and the Austrian school of economics." *Review of Austrian Economics* 5: 33–50.

———. 1996. "Calculation and the question of arithmetic." *Review of Austrian Economics* 9: 151–62.

Hicks, John R. 1939. *Value and Capital: An Inquiry into Some Fundamental Principles of Economic Theory.* Oxford: Clarendon Press. 1946.

———. 1967. *Critical Essays in Monetary Theory.* Oxford: Clarendon Press.

High, Jack C. 1980. "Maximizing, action, and market adjustment: An inquiry into the theory of economic disequilibrium." Ph.D. diss., University of California, Los Angeles, Department of Economics.

———. 1982. "Alertness and judgment: Comment on Kirzner." In Israel Kirzner, ed., *Method, Process, and Austrian Economics: Essays in Honor of Ludwig von Mises.* Lexington, Mass: D. C. Heath.

———. 1986. "Equilibrium and disequilibrium in the market process." In Israel Kirzner, ed., *Subjectivism, Intelligibility, and Economic Understanding.* New York: New York University Press.

Hill, Charles W. L., and David L. Deeds. 1996. "The importance of industry structure for the determination of firm profitability: a neo-Austrian perspective." *Journal of Management Studies* 33: 429–51.

Hills, Gerald E., G. T. Lumpkin, and Robert P. Singh. 1997. "Opportunity recognition: Perceptions and behaviors of entrepreneurs." *Frontiers of Entrepreneurship Research* 17: 168–82.

Hindle, K. 2004. "A practical strategy for discovering, evaluating, and exploiting entrepreneurial opportunities: Research-based action guidelines." *Journal of Small Business and Entrepreneurship* 17: 267–76.

Hirshleifer, Jack. 1956. "On the economics of transfer pricing." *Journal of Business* 29: 172–89.

Hite, Gailen L., James E. Owens, and Ronald C. Rogers. 1987. "The market for interfirm asset sales: Partial sell-offs and total liquidations." *Journal of Financial Economics* 18: 229–52.

Hoff, Trygve J. B. 1949. *Economic Calculation in the Socialist Society.* Indianapolis: Liberty Press. 1981.

Holcombe, Randall G. 2002. "Political entrepreneurship and the democratic allocation of economic resources." *Review of Austrian Economics* 15: 143–59.

Holmström, Bengt R. 1982. "Moral hazard in teams." *Bell Journal of Economics* 13: 324–40.

Holmström, Bengt R., and Jean Tirole. 1989. "The theory of the firm." In Richard Schmalensee and Robert D. Willig, eds., *Handbook of Industrial Organization.* Vol. 1. Amsterdam: North-Holland, 1989.

Hood, Jacqueline N., and John E. Young. 1993. "Entrepreneurship's areas of development: a survey of top executives in successful firms." *Journal of Business Venturing* 8: 115–35.

Hoppe, Hans-Hermann. 1996. "Socialism: A property or knowledge problem?" *Review of Austrian Economics* 9: 143–49.

———. 2007. "The limits of numerical probability: Frank H. Knight and Ludwig von Mises and the frequency interpretation." *Quarterly Journal of Austrian Economics* 10: 1–20.

Hubbard, R. Glenn, and Darius A. Palia. 1999. "A reexamination of the conglomerate merger wave in the 1960s: An internal capital markets view." *Journal of Finance* 54: 1131–52.

Hülsmann, Jörg Guido. 1997. "Knowledge, judgment, and the use of property." *Review of Austrian Economics* 10: 23–48.

———. 2000. "A realist approach to equilibrium analysis." *Quarterly Journal of Austrian Economics* 3: 3–51.

———. 2007. *Mises: The Last Knight of Liberalism.* Auburn, Ala.: Ludwig von Mises Institute.

Hülsmann, Jörg Guido, and Stephan Kinsella, eds. 2009. *Property, Freedom, and Society: Essays in Honor of Hans-Hermann Hoppe.* Auburn, Ala.: Ludwig von Mises Institute.

Hutchison, Terence W. 1981. "Austrians on philosophy and method (since Menger)." In Hutchison, *The Politics and Philosophy of Economics: Marxians, Keynesians and Austrians.* New York and London: New York University Press.

Jacobson, Robert. 1992. "The 'Austrian' school of strategy." *Academy of Management Review* 17: 782–807.

Jarrell, Gregg A., James A. Brickley, and Jeffry M. Netter. 1988. "The market for corporate control: the empirical evidence since 1980." *Journal of Economic Perspectives* 2: 49–68.

Jensen, Michael C. 1986. "Agency costs of free cash flow, corporate finance, and takeovers." *American Economic Review* 76: 323–29.

———. 1989. "Eclipse of the public corporation." *Harvard Business Review*: 61–74.

———. 1991. "Corporate control and the politics of finance." *Journal of Applied Corporate Finance* 6: 13–33.

———. 1993. "The modern industrial revolution, exit, and the failure of internal control systems." *Journal of Finance* 48: 831–80.

Jensen, Michael C., and William Meckling. 1976. "Theory of the firm: Managerial behavior, agency costs, and capital structure." *Journal of Financial Economics* 3: 305–60.

———. 1992. "Specific and general knowledge, and organizational structure." In Lars Werin and Hans Wijkander, eds., *Contract Economics.* Oxford: Blackwell.

Jensen, Michael C., and Richard S. Ruback. 1983. "The market for corporate control: The scientific evidence." *Journal of Financial Economics* 11: 5–50.

Jensen, Michael C., and Karen Wruck. 1994. "Science, specific knowledge and total quality management." *Journal of Accounting and Economics* 18: 247–87.

John, Kose and Eli Ofek. 1995. "Asset sales and increase in focus." *Journal of Financial Economics* 37: 105–26.

Joskow, Paul L. 1985. "Vertical integration and long-term contracts: The case of coal-burning electric generating plants." *Journal of Law, Economics, and Organization* 1: 33–80.

———. 1987. "Contract duration and relationship-specific investments: Empirical evidence from coal markets." *American Economic Review* 77: 168–85.

———. 1988. "Price adjustment in long-term contracts: The case of coal." *Journal of Law and Economics* 31: 47–83.

———. 1990. "The performance of long-term contracts: Further evidence from the coal markets." *Rand Journal of Economics* 21: 251–74.

———. 1991. "The role of transaction cost economics in antitrust and public utility regulatory policies." *Journal of Law, Economics, and Organization* 7: 53–83.

Judd, Kenneth L., Karl Schmedders, and Sevin Yeltekin. 2003. "Optimal rules for patent races." CMS-EMS discussion paper 1343. Northwestern University.

Kaish, Stanley, and Benjamin Gilad. 1991. "Characteristics of opportunities search of entrepreneurs versus executives: Sources, interest, general alertness." *Journal of Business Venturing* 6: 45–61.

Kaplan, S. N., and P. Strömberg. 2003. "Financial contracting theory meets the real world: an empirical analysis of venture capital contracts." *Review of Economic Studies* 70: 281–315.

Kaplan, Steven N., and Michael S. Weisbach. 1992. "The success of acquisitions: Evidence from divestitures." *Journal of Finance* 47: 107–38.

Keynes, John Maynard. 1921. *A Treatise on Probability*. London: Macmillan.

Kihlstrom, R. E., and J. J. Laffont. 1979. "A general equilibrium entrepreneurial theory of firm formation based on risk aversion." *Journal of Political Economy* 87: 719–48.

Kim, Jongwook, and Joseph T. Mahoney. 2002. "Resource-based and property rights perspectives on value creation: the case of oil field unitization." *Managerial and Decision Economics* 23: 225–45.

———. 2005. "Property rights theory, transaction costs theory, and agency theory: an organizational economics approach to strategic management." *Managerial and Decision Economics* 26: 223–42.

King, Elizabeth A. 1994. *Transfer Pricing and Valuation in Corporate Taxation: Federal Legislation vs Administrative Practice.* Boston: Kluwer Academic Publishers.

Kirzner, Israel M. 1963. *Market Theory and the Price System.* Princeton N.J.: D. Van Nostrand.

———. 1966. *An Essay on Capital.* New York: Augustus M. Kelley.

———. 1973. *Competition and Entrepreneurship.* Chicago: University of Chicago Press.

———. 1979. *Perception, Opportunity, and Profit: Studies in the Theory of Entrepreneurship.* Chicago and London: University of Chicago Press. 1983.

———. 1985a. "The perils of regulation." In Kirzner, *Discovery and the Capitalist Process.* Chicago: University of Chicago Press. 1985.

———. 1985b. *Discovery and the Capitalist Process.* Chicago: University of Chicago Press.

———. 1988a. "The economic calculation debate: Lessons for Austrians." *Review of Austrian Economics* 2: 1–18.

———. 1988b. "Welfare economics: A modern Austrian perspective." In Walter Block and Llewellyn H. Rockwell, Jr., eds., *Man, Economy and Liberty: Essays in Honor of Murray N. Rothbard.* Auburn, Ala: Ludwig von Mises Institute.

———. 1992. *The Meaning of Market Process.* London: Routledge.

———. 1994. "Introduction" in Kirzner, ed., *Classics in Austrian Economics: A Sampling in the History of a Tradition.* London: William Pickering.

———. 1995. "Review of Jack Birner and Rudy van Zijp, Hayek, co-ordination, and evolution." *Southern Economic Journal* 61: 1243–44.

———. 1996. "Reflections on the Misesian legacy in economics." *Review of Austrian Economics* 9: 143–54.

———. 1997. "Entrepreneurial discovery and the competitive market process: An Austrian approach." *Journal of Economic Literature* 35: 60–85.

———. 1999. "Mises and his understanding of the capitalist system." *Cato Journal* 19: 215–32.

———. 2000. "Hedgehog or fox? Hayek and the idea of plan-coordination." In Kirzner, *The Driving Force of the Market Economy: Essays in Austrian Economics*. London: Routledge.

Klein, Benjamin, Robert A. Crawford, and Armen A. Alchian. 1978. "Vertical integration, appropriable rents, and the competitive contracting process." *Journal of Law and Economics* 21: 297–326.

Klein, Daniel B. 1997. "Convention, social order, and the two coordinations." *Constitutional Political Economy* 8: 319–335.

———. 2008. "Toward a public and professional identity for our economics." *Econ Journal Watch* 5: 358–372.

Klein, Daniel B., and Aaron Orsborn. 2009. "Concatenate coordination and mutual coordination." *Journal of Economic Behavior and Organization* 72: 176–87.

Klein, Daniel B., and Charlotta Stern. 2006. "Economists' policy views and voting." *Public Choice* 126: 331–42.

Klein, Peter G. 1992. "Introduction" in Hayek, *The Fortunes of Liberalism: Essays on Austrian Economics and the Ideal of Freedom*. Vol. 4 of *The Collected Works of F. A. Hayek*. Chicago: University of Chicago Press. Peter G. Klein (ed.)

———. 1996. "Economic calculation and the limits of organization." *Review of Austrian Economics* 9: 3–28

———. 1999. "Entrepreneurship and corporate governance." *Quarterly Journal of Austrian Economics* 2: 19–42.

———. 2000. "New institutional economics." In Boudewin Bouckeart and Gerrit de Geest, eds., *Encyclopedia of Law and Economics*. Cheltenham, U.K.: Edward Elgar.

———. 2001. "Were the acquisitive conglomerates inefficient?" *RAND Journal of Economics* 32: 745–61.

———. 2005. "The make-or-buy decision: Lessons from empirical studies." In Claude Ménard and M. Shirley, eds., *Handbook of New Institutional Economics*. New York: Springer.

———. 2006. "Foreword" in Carl Menger, *Principles of Economics*. Auburn, Ala.: Ludwig von Mises Institute, 2006 [1871].

Klein, Peter G., and Sandra K. Klein. 2008. "Are divestitures predictable? A duration analysis." Working paper. Contracting and Organizations Research Institute, University of Missouri.

Klein, Peter G., and George A. Selgin. 2000. "Menger's theory of money: Some experimental evidence." In John Smithin, ed., *What Is Money?* London: Routledge.

Knight, Frank H. 1921. *Risk, Uncertainty, and Profit*. New York: Hart, Schaffner and Marx.

———. 1936. "The quantity of capital and the rate of interest." *Journal of Political Economy* 44: 433–463, 612–642.

Koch, Charles G. 2007. *The Science of Success: How Market-Based Management Built the World's Largest Private Company*. New York: Wiley.

Koppl, Roger. 2006. "Austrian economics at the cutting edge." *Review of Austrian Economics* 19: 231–41.

Koppl, R., and Richard N. Langlois. 2001. "Organizations and language games." *Journal of Management and Governance* 5: 287–305.

Kor, Yasemin Y., and Joseph T. Mahoney. 2000. "Penrose's resource-based approach: the process and product of research creativity." *Journal of Management Studies* 37: 109–39.

Kor, Yasemin Y., Joseph T. Mahoney, and Steven C. Michael. 2007. "Resources, capabilities, and entrepreneurial perceptions." *Journal of Management Studies* 44: 1187–1212.

Kornai, János. 1986. "The soft budget constraint." *Kyklos* 39: 3–30.

Kreps, David M. 1990. "Corporate culture and economic theory." In James E. Alt and Kenneth A. Shepsle, eds., *Perspectives on Positive Political Economy*. New York: Cambridge University Press.

———. 1990. *A Course in Microeconomic Theory*. Princeton, N.J.: Princeton University Press.

Lachmann, Ludwig M. 1956. *Capital and its Structure*. London: G. Bell & Sons.

————. 1977. *Capital, Expectations, and the Market Process*. Kansas City: Sheed Andrews and McMeel.

Lang, Larry H. P., Annette B. Poulsen, and Rene M. Stulz. 1994. "Firm performance, asset sales, and the costs of managerial discretion." *Journal of Financial Economics* 37: 3–37.

Lang, Larry H. P., and Rene M. Stulz. 1994. "Tobin's q, corporate diversification, and firm performance." *Journal of Political Economy* 102: 1248–80.

Lang, Larry H. P., René M. Stulz, and Ralph Walkling. 1991. "A test of the free cash flow hypothesis: The case of bidder returns." *Journal of Financial Economics* 28: 315–35.

Lange, Oskar. 1936–37. "On the economic theory of socialism." *Review of Economic Studies* 4: 53–71, 123–42.

————. 1958. "The role of planning in socialist economy." In Morris Bornstein, ed., *Comparative Economic Systems*. Homewood, Ill.: Richard D. Irwin, 1969.

————. 1965. "The computer and the market." In Alec Nove and D. M. Nuti, eds., *Socialist Economics*. London: Penguin Books, 1972.

Langlois, Richard N. 1982. "Subjective probability and subjective economics," C.V. Starr Center for Applied Economics Research Report #82-09, Faculty of Arts and Science, New York University.

————. 1992. "Transaction cost economics in real time." *Industrial and Corporate Change* 1: 99–127.

————. 1994a. "The boundaries of the firm." In Peter J. Boettke, ed., *The Elgar Companion to Austrian Economics*. Aldershot, UK: Edward Elgar.

————. 1994b. "The 'new' institutional economics." In Peter J. Boettke, ed., *The Elgar Companion to Austrian Economics*. Aldershot, UK: Edward Elgar.

————. 1998. "Personal capitalism as charismatic authority: the organizational economics of a Weberian concept." *Industrial and Corporate Change* 7: 195–214.

————. 2001. "Strategy and the market process: Introduction to the special issue." *Managerial and Decision Economics* 22: 163–68.

————. 2002. "Modularity in technology and organization." *Journal of Economic Behavior and Organization* 49: 19–37.

Langlois, Richard N., and M. Cosgel. 1993. "Frank Knight on risk, uncertainty, and the firm: a new interpretation." *Economic Inquiry* 31: 456–65.

Langlois, Richard N., and Nicolai J. Foss. 1999. "Capabilities and governance: the rebirth of production in the theory of economic organization." *Kyklos* 52: 201–18.

Langlois, Richard N., and Paul L. Robertson. 1995. *Firms, Markets, and Economic Change: A Dynamic Theory of Business Institutions*. London and New York: Routledge.

Lavoie, Don. 1985. *Rivalry and Central Planning: The Socialist Calculation Debate Reconsidered*. Cambridge: Cambridge University Press.

Lawson, Tony. 1997. *Economics and Reality*. Routledge: London, U.K.

Lazear, Edward P. 2004. "Balanced skills and entrepreneurship." *American Economic Review* 94: 208–11.

———. 2005. "Entrepreneurship." *Journal of Labor Economics* 23: 649–80.

Lee, Dwight R. 1994. "Go to Harvard and turn left: The rise of socialist ideology in higher education." In T. William Boxx and Gary M. Quinlivan, eds., *The Cultural Context of Economics and Politics*. Lanham, MA: University Press of America.

Lerner, Abba. 1934. "Economic theory and socialist economy." *Review of Economic Studies* 2: 51–61.

Lewin, Peter. 1999. *Capital in Disequilibrium: the Role of Capital in a Changing World*. London: Routledge.

———. 2005. "The firm in disequilibrium: Contributions from the Austrian tradition." Working Paper. Department of Management, University of Texas at Dallas.

Lewin, Peter, and Steven E. Phelan. 1999. "Firms, strategies, and resources: Contributions from Austrian economics." *Quarterly Journal of Austrian Economics* 2: 3–18.

———. 2002. "Rent and resources: a market process perspective." In Nicolai J. Foss and Peter G. Klein, eds., *Entrepreneurship and the Firm: Austrian Perspectives on Economic Organization*. Aldershot: Edward Elgar.

Liebowitz, Stanley J., and Stephen E. Margolis. 1990. "The fable of the keys." *Journal of Law and Economics* 33: 1–26.

———. 1995. "Path dependence, lock-in and history." *Journal of Law, Economics, and Organization* 11: 205–26.

———. 1999. *Winners, Losers, and Microsoft: Competition and Antitrust in High Technology*. Oakland: Independent Institute.

Lindahl, Erik. 1939. *Studies in the Theory of Money and Capital*. London: George Allen & Unwin.

Lippman, Steven A., and Richard P. Rumelt. 2003. "The payments perspective: Micro-foundations of resource analysis." *Strategic Management Journal* 24: 903–27.

Littlechild, Steven C. 1986. "Three types of market process." In Richard N. Langlois, ed., *Economics as a Process*. Cambridge: Cambridge University Press.

Long, Roderick T. 2006. "Realism and abstraction in economics: Aristotle and Mises versus Friedman." *Quarterly Journal of Austrian Economics* 9: 3–23.

Long, W., and W. E. McMullan. 1984. "Mapping the new venture opportunity identification process." In John A. Hornaday, ed., *Frontiers of Entrepreneurship Research*. Wellesley, Mass: Babson College.

Loury, Glenn L. 1979. "Market structure and innovation." *Quarterly Journal of Economics* 93: 395–410.

Lucas, Robert E., Jr. 1972. "Expectations and the neutrality of money." *Journal of Economic Theory* 4: 103–24.

———. 1977. "Understanding business cycles." In Lucas, *Studies in Business-Cycle Theory*. Cambridge, Mass: MIT Press, 1981.

Lumpkin, G. T., and Gregory G. Dess. 1996. "Clarifying the entrepreneurial orientation construct and linking it to performance." *Academy of Management Review* 21: 135–72.

Lundberg, Erik. 1937. *Studies in the Theory of Economic Expansion*. London: P. S. King & Son.

Lynch, Harry H. 1971. *Financial Performance of Conglomerates*. Boston: Harvard University Press.

Macher, Jeffrey T., and Barak D. Richman. 2008. "Transaction cost economics: An assessment of empirical research in the social sciences." *Business and Politics* 10, Article 1.

Machlup, Fritz. 1934. *Führer durch die Krisenpolitik.* Vienna: J. Springer.

———. 1958. "Equilibrium and disequilibrium: Misplaced concreteness and disguised politics." In Machlup, *Essays in Economic Semantics*, second edition. Brunswick, N.J.: Transaction, 1991.

———. 1974. "Integrationshemmende integrationspolitik." In Herbert Giersch, ed., *Bernhard-Harms-Vorlesungen.* Kiel: Institut für Weltwirtschaft.

———. 1976a. "Discussion of the four papers." In Laurence S. Moss, ed., *The Economics of Ludwig von Mises: Toward a Critical Reappraisal.* Kansas City: Sheed and Ward.

———. 1976b. "Hayek's contributions to economics." In Machlup, ed., *Essays on Hayek.* Hillsdale, Mich: Hillsdale College Press.

Machovec, Frank M. 1995. *Perfect Competition and the Transformation of Economics.* London: Routledge.

MacKenzie, Douglas W. 2008. "The equilibrium analysis of Mises, Hayek, and Lachmann." Working Paper, Department of Economics, SUNY–Plattsburgh.

Mahoney, Joseph T. 1995. "The management of resources and the resource of management." *Journal of Business Research* 33: 91–101.

Mäki, Uskali. 1996. "Scientific realism and some peculiarities of economics." *Boston Studies in the Philosophy of Science* 169: 425–45.

Malkiel, Burton G. 1990. *A Random Walk Down Wall Street.* New York: W.W. Norton.

Manne, Henry G. 1965. "Mergers and the market for corporate control." *Journal of Political Economy* 73: 110–20.

Marchal, Jean. 1951. "The construction of a new theory of profit." *American Economic Review* 41: 549–65.

Marget, Arthur W. 1938–42. *The Theory of Prices: An Examination of the Central Problem of Monetary Theory.* New York: Augustus M. Kelley. 1966.

Mathews, Don. 1998. "Management vs. the market: An exaggerated distinction." *Quarterly Journal of Austrian Economics.* 1: 41–46.

Mathews, John A. 2006. "Ricardian rents or Knightian profits? More on Austrian insights on strategic organization." *Strategic Organization* 4: 97–108.

Matsusaka, John G. 1993. "Takeover motives during the conglomerate merger wave." *Rand Journal of Economics* 24: 357–379.

————. 2001. "Corporate diversification, value maximization, and organizational capabilities." *Journal of Business* 74: 409–31.

Mayer, Hans. 1932. "The cognitive value of functional theories of price." In Israel M. Kirzner, ed., *Classics in Austrian Economics: A Sampling in the History of a Tradition*. London: William Pickering, 1994.

Mayer, Kyle J., and Nicholas S. Argyres. 2004. "Learning to contract: Evidence from the personal computer industry." *Organization Science* 15: 394–410.

McCormick, Brian J. 1992. *Hayek and the Keynesian Avalanche*. New York: St. Martin's Press.

McGrath, R. G., and I. C. MacMillan. 2000. *The Entrepreneurial Mindset*. Cambridge, Mass: Harvard Business School Press.

McMullen, Jeffrey, Lawrence A. Plummer, and Zoltan J. Acs. 2007. "What is an entrepreneurial opportunity?" *Small Business Economics* 28: 273–83.

McMullen, Jeffrey, and Dean A. Shepherd. 2006. "Entrepreneurial action and the role of uncertainty in the theory of the entrepreneur." *Academy of Management Review* 31: 132–52.

Meese, Alan. 1997. "Price theory and vertical restraints: A misunderstood relation." *UCLA Law Review* 143: 143–204.

Ménard, Claude, and M. Shirley, eds. 2005. *Handbook of New Institutional Economics*. New York: Springer.

Menger, Carl. 1871. *Principles of Economics*. Trans James Dingwall and Bert Hoselitz. Auburn, Ala.: Ludwig von Mises Institute, 2006.

————. 1883. *Investigations into the Method of the Social Sciences with Special Reference to Economics*. New York: New York University Press. 1981.

————. 1892. "On the origin of money." *Economic Journal* 2: 239–55.

Meyer, David R. 2000. *Hong Kong as a Global Metropolis*. Cambridge, UK: Cambridge University Press

Milgrom, Paul A., and John Roberts. 1992. *Economics, Organization, and Management*. Englewood Cliffs, N.J.: Prentice-Hall.

Milhaupt, Curtis J. 1997. "The market for innovation in the United States and Japan: Venture capital and the comparative corporate governance debate." *Northwestern University Law Review* 91: 865–98.

Miller, Kent D. 2007. "Risk and rationality in entrepreneurial processes." *Strategic Entrepreneurship Journal* 1: 57–74.

Minkler, Alanson P. 1993a. "The problem with dispersed knowledge: Firms in theory and practice." *Kyklos* 46: 569–87.

———. 1993b. "The problem with dispersed knowledge: Firms in theory and practice." *Kyklos* 46: 569–587.

Mises, Ludwig von. 1912. *The Theory of Money and Credit.* London: Jonathan Cape. 1934.

———. 1920. *Economic Calculation in the Socialist Commonwealth.* Trans. S. Adler. Auburn, Ala.: Ludwig von Mises Institute, 1990.

———. 1922. *Socialism: An Economic and Sociological Analysis.* Trans. J. Kahane. New Haven: Yale University Press, 1951.

———. 1933. *Epistemological Problems of Economics.* Auburn, Ala.: Ludwig von Mises Institute. 2003.

———. 1944. *Bureaucracy.* New Haven: Yale University Press.

———. 1947. *Planned Chaos.* Irvington-on-Hudson, N.Y.: Foundation for Economic Education.

———. 1949. *Human Action: A Treatise on Economics,* scholar's edition. Auburn, Ala: Ludwig von Mises Institute. 1998.

———. 1951. "Profit and loss." In Ludwig von Mises, *Planning for Freedom,* fourth edition. Spring Mills, Penn.: Libertarian Press, 1980.

———. 1962. *The Ultimate Foundation of Economic Science: An Essay on Method.* Princeton, N.J.: Van Nostrand.

Mises, Margit von. 1984. *My Years with Ludwig von Mises,* second enlarged edition. Cedar Falls, Iowa: Center for Futures Education.

Mises, Richard von. 1939. *Probability, Statistics and Truth.* New York: Dover Publications. 1957.

Mitchell, Mark, and J. Harold Mulherin. 1996. "The impact of industry shocks on takeover and restructuring activity." *Journal of Financial Economics* 41: 193–229.

Mitchell, Mark L., and Kenneth Lehn. 1990. "Do bad bidders become good targets?" *Journal of Political Economy* 98: 372–98.

Montgomery, Cynthia A., and Birger Wernerfelt. 1988. "Diversification, Ricardian rents, and Tobin's q." *Rand Journal of Economics* 19: 623–32.

Montias, J. Michael. 1976. *The Structure of Economic Systems*. New Haven, Conn.: Yale University Press.

Morck, Randall, Andrei Shleifer, and Robert W. Vishny. 1988. "Management ownership and market valuation: An empirical analysis." *Journal of Financial Economics* 20: 293–315.

Morgenstern, Oskar. 1935. "Perfect foresight and economic equilibrium." In Andrew Schotter, ed., *Selected Economic Writings of Oskar Morgenstern*. New York: New York University Press, 1976.

Moroney, John R. 1972. "The current state of money and production theory." *American Economic Review* 62: 335–43.

Mosakowski, Elaine. 1997. "Strategy making under causal ambiguity: Conceptual issues and empirical evidence." *Organization Science* 8: 414–42.

———. 1998. "Entrepreneurial resources, organizational choices, and competitive outcomes." *Organization Science* 9: 625–43.

Musgrave, Alan. 1981. " 'unreal assumptions' in economic theory: The f-twist untwisted." *Kyklos* 34: 377–87.

Myers, Stewart C., and Nicholas S. Majluf. 1984. "Corporate financing and investment decisions when firms have information that investors do not have." *Journal of Financial Economics* 13: 187–221.

Nelson, Richard R. 1991. "Why do firms differ, and how does it matter?" *Strategic Management Journal* 12: 61–74.

Nelson, Richard R., and Sidney G. Winter. 1982. *An Evolutionary Theory of Economic Change*. Cambridge, Mass.: Harvard University Press.

Ng, Desmond. 2005. "Strategic entrepreneurship: An Austrian economic approach to competitive strategy." *Journal of International Business Strategy* 1: 75–84.

Oakley, Allen. 1999. *The Revival of Modern Austrian Economics: A Critical Assessment of Its Subjectivist Origins.* Aldershot, U.K.: Edward Elgar.

O'Brien, Dennis. 1984. "The evolution of the theory of the firm." In O'Brien, *Methodology, Money and the Theory of the Firm.* Aldershot: Edward Elgar, 1994.

O'Driscoll, Gerald P. 1977. *Economics as a Coordination Problem: The Contributions of Friedrich A. Hayek.* Kansas City: Sheed Andrews and McMeel.

O'Driscoll, Gerald P., and Mario J. Rizzo. 1985. *The Economics of Time and Ignorance.* London: Basil Blackwell.

Olson, M. 1965. *The Logic of Collective Action: Public Goods and the Theory of Groups.* Cambridge, Mass: Harvard University Press.

Parker, S. C. 2004. *The Economics of Self-employment and Entrepreneurship.* Cambridge, U.K.: Cambridge University Press.

———. 2008. "The economics of formal business networks." *Journal of Business Venturing* 23: 627–40.

Pasour, E. C., Jr. 2004. "Agricultural economists and the state." *Econ Journal Watch* 1: 106–33.

Penrose, Edith T. 1959. *The Theory of the Growth of the Firm.* Third edition, New York: Oxford University Press, 1995.

Pierson, N. G. 1902. "The problem of value in the socialist community." In F. A. Hayek, ed., *Collectivist Economic Planning.* Clifton, N.J.: Augustus M. Kelley. 1975.

Pisano, Gary P. 1990. "Using equity participation to support exchange: Evidence from the biotechnology industry." *Journal of Law, Economics, and Organization* 5: 109–26.

Pisano, Gary P., Michael V. Russo, and David J. Teece. 1988. "Joint ventures and collaborative arrangements in the telecommunications equipment industry." In David Mowery, ed., *International Collaborative Ventures in U.S. Manufacturing.* Cambridge, Mass.: Ballinger, 1988.

Porter, Michael E. 1980. *Competitive Strategy.* New York: Free Press.

———. 1987. "From competitive advantage to corporate strategy." *Harvard Business Review*: 43–59.

Ravenscraft, David, and F. M. Scherer. 1987. *Mergers, Sell-Offs, and Economic Efficiency.* Washington, D.C.: Brookings Institution.

———. 1991. "Divisional sell-offs: A hazard function analysis." *Managerial and Decision Economics* 12: 429–38.

Read, Leonard. 1958. *I, Pencil: My Life Story as Told to Leonard Read.* Irvington-on-Hudson, N.Y.: Foundation for Economic Education.

Reece, James S., and William R. Cool. 1978. "Measuring investment center performance." *Harvard Business Review* 56: 28–30.

Richardson, G. B. 1972. "The organisation of industry." *Economic Journal* 82: 883–96.

Ricketts, Martin. 1987. *The New Industrial Economics: An Introduction to Modern Theories of the Firm.* New York: St. Martin's Press.

Rizzo, Mario J. 1978. "Praxeology and econometrics: A critique of positivist economics." In Louis M. Spadaro, ed., *New Directions in Austrian Economics.* Kansas City, Mo.: Sheed Andrews and McMeel.

Robbins, Lionel. 1934. *The Great Depression.* New York: Macmillan.

Roberts, Peter W., and Kathleen M. Eisenhardt. 2003. "Austrian insights on strategic organization: from market insights to implications for firms." *Strategic Organization*: 345–352.

Roe, Mark J. 1994. *Strong Managers, Weak Owners: The Political Roots of American Corporate Finance.* Princeton: Princeton University Press.

Rogerson, William P. 1992. *Overhead Allocation and Incentives for Cost Minimization in Defense Procurement.* Santa Monica, Calif.: Rand Corporation.

Roll, Richard. 1988. "Empirical evidence on takeover activity and shareholder wealth." In John C. Coffee, Jr., Louis Lowenstein, and Susan Rose-Ackerman, eds., *Knights, Raiders, and Targets: the Impact of the Hostile Takeover.* New York: Oxford University Press.

Romano, Roberta. 1992. "A guide to takeovers: Theory, evidence, and regulation." *Yale Journal on Regulation* 9: 119–80.

Rothbard, Murray N. 1956. "Toward a reconstruction of utility and welfare economics." In Mary Sennholz, ed., *On Freedom and Free Enterprise: Essays in Honor of Ludwig von Mises.* Princeton: Van Nostrand.

————. 1962. *Man, Economy, and State: A Treatise on Economic Principles*, scholar's edition. Auburn, Ala.: Ludwig von Mises Institute. 2004.

————. 1963a. *America's Great Depression*, second revised edition. New York: Richardson and Snyder. 1983.

————. 1963b. *What Has Government Done to Our Money?* Auburn, Ala: Ludwig von Mises Institute. 1990.

————. 1976. "Ludwig von Mises and economic calculation under socialism." In Laurence S. Moss, ed., *The Economics of Ludwig von Mises: Toward a Critical Reappraisal.* Kansas City: Sheed and Ward.

————. 1985. "Professor Hébert on entrepreneurship." *Journal of Libertarian Studies* 7: 281–86.

————. 1991. "The end of socialism and the calculation debate revisited." *Review of Austrian Economics* 5: 51–76.

————. 1993. "Letter to Sandra K. Johnson." January 20.

————. 1994. "Review of Bruce Caldwell and Stephan Boehm, eds., Austrian Economics: Tensions and New Directions." *Southern Economic Journal* 61: 559–60.

————. 1995. "The present state of Austrian economics." In Rothbard, *The Logic of Action One: Method, Money, and the Austrian School.* Cheltenham, U.K.: Edward Elgar, 1997.

Rubin, Paul H. 1990. *Managing Business Transactions: Controlling the Cost of Coordinating, Communicating, and Decisionmaking.* New York: Macmillan.

Rumelt, Richard P. 1974. *Strategy, Structure and Economic Performance.* Boston: Graduate School of Business Administration, Harvard University.

————. 1982. "Diversification strategy and profitability." *Strategic Management Journal* 3: 359–69.

Salerno, Joseph T. 1990a. "Postscript: Why a Socialist Economy Is 'Impossible'." In Ludwig von Mises, *Economic Calculation in the Socialist Commonwealth.* Auburn, Ala.: Ludwig von Mises Institute.

————. 1990b. "Ludwig von Mises as social rationalist." *Review of Austrian Economics* 4: 26–54.

————. 1991. "Commentary: The concept of coordination in Austrian macroeconomics." In Richard Ebeling, ed., *Austrian Economics*. Hillsdale, Mich.: Hillsdale College Press.

————. 1993. "Mises and Hayek dehomogenized." *Review of Austrian Economics* 6: 113–46.

————. 1994a. "Reply to Leland B. Yeager." *Review of Austrian Economics* 7: 111–25.

————. 1994b. "Ludwig von Mises's monetary theory in the light of modern monetary thought." *Review of Austrian Economics* 8: 71–115.

————. 1996a. "Why we're winning: An interview with Joseph T. Salerno." *Austrian Economics Newsletter* 16: 1–8.

————. 1996b. "A final word: Calculation, knowledge, and appraisement." *Review of Austrian Economics* 9: 141–42.

————. 1999a. "Carl Menger: The founder of the Austrian school." In Randall G. Holcombe, ed., *Fifteen Great Austrian Economists*. Auburn, Ala.: Ludwig von Mises Institute.

————. 1999b. "The place of Mises's *Human Action* in the development of modern economic thought." *Quarterly Journal of Austrian Economics* 2: 35–65.

————. 2002. "The rebirth of Austrian economics—in light of Austrian economics." *Quarterly Journal of Austrian Economics* 5: 111–28.

————. 2006. "Mises's favorite Anglo-American economists." Mises.org Daily Article, Oct. 18 2006.

Samuelson, Paul A. 1947. *Foundations of Economic Analysis*. Cambridge, Mass.: Harvard University Press.

Sanchez, Ron, Aimé Heene, and Howard Thomas. 1996. "Introduction: Towards the theory and practice of competence-based competition." In Sanchez, Heene and Thomas, eds., *Dynamics of Competence-Based Competition: Theory and Practice in the New Strategic Management*. London: Elsevier, 1996.

Sarasvathy, Saras. 2001. "Causation and effectuation: Toward a theoretical shift from economic inevitability to entrepreneurial contingency." *Academy of Management Review* 26: 243–63.

Saussier, Stéphane. 2000. "Transaction costs and contractual incompleteness: the case of Électricitié de France." *Journal of Economic Behavior and Organization* 42: 189–206.

Sautet, Frederic. 2001. *An Entrepreneurial Theory of the Firm*. London, U.K.: Routledge.

Scharfstein, David. 1988. "The disciplinary role of takeovers." *Review of Economic Studies* 55: 185–99.

Schelling, Thomas C. 1978. *Micromotives and Macrobehavior*. New York: Norton.

Schlingemann, Frederik P., Rene M. Stulz, and Ralph A. Walkling. 2002. "Divestitures and the liquidity of the market for corporate assets." *Journal of Financial Economics* 64: 117–44.

Schultz, T. W. 1975. "The value of the ability to deal with disequilibria." *Journal of Economic Literature* 13: 827–46.

———. 1980. "Investment in entrepreneurial ability." *Scandinavian Journal of Economics* 82: 437–48.

Schumpeter, Joseph A. 1911. *The Theory of Economic Development: An Inquiry into Profits, Capital, Credit, Interest, and the Business Cycle*. Trans. Redvers Opie. Cambridge, MA: Harvard University Press, 1934.

———. 1942. *Capitalism, Socialism and Democracy*. New York: Harper and Row.

Selgin, George A. 1988. "Praxeology and understanding: An analysis of the controversy in Austrian economics." *Review of Austrian Economics* 2: 19–58.

Servaes, Henri. 1996. "The value of diversification during the conglomerate merger wave,." *Journal of Finance* 51: 1201–25.

Shane, Scott A. 2003. *A General Theory of Entrepreneurship: The Individual–Opportunity Nexus*. Cheltenham, U.K.: Edward Elgar.

Shane, Scott A., and S. Venkataraman. 2000. "The promise of entrepreneurship as a field of research." *Academy of Management Review* 25: 217–26.

Shapiro, Carl, and Hal R. Varian. 1998. *Information Rules: A Strategic Guide to the Network Economy*. Boston: Harvard Business School Press.

Shapley, Deborah. 1993. *Promise and Power: The Life and Times of Robert McNamara*. Boston, MA: Little, Brown and Company.

Shaver, Kelly G., and Linda R. Scott. 1991. "Person, process, choice: the psychology of new venture creation." *Entrepreneurship Theory and Practice* 16: 23–45.

Shelanski, Howard A. 1993. "Transfer pricing and the organization of intrafirm exchange." Ph.D. diss., University of California, Berkeley, Department of Economics.

Shelanski, Howard A., and Peter G. Klein. 1995. "Empirical research in transaction cost economics: A review and assessment." *Journal of Law, Economics, and Organization* 11: 335–61.

Shleifer, Andrei, and Robert W. Vishny. 1989. "Management entrenchment: The case of manager-specific investments." *Journal of Financial Economics* 25: 123–39.

———. 1991. "Takeovers in the '60s and '80s: Evidence and implications." *Strategic Management Journal* 12: 51–59.

———. 1997. "A survey of corporate governance." *Journal of Finance* 52: 737–83.

Shook, Christopher L., Richard L. Priem, and Jeffrey E. McGee. 2003. "Venture creation and the enterprising individual: a review and synthesis." *Journal of Management* 29: 379–99.

Simon, Herbert A. 1951. "A formal theory of the employment relationship." *Econometrica* 19: 293–305.

———. 1961. *Administrative Behavior*. Second edition, New York: Macmillan.

Skocpol, Theda. 1996. "Delivering for young families: The resonance of the GI Bill." *American Prospect* 28: 66–72.

Smit, Hans T. J. 2001. "Acquisition strategies as option games." *Journal of Applied Corporate Finance* 14: 79–89.

Smith, Adam. 1776. *An Inquiry into the Nature and Causes of the Wealth of Nations*. Edited by R. H. Campbell, A. S. Skinner, and W. B. Todd. Indianapolis: LibertyClassics. 1981.

Smith, Clifford W., Jr. and Ross L. Watts. 1992. "The investment opportunity set and corporate financing, dividend, and compensation policies." *Journal of Financial Economics* 32: 263–92.

Smith, Kenneth W., and Alexander J. Triantis. 1994. "The value of options in strategic acquisitions." In Lenos Trigeorgis, ed., *Real Options in Capital Investment Models, Strategies, and Applications*. New York: Praeger.

Sobel, Robert. 1984. *The Rise and Fall of the Conglomerate Kings*. New York: Stein and Day.

Solow, R. 1957. "Technical change and the aggregate production function." *Review of Economics and Statistics* 39: 312–20.

Spadaro, Louis M., ed. 1978. *New Directions in Austrian Economics*. Kansas City, Mo.: Sheed Andrews and McMeel.

Spender, J. C. 2006. "The RBV, methodological individualism, and managerial cognition: Practicing entrepreneurship." Working paper, Leeds University.

Spulber, Daniel F. 1992. "Economic analysis and management strategy: A survey." *Journal of Economics and Management Strategy* 1: 535–74.

Stalebrink, Odd J. 2004. "The Hayek and Mises controversy: Bridging differences." *Quarterly Journal of Austrian Economics* 7: 27–38.

Standage, Tom. 1998. *The Victorian Internet*. New York: Walker.

Staubus, George J. 1986. "The market simulation theory of accounting measurement." *Accounting and Business Research* 16: 117–32.

Stein, Jeremy C. 1997. "Internal capital markets and the competition for corporate resources." *Journal of Finance* 52: 111–33.

Stern, Joel M., G. Bennett Stewart III, and Donald H. Chew, Jr. 1995. "The EVA financial management system." *Journal of Applied Corporate Finance* 8: 32–46.

Stewart, A. 1989. *Team Entrepreneurship*. Newbury Park, CA: Sage.

Stigler, G. J. 1961. "The economics of information." *Journal of Political Economy* 69: 213–25.

———. 1962. "Information in the labor market." *Journal of Political Economy* 70: 94–105.

Strigl, R. 1934. *Capital and Production*. Auburn, AL: Ludwig von Mises Institute. 2000.

Stromberg, Joseph A. 2004. "Introduction" in Murray N. Rothbard, *Man, Economy, and State: A Treatise on Economic Principles*, scholar's edition. Auburn, Ala.: Ludwig von Mises Institute.

Taylor, Fred M. 1929. "The guidance of production in a socialist state." In Benjamin E. Lippincott, ed., *On the Economic Theory of Socialism*. New York: McGraw-Hill, 1964.

Teece, David J. 1980. "Economies of scope and the scope of the enterprise." *Journal of Economic Behavior and Organization* 1: 223–47.

———. 1982. "Towards an economic theory of the multi-product firm." *Journal of Economic Behavior and Organization* 3: 39–64.

Thornton, Mark. 1999. "Review of Vaughn, Austrian Economics in America." *Public Choice* 98: 467–69.

Tullock, Gordon. 1969. "The new theory of corporations." In Erich Streissler, ed., *Roads to Freedom: Essays in Honor of Friedrich A. von Hayek*. Routledge and Kegan Paul.

US Department of Education. 1996. "Financial statistics of institutions of higher education."

Vanberg, Viktor J. 1994. "Spontaneous market order and social rules: A critical examination of F. A. Hayek's theory of cultural evolution." In Vanberg, *Rules and Choice in Economics*. London and New York: Routledge.

Vaughn, Karen I. 1994. *Austrian Economics in America: The Migration of a Tradition*. Cambridge: Cambridge University Press.

Venkataraman, Sankaran. 1997. "The distinctive domain of entrepreneurship research." In Jerome R. Katz and Robert H. Brockhaus, eds. *Advances in Entrepreneurship, Firm Emergence, and Growth*. Greenwich, CT: JAI Press, 1993.

Vickers, Douglas. 1970. "The cost of capital and the structure of the firm." *Journal of Finance* 25: 1061–80.

———. 1987. *Money Capital and the Theory of the Firm Preliminary Analysis*. Cambridge: Cambridge University Press.

Walker, D. A. 1969. "Marshall's theory of competitive exchange." *Canadian Journal of Economics* 2: 590–98.

Weber, Max. 1921. *Economy and Society*. Berkeley: University of California Press. 1978.

Wernerfelt, Birger. 1984. "A resource-based view of the firm." *Strategic Management Journal* 5: 171–180.

Weston, J. Fred. 1989. "Divestitures: Mistakes or learning." *Journal of Applied Corporate Finance* 2: 68–76.

Weston, J. Fred, Kwang S. Chung, and Susan E. Hoag. 1990. *Mergers, Restructuring, and Corporate Control.* Englewood Cliffs, N.J.: Prentice-Hall.

White, Lawrence H. 1981. "Introduction" in Carl Menger, *Investigations into the Method of the Social Sciences with Special Reference to Economics.* New York: New York University Press. 1981 [1883].

————. 1996. "Hayek's pure theory of capital." Unpublished manuscript. Department of Economics, University of Georgia.

————. 1999. "Why didn't Hayek favor laissez-faire in banking?" *History of Political Economy* 34: 753–69.

White, Lawrence J. 2005. "The Federal Reserve System's influence on research in monetary economics." *Econ Journal Watch* 2: 325–54.

Wicksteed, Philip H. 1910. *The Common Sense of Political Economy.* London: George Routledge & Sons. 1933.

Wieser, Friedrich. 1914. *Social Economics.* London: Allen and Unwin. 1927.

Williamson, Oliver E. 1975. *Markets and Hierarchies: Analysis and Antitrust Implications.* New York: Free Press.

————. 1981. "The modern corporation: Origins, evolution, attributes." *Journal of Economic Literature* 19: 1537–68.

————. 1985. *The Economic Institutions of Capitalism.* New York: Free Press.

————. 1991a. "Private ownership and the capital market." In Horst Siebert, ed., *Privatization: Symposium in Honor of Herbert Giersch.* Tübingen: J. C. B. Mohr, 1992.

————. 1991b. "Comparative economic organization: the analysis of discrete structural alternatives." *Administrative Science Quarterly* 36: 269–96.

————. 1991c. "Economic institutions: Spontaneous and intentional governance." *Journal of Law, Economics, and Organization* 1: 159–87.

————. 1991d. "Strategizing, Economizing, and Economic Organization." *Strategic Management Journal* 12: 75–94.

————. 1992. "Markets, hierarchies, and the modern corporation: An unfolding perspective." *Journal of Economic Behavior and Organization* 17: 335–52.

———. 1996. *The Mechanisms of Governance.* New York: Oxford University Press.

———. 2000. "The new institutional economics: Taking stock, looking ahead." *Journal of Economic Literature* 38: 595–613.

Winiecki, Jan. 1990. "Why economic reforms fail in the Soviet Union." *Economic Inquiry* 28: 195–221.

Winter, Sidney G. 1988. "On Coase, competence, and the corporation." *Journal of Law, Economics, and Organization* 4: 163–80.

Witt, Ulrich. 1998. "Imagination and leadership: The neglected dimension of an evolutionary theory of the firm." *Journal of Economic Behavior and Organization* 35: 161–77.

———. 2003. "Market opportunity and organizational grind: The two sides of entrepreneurship." *Advances in Austrian Economics* 6: 131–51.

Xue, J. H., and Peter G. Klein. 2010. "Regional determinants of technology entrepreneurship." *International Journal of Entrepreneurial Venturing* 1: 291–308.

Yeager, Leland B. 1994. "Mises and Hayek on calculation and knowledge." *Review of Austrian Economics* 7: 93–109.

———. 1995. "Rejoinder: Salerno on calculation, knowledge, and appraisement." *Review of Austrian Economics* 9: 137–39.

———. 1997. "Calculation and knowledge: Let's write *finis.*" *Review of Austrian Economics* 10: 133–36.

Yu, Tony Fu-Lai. 1999. "Toward a praxeological theory of the firm." *Review of Austrian Economics* 12: 25–41.

———. 2003. "A subjectivist approach to strategic management." *Managerial and Decision Economics* 24: 335–45.

Zijp, Rudy van. 1993. *Austrian and New Classical Business Cycle Theories: A Comparative Study Through the Method of Rational Reconstruction.* Brookfield, VT: Edward Elgar.

Zingales, Luigi. 1998. "Corporate governance." In John Eatwell, Murray Milgate, and Peter Newman, eds., *The New Palgrave Dictionary of Law and Economics.* London: Macmillan. 1998.

Index

About the Author

Peter G. Klein is an Associate Professor in the Division of Applied Social Sciences at the University of Missouri, Adjunct Professor at the Norwegian School of Economics and Business Administration, and Senior Scholar of the Ludwig von Mises Institute. His research focuses on the boundaries and internal organization of the firm, with applications to diversification, innovation, entrepreneurship, and financial institutions. He is author or editor of four books and author of over fifty scholarly articles. Klein holds a Ph.D. in economics from the University of California, Berkeley and a B.A. from the University of North Carolina, Chapel Hill. He blogs at organizationsandmarkets.com.